Facility Siting:

Risk, Power and Identity in Land Use Planning

Dedicated to the memory of Bengt T M Löfstedt

RISK, SOCIETY AND POLICY SERIES
Edited by Ragnar E Löfstedt

Facility Siting:
Risk, Power and Identity in Land Use Planning

Edited by
Åsa Boholm and Ragnar E Löfstedt

Routledge
Taylor & Francis Group
LONDON AND NEW YORK

First published 2004 by Earthscan in the UK and USA

2 Park Square, Milton Park, Abingdon, Oxon OX14 4RN
711 Third Avenue, New York, NY 10017, USA

Routledge is an imprint of the Taylor & Francis Group, an informa business

First issued in paperback 2016

A catalogue record for this book is available from the British Library

Library of Congress Cataloging-in-Publication Data

Boholm, Åsa.
Facility siting: risk, power and identity in land use planning / by Åsa Boholm and Ragnar Löfstedt.
p. cm.
Includes bibliographic references and index.

1. Land use–Planning–Case studies. I. Löfstedt, Ragnar. II. Title.

HD108.6.B65 2004
711l.4–dc22

2004016776

ISBN 978-1-138-99087-6 (pbk)
ISBN 978-1-84407-146-3 (hbk)

Typesetting by FiSH Books
Cover design by Yvonne Booth

Contents

List of Figures and Tables

Figures

Tables

List of Acronyms and Abbreviations

AAA	American Anthropological Association
ACHP	US Advisory Council for Historic Preservation
ACNW	NRC Advisory Committee on Nuclear Waste
AEA	Atomic Energy Authority
AONB	Area of Outstanding Natural Beauty
ASN	Autorité de Sûreté Nucléaire
BOR	US Bureau of Reclamation
BRGM	French Bureau of Geological and Mining Research
BSE	bovine spongiform encephalopathy
CAP	Common Agricultural Policy
CCC	US Civilian Conservation Corps
CEA	French Atomic Energy Commissariat
CEFOS	Centre for Public Sector Research
CLIS	local information and monitoring committee
CNE	French National Scientific Evaluation Committee
CO_2	carbon dioxide
dB	decibels
DOE	US Department of Energy
DOT	US Department of Transportation
EdF	Electricity of France
EIS	environmental impact statement
EPA	Swedish Environmental Protection Agency
EPA	US Environmental Protection Agency
EU	European Union
FHWA	US Federal Highway Administration
GIS	geographic information system
ha	hectare
HGV	heavy goods vehicle
HLW	high-level nuclear waste
hm3	cubic hectometre (1 hm3 = 1000 million litres)
HSE	UK Health and Safety Executive
INERIS	French Institute for the Industrial Environment and Risks
IRSN	Institute of Radiation Protection and Nuclear Safety
km	kilometres
LLRW	low-level radioactive waste
MP	member of parliament
NAS	National Academy of Science
NFFO	Non-Fossil Fuel Obligation programme

NGO	non-governmental organization
NIMBY	not in my backyard
NPS	US National Park Service
NRC	US National Research Council
NRCER	Network for Research into the Construction of Environmental Risk
NWD	Clark County Nuclear Waste Division
OPECST	French Parliamentary Office of Evaluation of Scientific and Technological Choices
PA	performance assessment
PRC	Clark County Peer Review Committee
RWM	radioactive waste management
SHPO	US State Historic Preservation Office
SKB	Swedish Nuclear Fuel and Waste Management Company
SJ	Swedish State Railways
TCP	traditional cultural property
TPA	total performance assessment
TRC	Nevada Technical Review Committee
UK	United Kingdom
URL	underground research laboratory
US	United States
USNRC	US Nuclear Regulatory Commission
WIPP	Waste Isolation Pilot Plant
YMP	Yucca Mountain Project

List of Contributors

Simone Abram, Department of Town and Regional Planning, University of Sheffield, UK

Per Binde, Centre for Public Sector Research, Göteborg University, Sweden

Åsa Boholm, Centre for Public Sector Research, Göteborg University and School of Public Administration, Göteborg University, Sweden

Alex Carrol, Bureau of Applied Research in Anthropology, University of Arizona, US

Amy Eisenberg, Bureau of Applied Research in Anthropology, University of Arizona, US

Ralph Heiefort, Centre for Public Sector Research, Göteborg University and School of Public Administration, Göteborg University, Sweden

Jamil Khan, Environmental and Energy Systems Studies, Department of Technology and Society, Lund University, Sweden

Ragnar E Löfstedt, King's Centre for Risk Management, King's College, London, UK

Gaspar Mairal, Department of Psychology and Sociology, University of Zaragoza, Spain

Claire Mays, Institute Symlog, Cachan, France

Eugene A Rosa, Department of Sociology, Washington State University, US

James F Short, Department of Sociology, Washington State University, US

Peter Simmons, Centre for Environmental Risk, University of East Anglia, UK

Annelie Sjölander-Lindqvist, Centre for Public Sector Research, Göteborg University and Human Ecology Division, Lund University, Sweden

Richard W Stoffle, Bureau of Applied Research in Anthropology, University of Arizona, US

Rebecca Toupal, Bureau of Applied Research in Anthropology, University of Arizona, US

Ylva Uggla, Man–Technology–Environment Research Centre, Department of Social and Political Sciences, Örebro University, Sweden.

Gordon Walker, Institute for Environment and Sustainability Research, Department of Geography, Staffordshire University, UK

M Nieves Zedeno, Bureau of Applied Research in Anthropology, University of Arizona, US

Preface

This volume is the outcome of an international research conference on facility siting held at Örenäs Castle in the southern Swedish town of Glumslöv in May 2001. The conference brought together academics from several countries to discuss some of the core themes of facility siting. The participants have diverse and robust field experience, coming from a range of disciplinary backgrounds, including social anthropology, sociology, psychology, geography, political science and decision sciences. The conference presented the following thematic sessions: conflicts on the margin – global versus local tensions; democratic principles, deliberation and authority; official discourses, public understandings and the framing of controversy; local dimensions, controversy and environmental resistance; and lessons from hazardous siting (efforts, accomplishments and public participation). Some of the papers presented at these thematic sessions have been published as a special issue of *Journal of Risk Research* (*Journal of Risk Research*, 2004), treating the theme of 'New Perspectives on Siting Controversy'. Another selection of papers, focusing on the political, social and cultural dimensions of facility siting in a local environment, are included as chapters in this edited volume.

We thank Per Binde, Max Boholm and Marcia Grimes for their invaluable editorial assistance. We are grateful to the anonymous reviewers who have read this volume, offering many constructive comments and suggestions to the authors. The New Perspectives on Siting Controversy conference and this book were made possible by support from the Swedish Council for Research in the Humanities and Social Sciences, the Swedish Transport and Communications Research Board, the National Swedish Rail Administration and the Centre for Public Sector Research, Göteborg University.

Åsa Boholm and Ragnar E Löfstedt
September 2004

Introduction

Åsa Boholm and Ragnar E Löfstedt

Overview

The contestation of local environments that often accompanies facility siting concerns the roles and meanings of land and land use within a setting of high modernist planning (Scott, 1998). James C Scott of Yale University has characterized the core of high modernism in the following way:

> ...a supreme self-confidence about continued linear progress, the development of scientific and technical knowledge, the expansion of production, the rational design of social order, the growing satisfaction of human needs, and, not least, an increasing control over nature (including human nature) commensurate with scientific understanding of natural laws (Scott, 1998, p90).

The foundation of high modernism, according to Scott, is that the state, in the guise of the 'welfare state', achieves a new role as a promoter of the 'common good'. The state adopts a new purpose: its ultimate rationale is to enhance the living conditions of the members of society. The state designs policies and administrations concerning health, education, work, family life, safety, production and consumption. To design such policies, society is treated as an external object harbouring populations who can be measured, assessed and investigated (Scott, 1998, p91). The deliberate design of society through scientific planning and social engineering is born as a practice and idea. 'It was possible to conceive of an artificial, engineered society designed, not by custom and historical accident, but according to conscious, rational scientific criteria' (Scott, 1998, p92).

So, in this sense high modernistic planning is blind to history and tradition. It lives in the present and is concerned only with the future, which it strives to improve by design schemas. High modernism values science-based technology and technological progress, prefers centralized solutions over local ones and acts in the name of broad communities – such as nation states or supra-national associations – rather than local communities or marginal populations. It favours large-scale over small-scale solutions, and values infrastructure and communication systems by means of which the distance between people in terms of space and habitus – that is to say, their 'socialized subjectivity' (Bourdieu, 1977) – can be conquered.

High modernism has given rise to tremendous technological achievements with respect to energy production and distribution, transportation of goods and people over vast distances, mass production of goods and services, and communication that surmounts geographical distance. The institutional and organizational features and constraints of large-scale technological projects or megaprojects include their political support and the rhetoric surrounding them, and their management, leadership, costs and performance in relation to stated goals (Latour, 1996; Corvellec, 2001; Flyvbjerg et al, 2002, 2003; Altschuler and Luberhoff, 2003). Facilities and infrastructures – including nuclear power plants, electric power dams, wind farms, oil refineries, power transmission lines and pipelines traversing continents, railways for high speed trains, motorways, air fields, large bridges or long tunnels through mountains or under the sea – although allegedly contributing to the greater good of society, do not, however, pass unnoticed. Indeed, in many cases the facilities and infrastructures have considerable impact on the surrounding environment and nearby communities.

Facilities of the kind enumerated have made life easier, safer and more comfortable for many people. On the other hand, they have produced negative side-effects in terms of waste products, hazardous impacts and risks for humans and the natural environment. Waste has to be placed somewhere for storage, destruction or recycling into something useful to society. No wonder the literature on facility siting (regarding its political, legal, economic and organizational dimensions, as well as its impact on the environment in terms of people, community, landscape and nature) is growing steadily. The early literature on facility siting referred mainly to hazardous waste, particularly high-level nuclear waste (Dunlap et al, 1993; Rabe, 1994). Hazardous waste management now has a broader range of connotations, encompassing many different technologies (for example, waste incinerators) and with many types of infrastructure having environmental or social impact (Goldman, 2000; US Environment Protection Agency, 2000).

Sometimes a facility siting process runs fairly smoothly, characterized by cooperation or dialogue between involved parties, leading to trust on all sides. In other cases, conflicts, driven more often than not by a perceived lack of fairness, proliferate and develop into drawn-out controversies that mobilize many groups and actors – such as stakeholders, citizens, governmental and non-governmental organizations (NGOs). Media exposure, expert disagreement, citizen mobilization, appeals, legal investigations and political turbulence follow suit. How can such conflicts be studied, understood and theorized? These are questions addressed by this volume. To grasp the dynamics of facility siting, we need to outline some of its basic social and organizational features. We have fields of alliances, which can shift over time as a project develops, among a variety of actors, whether individuals, organizations or institutions (Latour, 1996). There may be many competing interpretations – in agreement or disagreement – as to the utility of the project, its legitimacy and impacts and what the priorities should be (Corvellec, 2001). There are, for example, technological failures or accidents, high-stakes risk issues, experts making diverging risk assessments and authorities who fail to communicate adequately with the concerned public, either by withholding information or by making contradictory statements. In addition, public distrust of relevant authorities or companies plays a significant role, as does the issue regarding whether the affected public perceives the need for the facility. Experts and stakeholders often disagree as to what the negative externalities are with regard to the facility in question and how they should best be regulated (see Kasperson et al, 1992; Petts, 1992; Mazur, 1998).

The broad label 'facility siting' encompasses a web of issues involving benefits for individuals and the community, potential new risks or negative consequences, the trust and legitimacy of those involved in planning and management, and possible compensation for negatively affected stakeholders. Furthermore, it brings to the fore the strengths and weaknesses of institutional frameworks in decision-making, communication and deliberation, and the exchange of viewpoints, arguments and values (Kunreuther et al, 1993; Renn et al, 1995, 1996). Controversial cases are characterized by interplay between a range of organizational actors with diverging perspectives: technical experts, representatives of governmental authorities, elected political representatives, lawyers, academics from various disciplines being consulted as specialists and representatives of interest based organizations, and members of the local public, including those directly affected. What, then, can be learnt from the study of cases that some actors regard as failures of planning, 'failures' that others regard as victories of the interests of the weak, be it local communities or nature, over those of the mighty?

Although the settings and objectives of facility siting are diverse, there are certain common threads (see Owens, 2004). The placing of large-scale technological facilities in local environments can be a point of contention between, for example, experts and lay persons, politicians and ordinary citizens, spokespeople from industry, environmental stakeholders and homeowners. A projected facility often embodies global, modern and large-scale values, which construe growth and change as inherently good. However, the facility can also be understood as a threat to local identity, tradition, social and cultural continuity and local citizenship, eroding the perceived authority of communities over decisions pertaining 'their' land and their accustomed way of life vis-à-vis the land (Hornborg, 1994; Mairal Buil and Bergua Amores, 1998).

Controversy concerning facility siting has caused serious difficulties for the waste and chemical industries in North America and Europe (Kunreuther et al, 1993; Petts, 1995, 2001, 2004; Löfstedt, 1997). In the US, where around 300 million tonnes of hazardous waste is produced per year, no large freestanding hazardous waste facility has been sited anywhere since 1980 (Piller, 1991; Rabe, 1994). It is even becoming difficult to site and build renewable energy plants in some nations owing to public opposition or institutional constraints (Hargreaves, 1996; Wolsink, 1996, 2000; Henning, 2000; Khan, 2003). In the UK, only 35 per cent of the wind farms supported by the national programme that promotes renewable energy, Non-Fossil Fuel Obligation (NFFO), have been built (Jackson and Löfstedt, 1998). The same holds for waste incinerators in the UK (Petts, 1995, 2001), where new plants, as a rule, encounter opposition from the public. In countries such as Sweden and Holland, planned renewable energy facilities such as wind farms and solar energy fields have been opposed by institutional actors and governmental agencies. They claim that such facilities are detrimental to landscape aesthetics or to historic sites (Henning, 2000; Wolsink, 2000; Khan, 2003).

Local residents often protest against the prospect of having a large-scale facility located nearby, a facility with possible negative repercussions in terms of smell, noise, ugliness or other degradation of quality of life, or posing potential health risks for those living nearby. This attitude is sometimes labelled the 'not in my backyard' or NIMBY attitude. The term 'NIMBYism' as used by technical experts, representatives of industry and government and even, occasionally, by social scientists refers alternately to an emotional/irrational or calculated/selfish response to facility siting. Irrespective as to what interpretation is chosen, simply labelling a case of resistance to facility siting as an example of NIMBYism is an implicit accusation that assumes that there is a right and a wrong way. Simplistic, normative judgements as to the shortcomings of human behaviour have little to offer if we wish to explain adequately contestations of facility siting (Freudenberg and Pastor, 1992; McAvoy, 1999; Boholm, 2000). Conflict over local environments involving individuals and institutions in the context of facility siting is far more complex than the NIMBY theory of resistance assumes (Wolsink, 2000). Policy dissemination and implementation often collide with the structures and infrastructures according to which life is organized, with people's collective everyday experiences, their notions of righteousness, morality and obligation and, not least, their conception of themselves (Shore and Wright, 1997). To arrive at a more nuanced social science-based understanding of facility siting, we need new theoretical and methodological approaches.

Broadly speaking, we distinguish two strands of research pertinent to facility siting. On the one hand, there is a large amount of planning literature, mainly within economics, geography and political science (for example, Miller, 2001; Owens and Cowell, 2002). On the other hand, there is research focusing on individuals that takes account of opinions rather than organizational dimensions, and seeks to ascertain how individuals perceive benefits and adverse effects, how they assess fairness, and how they weigh the costs and benefits of facility siting proposals or actual facilities in operation (for example, Sjöberg and Drottz-Sjöberg, 2001). In what follows, we will give a brief overview of some current research trends. These trends concern risk, environmental stigma, decision-making procedures and political legitimacy, and landscape and place attachment.

The role of risk issues in facility siting

Controversies about facility siting often, but not necessarily, relate to risk issues in the sense of potentially negative consequences for health, the economy, people's social status or for general quality of life. Since the 1970s, questions regarding how members of the public conceive of and react to various risks have received increasing attention from researchers and policy-makers. An assumption made early on in psychometric research of risk perceptions was that risk assessment builds on matters other than calculations of probabilities and outcomes. When people assess risks, they take into account various qualitative attributes, such as the immediacy of an adverse effect, available alternatives, the state of knowledge, and familiarity and control of a hazard (von Winterfeldt and Edwards, 1984; Slovic, 1987).

Research by psychologists has demonstrated that there are mental guidelines with regard to what knowledge of any risk is readily accessible, and that these guidelines preclude full exploration of the information concerning available options (Tversky and Kahnemann, 1973; Fischhoff et al, 1981; Slovic, 1987, 2000). In reasoning and making decisions about risk, people employ tacit knowledge, decision-making rules and heuristic criteria, and also pay attention to the social context, social justification and warrantability of ideas and actions (for example, Slovic, 2000). Whether risks are voluntary or forced, considered to be known or new, controllable or beyond personal agency, and whether they are personal or are understood to affect people, in general – all these issues exemplify qualitatively distinguishing features of meaning that influence the assessment of risk magnitude and gravity or the saliency of certain risk issues above others.

The extent to which new technologies are acceptable to the general public is not, however, reducible to cognitive dimensions pertaining to individual psychology (von Winterfeldt and Edwards, 1984). Technology is socially and politically embedded; vested interests of social actors, public debate and dispute regarding risks and benefits all influence public opinion. Risks are socially amplified by social, institutional and cultural processes in ways that influence risk perception, and shape individual and social action in the face of uncertainty (Kasperson et al, 1988; Renn, 1991; Pidgeon et al, 2003). The media plays an important role in this process (Boholm, 1998; Ferreira et al, 2001; Flynn et al, 2001). In order to understand controversies about technology, our perspective therefore needs to be broadened to take into account not only the psychology of individuals, but also socially and culturally construed values and moral considerations, as well as political, social and ideological concerns. These points have been addressed by advocates of cultural theory (see Douglas and Wildavsky, 1982; Rayner and Cantor, 1987; Thompson et al, 1990; Wildavsky and Dake, 1990; Dake, 1991; Douglas, 1992; Tansey and O'Riordan, 1999; Tansey, 2004; see also critique by Boholm, 1996, and Sjöberg, 1997), as well as by others pursuing 'constructivist' approaches to risk perception (Hilgartner, 1992; Short and Clarke, 1992; Clarke and Short, 1993, pp379–382). The meanings, ontological premises and moral implications of risk are socially and culturally construed by collectively shared representations. This means that risks should be viewed as embedded in culturally and historically situated ideas, practices and events. Risks – that is, hazards with which people are concerned, not objective dangers – are formulated contextually by local communities, interest groups and organizations (Boholm, 2003; Ferreira, 2004).

THE 'HOW' OF FACILITY SITING

One outcome of research by psychologists into risk perception was the development of communication programmes through which the public can be better informed of various risks and, it was hoped, perhaps make better decisions. With regard to facility siting, especially in the US, industry and regulatory bodies are increasingly taking local concerns more seriously (see, for example, initiatives by US National Research Council 1989, 1996; the US Environment Protection Agency, 2000; the US Department of Health and Human Services, 2002). However, local concern about facility-siting projects has been mainly interpreted as a product of communication failure. By using pedagogically designed risk-communication programmes, project proponents and risk communicators hoped for a better educated public more willing to tolerate the siting of a facility in their neighbourhood. Under the assumption that public reactions to risks can be steered from above by means of detailed factual (scientifically framed) information, technical experts have been given a central role in the communication process. The various risk communication programmes that have been recently implemented in Europe and the US have, however, been ineffective: members of the local public continue to be critical of planned waste incinerators, tunnels, highways and nuclear waste storage facilities (for example, Kasperson et al, 1992; Boholm, 2000).

Risk communication initiatives often fail since what is at stake is not merely the form and content of the message – that is, what information is communicated about the risks and even the benefits (Leiss, 1996). Trust in those responsible for providing the information is highly relevant (Renn and Levine, 1991; Kasperson et al, 1992; Slovic, 1993; Slovic and McGregor, 1994; Earle and Cvetkovich, 1995; Leiss, 1996; Löfstedt, 1996a, 1996b; Cvetkovich and Löfstedt, 1999). Failure to successfully implement risk communication programmes often stems from public distrust of policy-makers and industrial officials (see Löfstedt and Horlick-Jones, 1998). It is far easier to destroy trust than to build it, particularly as negative trust-undermining events tend to take the form of unusual events or dramatic accidents that are more easily remembered, whereas positive trust-building events are more long term and, therefore, also more indistinct (Slovic, 1993).

In a facility-siting conflict, opponents and proponents tend to distrust each other (Smith and Marquez, 2000). A lack of trust in policy-makers and industrial officials contributes to difficulties in siting industrial plants (Dunlap et al, 1993) and in managing environmental crises (for example, chemical spills or the proposed decommissioning by Shell of the Brent Spar oil storage platform in 1995; Löfstedt and Renn, 1997). If the public believes that governments work closely with industry, and the latter is seen as a ruthless, economically based vested interest, distrust of regulation and legislative controls may result (Kunreuther et al, 1993; Linneroth-Bayer and Fitzgerald, 1996). Inappropriate handling of crises may lead to further loss of trust in the risk regulators. In fact, researchers have shown that siting controversies such as that surrounding Brent Spar, apart from having profound financial implications, further decrease general public trust and confidence in policy-makers (Löfstedt and Renn, 1997). One reason for this is that trust tends to be asymmetrical: if trust is low, new information about a person or organization will make already weak trust even weaker. If information is positive, this does not mean that trust is automatically strengthened since there is an a priori judgement of the character of the other as deceitful, incompetent, selfish or the like, which motivates a distrustful stance. If trust is high, however, things are different: new information, even if negative, will be assessed in a much more favourable light and will not immediately destroy trust (Cvetkovich et al, 2002).

A considerable portion of the literature on facility siting is policy related, it aims to offer practical advice on how to reach better and more cooperative solutions and how to handle conflicts. Issues of procedural and substantial fairness have been central (Albin, 1993; Young, 1994; Renn et al, 1995, 1996; Linneroth-Bayer and Fitzgerald, 1996). Such literature has a normative and applied outlook, suggesting forms for public participation in decision-making and for deliberative communication processes that promise to be more democratic and fair by accounting for various perspectives and viewpoints (Kunreuther et al, 1993; Renn et al, 1995). It addresses questions such as under what conditions facilities can be built and under what conditions plans fail (for example, Petts, 1995, 2001; Löfstedt, 1996a, 1996b, 1997, 2003). Various bottom-up approaches, specifically for the risk characterization stage when involving a multitude of stakeholders, have been proposed as an alternative to the outdated technocratic model of decision-making. Such bottom-up approaches are more sensitive to local perspectives and concerns, and encourage trust building; whether they are actually successful or not is another matter (Fischhoff, 1995; Renn et al, 1995; Renn, 1998; Löfstedt, 1999).

Facility siting in Europe and the US is regulated by a series of laws. There are standard procedures for how interests should be weighed in order to allow the relevant authorities (county and regional boards, as well as national agencies, according to various defined interests – environment, economic growth, security and public health) to have their say in accordance with established planning procedures, institutional schemes and procedures for decision-making and deliberation. The democratic jurisdiction of these institutions, including which actors are invited to participate and in what manner, are a topical issue in much current work on facility siting (Renn et al, 1995; Hunold and Young, 1998; Löfstedt, 1999). From a political perspective, controversy over localization can, broadly speaking, be understood as a power contest over territory and land use; as such, it is always a potential source of conflict in society (Strandberg, 2000). However, this is not to say that conflicts over facility siting are essentially an issue of 'national need versus local interest' (Owens, 2004). According to this common meta-narrative of siting controversy, conflicts arise due to defects in the policy implementation process. Alternatively, conflicts could be conceptualized as contestation (although articulated in a local context) of national policies and priorities regarding vital issues concerning sustainable development, environmental values, economic growth, distribution and use of resources (Owens, 2004).

Contaminated communities and environmental stigma

Risks from pollution, stemming from technology driven by human agency and affecting people in their home environment, can create a dramatic shift in the evaluation of the everyday context of living (Fitchen, 1989). The experience of being made a victim of unjustified intrusion into one's place of living can degrade one's perception of home and the accustomed home environment. Several recent studies of this matter (see, for example, Edelstein, 1998; Flynn et al, 2001) have drawn on the seminal work of Ervin Goffman, *Stigma: Notes on the Management of Spoiled Identities* (Goffman, 1963). Focusing on people with physical handicaps, deviant sexual identities or prior histories as inmates in prisons or mental asylums, Goffman argues that 'stigma' is a spoiled social identity. The stigma bearer is classified as a person who has been given a particular, but deviant and abnormal, role and status in society. The theoretical perspective developed by Goffman 40 years ago is still highly relevant. Goffman discusses how actors manage spoiled social identities in contexts of interaction, how they communicate and express deviance, act to hide or reveal stigma and how personal identity as a 'spoiled' person is construed by means of expressing denial, confirmation, pride, shame or using strategies of secrecy or blatant openness.

In American risk research into public resistance to facility siting, Goffman's work has undergone something of a renaissance: 'the concept of stigma can clearly be generalized from persons to environments' (Slovic et al, 1991, p686). It is fair to say that research into environmental stigma has largely been carried out in the US; American studies include examinations of, for example, the Hanford nuclear complex, the toxic spills at Love Canal and Legler and the high-level waste depository at the Nevada nuclear test site (Edelstein, 1988; Slovic et al, 1991, 1994; Dunlap et al, 1993; Slovic, 1993; Gregory et al, 1995, 1996; US National Research Council, 1996; Flynn et al, 2001; Gregory and Satterfield, 2002). The notion of stigma may be generalized from an actual catastrophe to the risks introduced by a facility. Imagery of a stigmatized place (Boholm, 1998; Ferreira et al, 2001) may have consequences in terms of decisions, and could influence whether or not one visits a particular place, purchases a house there or buys products from the area (Easterling, 1997).

Stigmatization is closely associated with processes of blaming (Edelstein, 1988, pp114–115), as a spoiled identity has a moral dimension. In an American study of Legler, New Jersey, a community where the communal water system was contaminated by toxic chemicals from a dilapidated waste dump, Edelstein reports how residents felt awkward when confronted with strangers asking in pitying tones if they lived in the so-called 'water area'. The toxic contamination of the surrounding environment created a mark of abnormality on the victims, a spoiled identity which gave rise to several interrelated social problems. How do others relate to residents of a 'contaminated' community? How do residents themselves construe their new and 'spoiled' identities? Increasing publicity and exposure by the media might increase this process of stigmatization, of singling out a particular community from what are expected to be normal social conditions (Flynn et al, 2001). When applied to 'contaminated communities' – that is to say, communities affected by a hazardous site or toxic exposure – stigma acquires a double meaning, being 'both an attribute of the hazardous project and a potential adverse impact of the project on the community' (Edelstein, 1988, p180).

What are the effects on the community of environmental pollution, intrusion and consequent disruption of 'life-scape' – the taken-for-granted future prospect of 'good living' (see Edelstein, 1988)? In such a changed situation where damage has been done, processes of restitution are set in motion to compensate people who have been burdened in various ways (see Sjölander-Lindqvist et al, 2000). Such processes, which might involve legal process, considerable sums of money and new benefits for some, but might cause others to feel unjustly treated, can be expected to affect seriously the social order of the community. Communities affected by environmental stigma, whether deriving from toxic contamination or risks stemming from a facility in the neighbourhood, tend to become marginalized and distrustful of government and administration (Edelstein, 1988; Fitchen, 1989, 1991; Sjölander-Lindqvist et al, 2000). Under such conditions, members of local communities construe themselves as victims, unfairly used and disrespectfully treated by the state, by authorities and even society, as a whole. Hostility grows towards authorities, companies and other stakeholders understood to be responsible for their plight. Marginalization can also become a driving force in a process of social mobilization – for example, in the formation of citizens' groups, special interest societies or other collective actions – to protect interests and values felt to be threatened (Ostrom, 1990).

The role of landscape, place and identity

Research into environmental stigma raises the issue of the role of place and identity in facility siting. Local communities are products of cultural, historical and geographical conditions. Studies by social anthropologists, geographers and others have shown how landscape and place are forceful symbols in building social identity (for example, Firey, 1945; Entrikin, 1991; Bender, 1993; Hirsch and O'Hanlon, 1995; Lovell, 1998). The concept of local identity helps us to understand how members of a local community might relate to facility siting. The construction of such identities should be understood against a historical background. The local environment, with its landscape, natural environment, houses, buildings, landmarks and monuments, constitutes an important resource for shared experiences, memories and collective identification (Halbwachs, 1992; Zonabend, 1993). Landscapes are imbued with cultural meanings that speak of history and the future; landscapes are bearers of continuity (see, for example, Lovell, 1998). In the Swedish Hallandsås train tunnel case (see Chapters 7 and 11), the project raised questions about people's continued existence not only as farmers – often on family farms that have run in families for several generations – but as individuals with strong senses of attachment to their local place of living.

A prospective large-scale industrial facility with uncertain consequences for the future threatens to alter the landscape drastically. Well-known places, scenery and landmarks connected with shared memories and the life and works of earlier generations of inhabitants might be drastically altered or even destroyed. Facility siting is therefore not merely a question of new opportunities in terms of work or economy. From a perspective that takes account of the cultural value of place and its singular and irreplaceable values (Kopytoff, 1986), local reactions of protest, such as NIMBYism, can be regarded as rational responses to large-scale technologies that intrude, spatially and culturally, on accustomed ways of life (Hornborg, 1994; Mairal Buil et al, 1997; Mairal Buil and Bergua Amores, 1998; Sjölander-Lindqvist, 2004).

High modernism, it has been argued (Giddens, 1991), disrupts the traditional link between time and space and results in 'disembedding' or 'time–space compression' (Beck et al, 1994; Giddens, 1994; Bauman, 1998), where local contexts loose much of their traditionally given significance. Time and space are no longer connected as they once were through the 'situatedness' of place (Bauman, 1998, p16) when people lived their lives in places where their social relations and experiences were embedded. Modernity as a process of 'disembedding' means that autonomous individuals must create for themselves significance and trust in social relations within a global context of indefinite spans of time–space (Giddens, 1991). Far from creating a homogeneous global transnational culture, however, globalization effectively shapes new conditions of social marginalization and structural inequality. New boundaries are created between local and global orders and as the global order gains strength, so does the local (Bauman, 1998). According to this trend of 'glocalization' (Bauman, 1998, p70), members of local communities or regions articulate themselves emphatically by means of claims to local belonging and solidarity, enforcing a sense of ethnic identity based on beliefs about common heritage and destiny (see Smith, 1991).

The local community's movement towards modernity implies that values central to the community's identity and self-understanding will be challenged (Fitchen, 1991). Social relations are redefined as a result of the restructuring of economic and political power relations. In the face of uncertainty, communities entering a rapid process of change – involving new forms of leadership and new leaders, entrepreneurs and groups – mobilize and new kinds of social rhetoric emerge. What are the effects on the community of an uncertain situation deriving from an instance of toxic contamination of the environment, the pending establishment of a huge dam that will flood the community and force villagers to relocate (see Chapter 9) or the threat of destroying sites in a traditional ceremonial landscape due to new road traffic infrastructure (see Chapter 8)? What will happen to social identities when people's 'life-scapes' are disrupted and the prospect of 'good living' no longer exists (see Edelstein, 1988, Chapter 3)?

This volume

This book is a collection of case studies, each focusing on the establishment in a specific geographic setting of a large-scale technological project, motivated by broad national and regional interests. These cases highlight a mosaic of possible future effects, some positive, some negative and some more uncertain. The authors represent several social science disciplines, including geography, political science, sociology, social psychology and social anthropology, and they all have extensive research experience of discordant planning for large-scale facilities or of controversies over facilities already in operation. Deriving from the

US and several European countries (Sweden, England, Spain and France), the cases refer to radioactive and toxic waste storage facilities, a renewable energy plant, a food processing factory, a chemical plant, a railway tunnel, a railway for high speed trains, a highway bridge and dams. All of the studies share a reliance on ethnographic approaches where information is gathered in situ in direct contact with the actors, organizations, institutions and localities concerned. The empirical material draws on participant observations, interviews, analyses of official documents and newspaper articles and innovative methodologies, such as collaborative photography.

Some of the contributions deal with state-driven long-term policy issues of toxic waste disposal. The high-level nuclear waste issue and the politics involved marked the birth of facility-siting research in the US during the late 1970s and early 1980s. This issue has been hotly debated for many years, as well as resisted by potential host communities. These cases concerning radioactive waste siting reflect the frequently long-term nature of facility siting conflicts, where – in the process of finding host communities willing to accept waste storage facilities – policies change, moving from top-down hierarchical and technocratic approaches to bottom-up, voluntary schemes emphasizing stakeholder involvement in planning and decision-making. In Chapter 1, Eugene Rosa and James Short discuss the role of the organizational and institutional context of high-level nuclear waste disposal in the US – a paradigm case of low probability, high consequence and dreaded risks. One of their main conclusions is that 'organizational and institutional contexts, representing cultural, economic and political interests, largely determine the course of deliberation and decision-making within which public policies are forged'. In Chapter 2, Claire Mays deals with the parallel development regarding high-level radioactive management in France. As in the US, opposition has been very strong from local communities and local governments in the vicinity of the planned location of the waste management facility. Mays analyses opposition as not only a political act, but also as a culturally appropriate act of risk identification. She gives a new interpretation of stigma, and considers what might be needed to alter the dominant social representation of radioactive waste as unmanageable.

In Chapter 3, Ylva Uggla focuses on the deep disposal of toxic waste – mercury – in an old Swedish mine. This is part of a national strategy to dispose of mercury, and the company in charge (a partially state-owned corporation) is also the body responsible for finding a solution to nuclear waste disposal in Sweden. Environmental organizations claim that mercury could leak from the underground storage facility and contaminate groundwater, while the company claims that the storage solution is safe. This study demonstrates how the conflict revolves around diverging institutional logics, including the attribution of social features to the opponent: while the environmentalists, for example, construe the conflict in terms of an opposition between exploited and exploiter, the company sees it as a conflict between laypeople and experts. Depending upon how the conflict is construed, the parties involved embark on conflicting strategies of action.

Other chapters deal with less salient risk issues, but with controversies concerning the perceived negative externalities of facilities. In Chapter 4, Jamil

Khan discusses a Swedish case regarding a proposed renewable energy project – a biogas plant – to be sited in a small rural town. In this case the debate – in contrast to cases of hazardous waste facility siting that are typically driven by environmental organizations in cooperation with local citizens – focused upon intrusions on quality of life, such as odour, noise, traffic and impact on the landscape, rather than on risks and hazards. No biogas plant was built, an explanation being that the top-down planning process excluded local citizens, only including the municipal political and technocratic establishment and stakeholders already in favour of the project. In a similar case analysed by Simone Abram in Chapter 5, a spice manufacturing plant was planned to be sited and eventually built in a pastoral village in the English countryside. This led to strong local opposition from some of the inhabitants of this dormitory community, a community who counted many professionals and entrepreneurs among its inhabitants. The issues of smell and potentially increasing traffic were crucial to the protesters. Other villagers, together with the district council, were, however, in favour, expecting new job opportunities and development. A tacit 'cultural' dimension of this conflict was the idea that the smell of spices was foreign to the village, to the assumed identity of the villagers and to their sense of belonging in the British countryside.

In Chapter 6, Peter Simmons and Gordon Walker also address the impact of facility siting on local people's experience of place, focusing on a chemical works in the north of England. Although it was established as a fairly small operation in 1950, the site has grown dramatically in the size and scale of its operations through a process of incremental development. It, too, has had serious odour problems, and in 1992 there was a major fire that resulted in chemical contamination of the local river. As a consequence of the company's presence, many local people experience a sense of encroachment and of the identity of the neighbourhood being spoiled and stigmatized. Drawing upon discussions with local residents, the authors explore the implications of the site's presence for residents' sense of place and for their social identities.

A similar theme comes up in the case of a yet-to-be-completed railway tunnel through a nature reserve and a farming area in southern Sweden. This case includes technological failure, toxic exposure, environmental risks and the collective mobilization of a local community of farmers and villagers. In Chapter 7, Annelie Sjölander-Lindqvist explores how the tunnel is perceived to affect the local environment and its culturally valued assets. In this study, photographs taken by local residents of features, places and landmarks of value and significance serve as the point of departure for a discussion of local identity, belonging and sense of place evoked by the tunnel and the uncertainties associated with it. When values that are taken for granted in the course of everyday life become threatened, a process of active reflection is started by which local places, buildings or landmarks are reconsidered and assumed to have unique and valuable qualities.

The Hoover Dam was built during the 1930s to generate hydropower from the Colorado River. The canyon of the river and the surrounding mountains were considered an isolated wasteland. For the Southern Paiute, the Hualapai and other tribes who had lived there since time immemorial, things were different. For them the area is a ceremonial landscape, with a history dating back to the Creation. The surroundings of the Colorado River and the dam facility contain culturally significant caves, hot springs, trails and areas featuring minerals or plants essential for traditional ceremonial purposes. In Chapter 8, Richard Stoffle and his colleagues investigate a complicated planning procedure that involved several US federal agencies and the Southern Paiute and the Hualapai tribes in a consultation process regarding a new bridge for road traffic over the Hoover Dam. This case illustrates how facility siting can become an occasion for identity politics located within a broader framework of relations between a majority and an ethnic minority.

In Chapter 9, Gaspar Mairal presents a Spanish case concerning controversial dam-building schemes in the Pyrenees. These dams are part of a national water policy, the objective of which is to create a system of irrigation for arid lowlands. The negative impact of these mountain dams is that highland villages will be flooded, displacing entire communities. In this case there are clearly distinguishable winners and losers: villagers in the mountains stand against lowland farmers. Dam building in Spain has a long history as a national policy of modernization. Starting in the 1920s, dam building has been justified by rhetorical arguments about 'equity' and the common good. Today the conflict has set in motion an intricate process of identity politics in which globalization has become a local issue. Questions pivot around notions of minority versus majority: who and what is a minority and does minority status entail special rights? The mobilization of protest against the national dam schemes has created relationships between local communities in the Pyrenees and other minority communities threatened by big dams – for example, in Chile. Proponents and opponents of large dams argue by means of 'culturalism' – historicized schemes essentializing 'what we are' and 'what we are becoming'.

The use of arguments about risk in public debate is discussed by Per Binde and Åsa Boholm in Chapter 10, with reference to a Swedish railway modernization project. In this case, which involves two Swedish towns along the route of the West Coast Trunk Line, there has been intense debate about planning options and alternative placements of the new route. In one town, the authorities – the National Rail Administration and the city council – favour a new rail tunnel, including an underground railway station right under the city centre; opponents argue that a better alternative is to relocate the railway outside the city centre. In the other town, the planning alternative favoured by authorities is to move the tracks from the current route through the city centre and to build a new station east of the town. Here opponents argue that the status quo is a better option, since a city centre without a railway station would cause economic and cultural demise: businesses and shops would close down, tourism would be negatively affected and so forth. The dynamics of the debate take the form of a rhetorical battle in which arguments and counter arguments are used by opponents and proponents in such a way that the controversy has escalated in a schismogenetic manner, cementing stronger and stronger adversarial positions.

The building of a railway tunnel through the Hallandsås in Sweden has led to environmental consequences for the local community. Although some residents living near the construction site have been financially compensated, others have also experienced threats to their quality of life. As a result, both those directly affected by the construction of the railway tunnel and other locals – rightfully or wrongfully – perceive a discrepancy between the law, as exercised by the judicial system, and justice, as a taken-for-granted intuitive moral understanding. The legal aftermath of the tunnel construction has included several trials, among which are the district court trial concerning the acrylamide leakage and the environmental court's decision on the future of the tunnel project. These two judicial institutions have dealt with quite different aspects of the tunnel project, and in Chapter 11 Ralph Heiefort argues that this differentiation of state interests into multifarious judicial domains creates ambiguities and contradictions regarding what notions such as 'fairness', 'compensation', 'responsibility' and 'accountability' mean in a specific case of facility siting.

The contributions to this volume examine the organizational logic of actors, considered not as single individuals but as members of collectives. The case studies make it clear that there can be no single explanation of conflict or, for that matter, cooperation in cases of facility siting. Facility siting is not unicausal. The subject matter is located at the very intersection of agency-structure relations involving several societal subsystems: the economy, politics and culture (Bunge, 1998). Dimensions of structure and agency should be combined, and micro-events and macro-conditions must be accounted for. Rational choice theories – the NIMBY theory of resistance is one example – have limited explanatory power. Conflicts do not arise out of 'cold, and clever calculations of expected costs and benefits' alone (Bunge, 1998, p156). Although calculation and self-interest might certainly play a role, facility siting entails many other things – beliefs, values, ideals, norms, passions and emotions, not to mention organizational dimensions – that simply cannot be explained by means of rationalistic or normative assumptions about social life (Jaeger et al, 2001).

Social life is dynamic and complex; it is situated in time and space and consists of interactions between many different actors, groups, organizations and institutions, which each have their own perspectives and viewpoints. Decision-making in such a multifarious world is seldom clear cut and one dimensional, especially since the pay-offs of decisions in real life are more often assumed rather than known beforehand (Bunge, 1998, p179). The social, cultural and political dynamics of facility siting need to be studied as a bona fide area of social science research, drawing from systemic theories in disciplines such as sociology, organization studies, social psychology, business economics, political science, social anthropology and geography. We hope that the case studies presented in this volume will contribute to a better understanding of the contextual circumstances of facility siting. These circumstances affect facility siting in terms of its historical dimensions, the relations between political, economic and legal institutions, the role of cultural factors (such as symbols, values and belief systems), communication processes and, not least, the intentional agency of involved actors or groups of actors. Each of the included studies in its own way reveals the systemic nature of facility siting, and of the related contestation evolving over time in a complex field of situated relationships including individual actors, organizations and institutions.

1 The Importance of Context in Siting Controversies: The Case of High-Level Nuclear Waste Disposal in the US

Eugene A Rosa and James F Short

Introduction

That context matters is not only one of sociology's first principles but an enduring insight into the framing of social processes. Organizational and institutional contexts, representing cultural, economic and political interests, largely determine the course of deliberations and decision-making within which public policies are forged.

Controversies related to the siting of hazardous facilities provide many examples of this principle. Because such facilities entail serious risks, understanding the multiple contexts within which associated risks are presented to stakeholders, and the manner in which they are to be assessed and managed, is critical to successful siting projects.

Cognitive psychology has demonstrated the importance of context in framing individual perceptions and judgements under conditions of uncertainty (Kahneman et al, 1982). Less well understood, although addressed by a growing research literature, are the complex and multifaceted influences of organizational and institutional contexts that frame judgement and decision-making under conditions of uncertainty – that is, in short, frame the framing (see, for example, the essays in Erikson, 1994; Cohen, 2000).

Risks associated with the siting of a high-level nuclear waste (HLW) facility and their management could hardly be more complex or more daunting. This chapter examines the multiple contexts within which controversies concerning the siting of a HLW facility in the US have occurred. Our goal is to illustrate the pivotal role played by the intersecting contexts that shape the framing of issues, the definition and engagement of social and institutional actors, and the identity and actions of stakeholders.

We first review the history of US policy with regard to disposal of HLW, beginning with identification of multiple possible sites and the later decision by the US Congress to characterize a single site, located at Yucca Mountain in the state of Nevada. This legislative history is pivotal, for it led to the involvement of major institutional actors at all levels of government (federal, state and local), as well as the involvement of engineers and scientists – increasingly called the 'fifth branch' of government – in many disciplines, and of a variety of 'publics' and organizations. Social and behavioural scientists also became involved in the controversy in a variety of roles. We discuss the nature and the function of a few of these roles, and some personal experiences with them. Finally, we discuss the 'trust conundrum': the importance of trust relationships and involvement among those with technical expertise and the institutions and organizations with the responsibility for managing risks, and the many categories of stakeholders in the assessment and management of risks. We argue that these relationships, and these *social* contexts, rather than the many technical problems associated with the problem, largely explain the failure of the US to reach a working consensus regarding the disposal of HLW.

THE US CASE: WHAT WENT WRONG?

Management of HLW is one of the most challenging technological and political problems in human history. These wastes are highly lethal for at least 10,000 years, a period of time far exceeding the dynasty of any known civilization. And no nuclear nation anywhere has developed a management programme that approaches complete success.

For more than two decades the US has wrestled with the problem of HLW disposal. Yet, after the expenditure of billions of dollars and extended debate, bitter conflict continues, even though – on 9 July 2002 – Congress overrode the governor of Nevada's veto of the repository and – on 22 July 2002 – President George W Bush signed into law the bill authorizing Yucca Mountain as the nation's sole repository. Even in the light of these events, virtually no aspect of the debate has been settled – neither the technical nor the social acceptability of the proposed repository; and controversy is certain to continue. The state of Nevada has been preparing for both legal and technical battles of the Yucca Mountain Project (YMP) for nearly two decades and has already filed a number of lawsuits. State officials expect the nuclear industry to mount a strong lobbying/public relations campaign aimed at undermining those efforts; but they feel confident that the state's position will be upheld (State of Nevada, 2002). Why such intransigency?

US policy and the Nevada response

The basic premise of the Nuclear Waste Policy Act of 1982 was that HLW disposal should be based on scientific validity, fairness and equity in all of its many phases. The act called for a science-based, competitive process that would assess the suitability of three sites (all in western US states) for deep geological storage of HLW in such a way as to ensure the health and safety of affected parties. In 1987, however, amendments to the act abandoned this scientifically competitive strategy and the assessment effort was directed solely to characterization of a single site located approximately 145 kilometres north of Las Vegas, Nevada, at Yucca Mountain. Responsibility for the effort was vested in the YMP. Subsequently, a large number of institutional actors (official agencies, laboratories and academies, policy-makers and university scientists) became involved in the programme. The 1987 act was pivotal, and these actors have, since that time, spent countless hours and billions of dollars engaging in lively, often contentious, debate related to implementation of the provisions of this legislation. Actors include the Department of Energy (DOE), the US Nuclear Regulatory Commission (USNRC), the Environmental Protection Agency (EPA), the National Academy of Science (NAS) and its research arm, the National Research Council (NRC), various congressional committees and state agencies, most notably the state of Nevada and 'affected units of local government' (including Native American Indian tribes), as well as numerous research scholars in several disciplines. Much of this activity has been documented in official, professional and privately sponsored publications. Yucca Mountain Project expenditures, and funds spent on research related to the project, now total nearly US$7 billion. Yet the project remains controversial – scientifically, politically, ethnically and morally, and its success remains very much in question.[1]

Technical analyses

Perspectives of the NRC and scientists associated with universities and the national laboratory at Sandia, New Mexico, regarding the technical merits of the YMP are reviewed in the October 1999 issue of *Risk Analysis*, the major professional journal in the field (see Bonano and Leon, 1999; Budnitz, 1999; Eisenberg et al, 1999; Hechanova and Singh, 1999; Helton and Anderson, 1999; Helton et al, 1999; Pate-Cornell Rechard, 1999; Silva et al, 1999; Thompson, 1999).[2]

The authors of these articles disagree on the best procedures for conducting performance assessment (PA) of the YMP, but agree that this type of evaluation is appropriate for assessing the adequacy of the site for HLW[3] and agree on geological sequestration as the appropriate means of disposal. This view is controversial and vigorously disputed by the state of Nevada, which charges that PA abandons existing standards for radiation exposure that have been set by regulatory agencies and by legislation. That is, PAs look at performance of individual components of the project, as well as total performance (TPA), rather than assessing particular risks – for example, radiation standards via air, water and seismic risks, compared to specific standards for radiation exposure and seismic vulnerability. Moreover, congressionally proposed radiation standards for the YMP are considerably lower than existing standards set or recommended by regulatory agencies and the NRC.

PA defenders are not insensitive to controversy associated with the YMP, including the need to ensure the competence and independence of site and programme evaluators, and to convince the public of safety issues and project acceptability. Staff authors of the USNRC, the key oversight body evaluating the safety of the repository, note, for example, that 'a fundamental issue in waste system PA is the presentation of results to decision-makers and the public in a way that is understandable and allows one to discern the key elements of the analyses (ie their *transparency and clarity*)' (Eisenberg et al, 1999, p873, emphasis added to original). The NRC Advisory Committee on Nuclear Waste (ACNW) 'believes that exposure of the public to a PA process that is made more transparent could enhance public confidence in the ability of the repository to isolate waste effectively' (Eisenberg et al, 1999, p873). Garrick and Kaplan, writing from a decision theory perspective, argue that waste disposal should be replaced by a waste management approach because it 'leaves us in control' (more about this later) and 'may break the "paralysis of analysis" syndrome and allow us to move forward in a productive and relatively economical way' (Garrick and Kaplan, 1999, p912). Precisely how this is to be accomplished is not specified; but they argue that the 'fill-and-forget' implication of a disposal perspective (the original rationale for a geological solution) should be abandoned for a waste management philosophy which 'leaves us in control', and 'incremental confirmation and confidence-building of a permanent solution to the high-level waste problem based on science, engineering, and direct monitoring and observation' should be permitted (Garrick and Kaplan, 1999, pp912–913).[4]

Nevada responds

A major source of controversy between the state of Nevada, the federal government and the scientists referenced above is precisely the increased reliance on engineered, as opposed to natural, barriers for the isolation of HLW. Engineered barriers are also a fundamental change in the approach that was specified in the 1982 and 1987 Nuclear Waste Power Acts, both of which required that safety should be ensured primarily by the natural barriers inherent in the geology of the site, with engineered barriers as back-up measures only.

The most serious technical weakness of YMP PAs, in the view of the state of Nevada, and 'the most potentially explosive aspect of the federal programme', is 'the reality that tens of thousands of shipments (over 90,000 in all) of deadly spent nuclear fuel and high-level radioactive waste will travel the nations' highways and railroads – through 43 states and thousands of communities, day after day for upwards of 40 years' (Nevada Commission on Nuclear Projects, 2000, p4). The state charges that problems associated with the transport of waste to the Yucca Mountain site have been deliberately downplayed and that funding to investigate 'most transportation activities has been suspended' and ignored 'in notices for public hearings on the draft Yucca Mountain EIS [environmental impact statement] in communities outside Nevada where such hearings were held' (Nevada Commission on Nuclear Projects, 2000, p5).

The controversy has generated a good deal of bitterness and invective, including the charge that 'science has given way to raw politics' in the YMP:

> What began in 1983 as a noble piece of federal legislation that sought to place science ahead of politics, and fairness, equity and openness above congressional parochialism has degenerated into a technical and ethical quagmire, where facts are routinely

> twisted to serve predetermined ends and where 'might makes right' has replaced 'consultation, concurrence and cooperation' as the federal mantra for the programme (Nevada Commission on Nuclear Projects, 2000; see also, Treichel, 2000).

These charges reflect geographical as well as equity concerns. A key feature of the proposed repository is its location in relation to states operating nuclear power plants and its location within the state of Nevada (including its proximity to Las Vegas and to the state capital at Carson City). These features are presented in Figures 1.1 and 1.2.

Note that the state of Nevada has no commercial nuclear facilities. As a result, lacking the benefits of nuclear electricity but being asked to sequester nuclear waste challenged the spirit of the equity and fairness principles contained in the original act.

Another controversy, as noted above, centres on the transportation of nuclear waste from the 131 storage locations in 39 states around the country to Yucca Mountain. The transportation routes, whether by truck or rail (the only two modes of transportation anticipated), span long distances and cross numerous communities throughout the nation. Nevadans are deeply concerned about accidents in the transportation of HLW. Once transportation routes are finalized there is also the potential for the many communities along those routes to become equally concerned.

The necessary initial condition for meeting the criteria and the spirit of both the 1982 and 1987 Nuclear Waste Policy Acts was that technical and social domains of HLW disposal should be properly monitored. This required the collection and analysis of appropriate empirical data. To this end, the state of Nevada sought funds from the federal government to develop a two-pronged approach to the YMP:

1 technical monitoring of the site and the programme, including transportation; and
2 development of a comprehensive on-line data system that would serve as a baseline of the economic, demographic, social, health and cultural state of affairs in Nevada, against which to measure and project economic and social change.

When available funds proved to be inadequate for the latter purpose, the Nevada Agency for Nuclear Projects chose to focus on emergency management and transportation risks, and to devote particular attention to so-called 'special effects' – that is, effects on special populations (urban, rural, retirees, native tribes, local governments) and economies (property values, tourism, gaming) in Nevada due to the siting of the repository. The latter studies focused on such matters as risk perceptions and stigma attached to HLW and the YMP, and their impacts on property values, the tourist industry, state and local governmental agencies and other aspects of Nevada life, including public acceptability of a repository.

The primary strategy of the state relied on in-house funding of transportation studies and technical monitoring, while assigning the task of conducting special

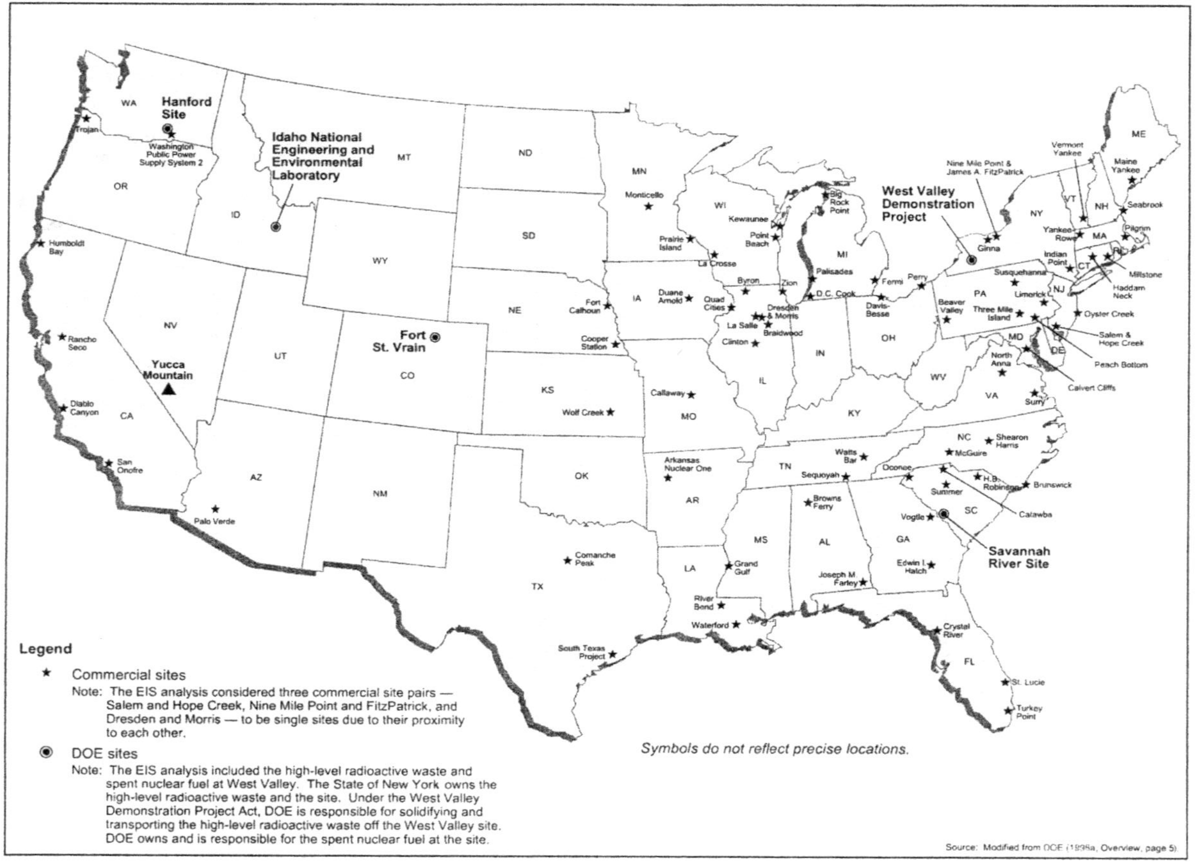

Source: State of Nevada Office for Nuclear Projects

Figure 1.1 *Location of commercial and DOE sites and Yucca Mountain*

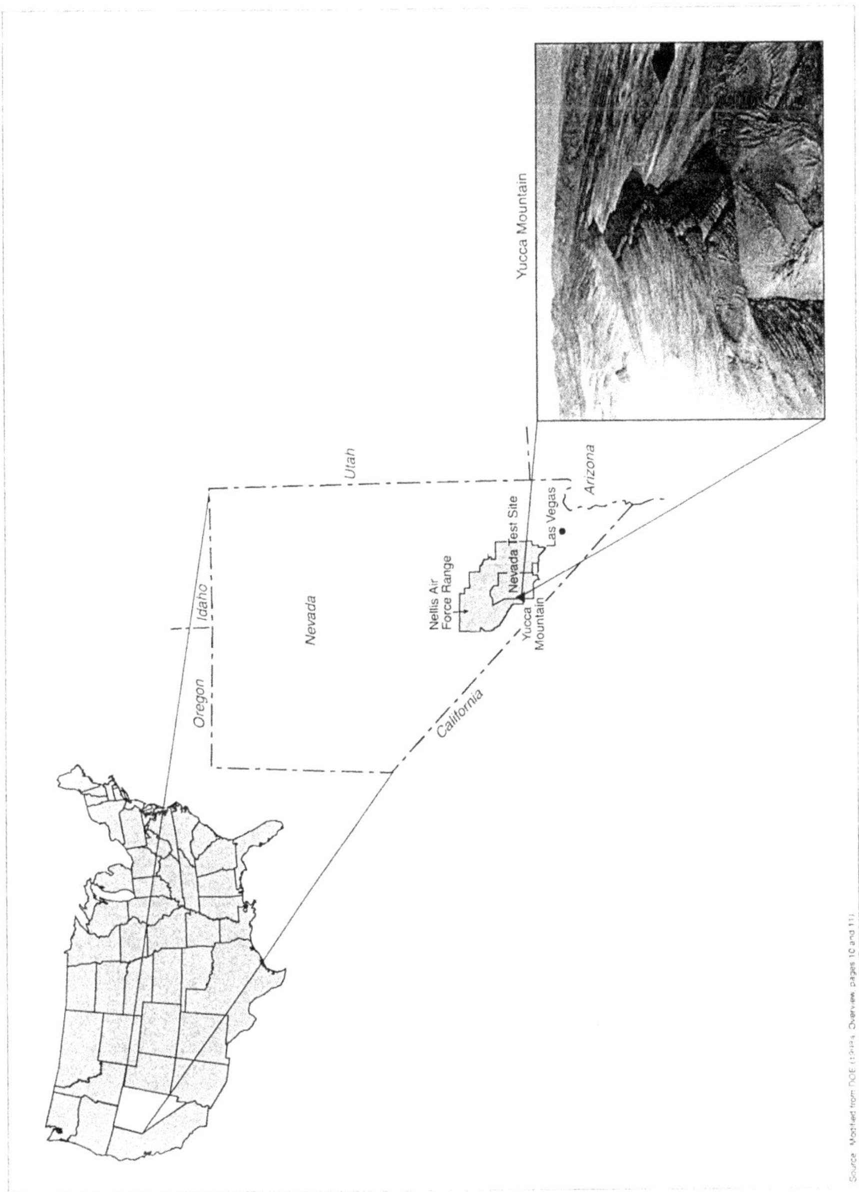

Source: State of Nevada Office for Nuclear Projects

Figure 1.2 *Yucca Mountain location*

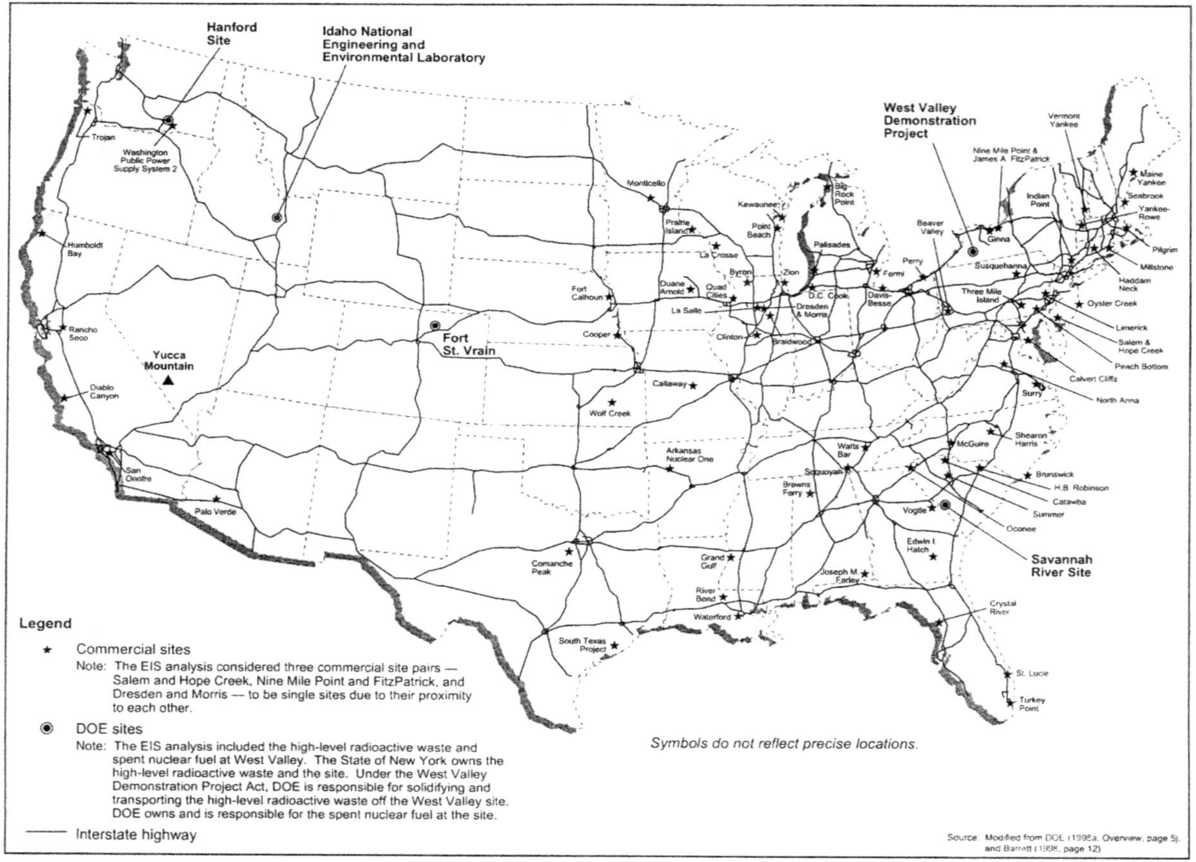

Source: State of Nevada Office for Nuclear Projects

Figure 1.3 *Commercial and DOE sites and Yucca Mountain in relation to the US interstate highway system*

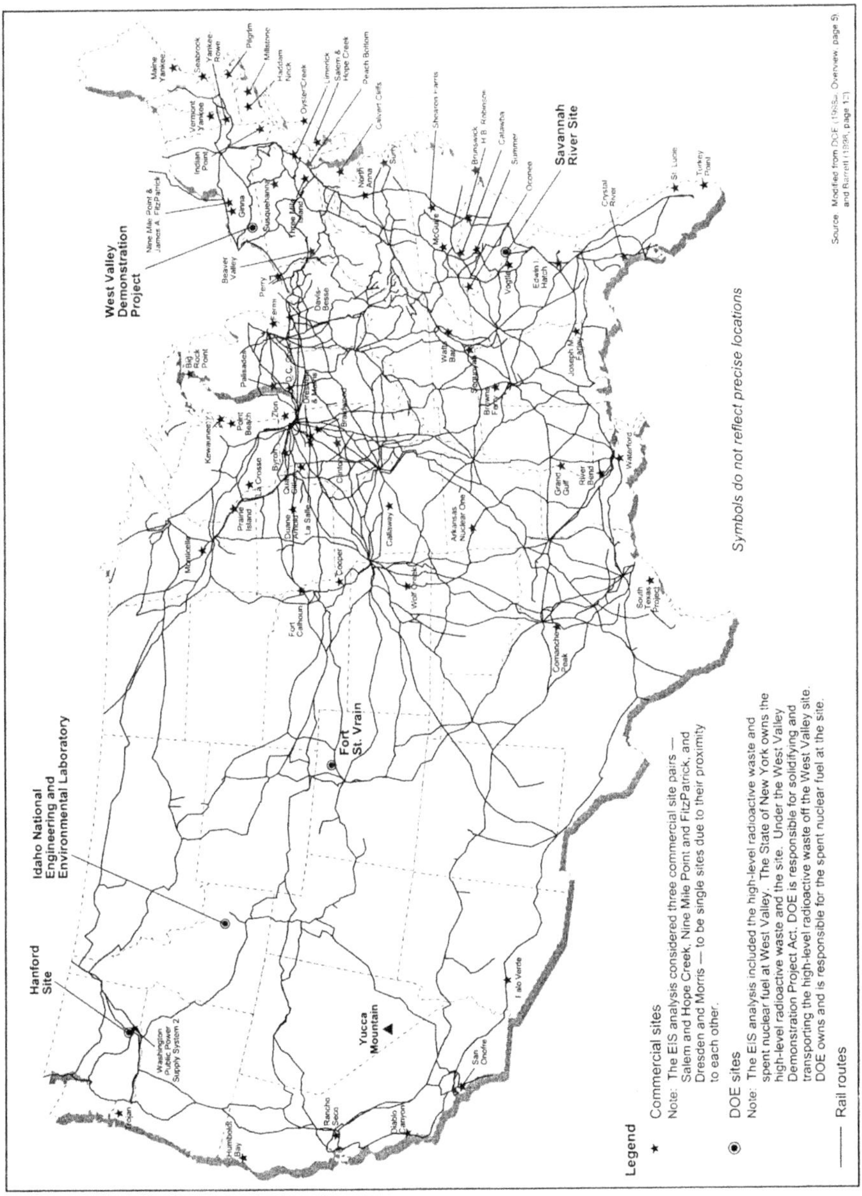

Source: State of Nevada Office for Nuclear Projects

Figure 1.4 *Commercial and DOE sites and Yucca Mountain in relation to the US railroad system*

effects research to a 'study team' of outside social scientists. This strategy yielded more than 300 reports, presentations, articles, books and chapters (Flynn et al, 1995, pxi), many of them pioneering studies of risk perceptions, possible stigma effects, the role of public trust in the acceptability of the YMP, variations in and contingencies associated with public acceptance, as well as studies of transportation and economic implications of the project.

The response of Clark County

Nevada counties followed quite different strategies from the state. Clark County, where the state's largest city and one of the most rapidly growing cities in the US (Las Vegas) is located, mounted by far the most ambitious effort.[5] The Clark County Nuclear Waste Division (NWD) was established as the official agency of the county for coordinating local efforts related to the proposed repository. Initially, the division relied largely on consultants and independent research contractors to guide a programme that was focused primarily on database development and management (such as demographic and economic characteristics, and transportation and emergency response systems) and on modelling the impacts of the YMP. Studies of social impacts were added somewhat later. At first, responsibility for most of these systems and for economic modelling, database management, emergency management, technical/environmental impacts, transportation, systems development, and socio-economic and socio-cultural areas was assigned to private contractors. As time went on, however, the NWD increasingly used the US DOE pass-through funds to build inhouse staff capability in all of these functions except for the socio-economic and cultural areas – the very areas that the growing literature on facility siting demonstrates is so crucial to success. A major effort was also devoted to coordinating databases and other activities with other institutional actors – county, city and University of Nevada Las Vegas offices.

Staff turnover proved to be a major problem for the Clark County effort – undoubtedly due, in part, to uncertain funding. Continuity suffered as a consequence and because the county was required to work with so many individual communities, including native tribes. Integration of research across areas of concern was a problem for both the state and the counties; but both continuity and integration were more problematic to the counties. The consultant 'study team' concept that was so important to the state effort was absent in the county programme.

The role of review committees

Both the state and county sought oversight by appointing review committees comprising distinguished social and physical scientists, and experts in transportation and emergency management. The state's Technical Review Committee (TRC) was created in 1986, at the same time as its study team was retained to conduct the research. The county effort did not get under way until 1991, when the US Department of Energy began funding affected units of local government, as well as the state. The TRC closely monitored study team research and met periodically with team members to discuss research findings and further research needs. Both the TRC and the study team issued reports and published independently of one another (see, for example, Erikson et al, 1994; Flynn et al, 1995).

A Peer Review Committee (PRC) – Clark County's counterpart of the state's TRC – was not appointed until spring 1991, shortly after Impact Assessment, Inc was retained as the primary contractor to carry out major portions of the research programme.[6] From the beginning, however, collaboration between PRC and the NWD funding proved to be a major stumbling block for both the state and county efforts, and in the final analysis was responsible for the demise of the TRC and, in part, of the PRC.

Not surprisingly, the state and county programmes differed considerably in the products of their efforts. The county NWD programme produced planning documents, contractor reports, and brief internal reports of staff activity that were designed for local consumption. These documents were of little interest to the broader audience of scholars, policy-makers, practitioners and others reached by the TRC and the state study team through professional publications and national news media. For the most part, this difference was to be expected since basic, often mundane, technical information is essential for planning purposes in such areas as emergency management, transportation, and economic and demographic planning. A state TRC member, in fact, first advised the county's NWD to adopt this strategy. Databases were compiled and excellent economic modelling was accomplished. The PRC was called upon to review such products mainly in the course of annual meetings.[7] However, discontinuation of the PRC after only four years of existence prevented independent evaluation of the effectiveness of its effort to involve local municipalities and county agencies. Those capabilities for managing social and economic change, and emergency preparedness – the ostensible purpose of the county's strategy – were never assessed.

For members of the PRC the experience was an extremely interesting, often frustrating, learning experience. The TRC, by contrast, met more frequently with study team members, reviewed ongoing work, and stayed together for more than a decade.

The chief frustration for social science members of the PRC was the slow pace, indeed, the reluctance, of the county programme to engage 'special effects' problems, to understand the impacts on special populations (for example, Native Americans) and other special features of the state (such as the gaming industry) – problems that were of key concern to affected publics. It was two and a half years after the PRC first met that the first such study was at last fielded. Ironically, despite the delay in getting started, studies in this area not only showed promise, but also had just begun to bear fruit when the PRC was abruptly terminated.

Surveys conducted in Las Vegas in 1993 and 1994 illustrate one of the 'social impact' studies that were fielded before termination of the PRC. The subtlety of the results, on the one hand, and their focus on organizational features, on the other, suggest their potential value for understanding such pivotal impacts. When respondents were asked in a completely open-ended fashion about problems and concerns, not surprisingly, Yucca Mountain was way down the list, behind such everyday concerns as crime, overpopulation and traffic, environmental quality and water problems. When the transportation and storage of nuclear waste were listed along with other problems, however, these concerns rose dramatically in importance. When the question was posed in terms of the next five years, HLW transportation and storage were two of the top four concerns.

One of the most promising features of Clark County's research was a focus on organizations – dominant actors in all siting decisions, but routinely ignored in the focus on individuals and on psychological factors. The study, initially with an open-ended format, sought simply to establish the nature of the membership, structures and purposes of a broad range of community organizations: environmental organizations, business organizations, service clubs, social movement organizations and others. Later, an attempt was made to examine organizational and individual members' behavioural responses to a wide range of issues, including nuclear waste transport and storage. Not surprisingly, for some organizations the Yucca Mountain was of major concern, while for others it was of only peripheral interest. However, individual members of most organizations reported that they had been, and intended to be, very active vis-à-vis nuclear matters. Based on the hypothesis that one of the best predictors of future behaviour is past behaviour, the PRC hoped to learn more about thresholds of action for both organizations and individuals, and to model sequences of perceived seriousness, as these affected individual and organizational behavioural responses to the schedule for acceptance of HLW by the Yucca Mountain Project. The goal was to move beyond measuring perceptions and stigma, which had dominated study of nuclear-related and other risks, to better understanding key social actors and processes that were more influential to outcomes – organizational behaviour, social movement activity, community mobilization and institutional-building processes.

It was not to be. In spring 1995, despite efforts to move things along, an impasse between the NWD and Impact Assessment, Inc, the primary contractor, could not be resolved and, with funding cuts looming and persistent resistance to special effects research that the PRC believed to be political in nature, the PRC chair resigned. The group was never again consulted or called together. For members of the PRC, the loss was less personal than a badly missed scientific and professional opportunity.

Withdrawal of major DOE funding in 1995 was a severe blow to both the state and Clark County. The NWD director was forced to cut his staff from about 20 to only 4 persons.[8] After two years, however, DOE funding was restored to the county (but not the state), and the staff was rebuilt. Importantly, although the gambling industry continued to resist scrutiny by researchers, the climate for research in the county was reported to have changed greatly. During the 'PRC period' (1991–1995), the director acknowledged that the division was severely constrained politically in the sorts of research that it could undertake or authorize. The PRC had been 'helpful', he reported; but he lacked the freedom to implement its recommendations. County officials and some NWD staff were resistant to studies that were recommended by the PRC – and supported by contractors.[9] Changes in county leadership and the support of sympathetic commissioners permitted new research initiatives to be undertaken in collaboration with the state. He still must 'be careful', the director reported; but the business community, including those involved in development, was now interested in the YMP and what it portended.

EXPLAINING GRIDLOCK: THE PUBLIC, ORGANIZATIONS AND INSTITUTIONS[10]

Stakeholders, the public, public opinion and public preferences are widely regarded as critical to the resolution of siting controversies. Indiscriminate use of these notions, however, often results in a great deal of misunderstanding. It is useful to know 'public opinion' and to study public attitudes towards problems or policies because such information provides one important context for debates over the legitimacy and acceptability of proposed solutions. It is quite another matter to speak of public understanding and how it relates to behaviour, or to predict how people will behave based on single – usually small – samples of general populations. No collective entity can be properly termed 'the public' if the term means an entity that perceives, apprehends, comprehends, or that will act with unity, or a reasonable degree of consensus or consistency. There are, course, many publics regarding matters of technological choice. Citizens – scientists, as well as non-scientists (scientists are hardly of one mind concerning even their own special disciplines, let alone issues concerning application of scientific knowledge and other complex social issues) – have a variety of interests and concerns – 'stakes' – that cannot be fully understood by characterizing 'public' concerns or behaviours so broadly.

Among those with special interests and concerns are 'stakeholders',[11] such as the organizations and institutions noted earlier. In addition, however, there are 'affected publics', defined simply as those persons, individually and collectively, who may be most affected by a technology, a project or a policy. Such affected publics are subspecies, as it were, of *the* public – consisting of a variety of organizations, institutions, individuals and groups who are most likely to experience untoward impacts.[12] Some of these stakeholders become directly involved in siting decisions; others do not.

Although those who become engaged might be expected to be driven solely by their special interest and ideologies, research reveals that many are neither so ill informed nor 'radical' as they are often portrayed. Freudenburg (1993) documents the surprisingly 'mainstream' nature of many of today's nuclear protesters and other groups of citizens concerned with environmental degradation, many of whom are knowledgeable, information-seeking, upstanding citizens who are eager to support solutions to complex problems that are based on reliable knowledge, with the proviso that decisions are arrived at by democratic means. Nuclear energy concerns, such as those with HLW, are neither narrowly self-centered nor primarily economically motivated (Kunreuther et al, 1990; Desvousges et al, 1993; Kempton et al, 1995). Indeed, stakeholders often expend considerable effort to increase their knowledge about topics in which they have special stakes (Couch and Kroll-Smith, 1998).[13]

Often these engaged or 'affected' publics are demographically representative of general populations; but they are distinguished from them by their activism, networking, and/or participation in social movements and social movement organizations. Because it is they who believe they are most 'at risk' – rather than the statistical aggregates of formal risk analysis – their opinions and their behaviours are especially salient to risk characterization (Shrader-Frechette, 1991; Stern and Fineberg, 1996). It follows that, when their interests and those of other affected publics coincide and when their legitimacy is sustained by wider public support, their power to effect policy and their legitimacy may be greatly enhanced, as in the case of the environmental justice movement (see Capek, 1999).

Broad consensus on values related to some social issues clearly is possible. Moreover, given the increasingly global nature of technological impacts, it is often the case that all of the world's peoples might be viewed as 'stakeholders' (Beck, 1992). This theoretical possibility is sustained by the work of Kempton and his colleagues (1995) who found a high degree of consensus on global environmental issues – ozone depletion, species loss and global warming – among people whom they interviewed. This finding is remarkable because their respondents were chosen for study as they were assumed to hold widely divergent views on environmental protection (for example, laid-off sawmill workers and Earth First! members). Kempton et al (1995, p214) argue that an environmental 'cultural consensus' has 'become integrated with core American values, such as parental responsibility, obligation to descendants and traditional religious teachings'. These findings bear significantly on technological risk problems – and on siting challenges.

Because they are rooted in networks of families, groups, organizations and institutions – and in values acquired in the course of experiences in these contexts – the concerns of affected publics are not merely the aggregated views of individuals. Behaviours, including information gathering and sharing, family protective measures, and economic and political decisions and actions, influence – and are influenced by – such connections between perceptions, attitudes, experiences and values. Actual behaviour thus remains problematic (see Clarke and Short, 1993). If, as Mary Douglas observes, 'individuals have no other way to make the big decisions except within the scope of institutions they build' (Douglas, 1986), it is no less the case that immediate, local and often mundane relationships are major influences on individual perceptions and beliefs, and that perceptions and beliefs thus acquired become part of discussions and other behaviours that impact upon networking and organizational decision-making. On a much broader scale, these processes and outcomes – in short, these social contexts – often give rise to new organizations and institutions. These social contexts and the social dynamics they embed must be understood if the goal of effective and democratic management of technological risks is to be realized.[14] They must be understood, in particular, if we are to develop a framework for the successful siting of hazardous facilities.

Reduction of uncertainty and vulnerability: The trust conundrum

As societies increasingly depend upon technical expertise and performance, acceptance of technologies, and of policies and practices of institutions, rests more and more on trust relationships between those with the expertise, the power and the responsibility for making decisions in a socially responsible way and those who are affected by such decisions (Rosa and Clark, 1999). Furthermore, with the growing gap between technological complexity, individual competence and system resiliency, social systems become more vulnerable. 'Recreancy', defined by Freudenburg (1993) as the failure of responsible agents and institutions to perform responsibly and in the common interest, lies behind much of the resistance to policy recommendations based on scientific enquiry and related technological applications. Freudenburg's study of attitudes toward a proposed low-level nuclear waste facility found that 'recreancy' variables more than tripled the amount of variance that could be explained by the socio-demographic and the ideological variables combined (Freudenburg, 1996). Howard Kunreuther and his colleagues (1990) found that trust in those who would be responsible for building and administering a high-level nuclear waste repository outweighed economic concerns – the basis of traditional cost–benefit analyses – among persons surveyed about their willingness to support such a facility in Nevada (see also Desvousges et al, 1993).

Trust relationships are complex. Building trust is more difficult than destroying it and trust, once destroyed, is difficult to restore (Rosa et al, 1993; Slovic, 1993). Yet, distrust often has positive value – for example, when it becomes the basis for greater vigilance or for fostering relationships that enhance vulnerability reduction and, ultimately, for building trust between parties with unequal resources and power to affect decisions (Heimer, 2001, p77). Carol Heimer's seminal work on solving trust problems notes that strategies based on trust work primarily by reducing uncertainty. By trusting the competency of the designers and builders of roadways, dams, bridges or nuclear facilities, anxieties regarding the safety of these hazardous facilities are allayed. Faced with intractable uncertainty – as surely is the case of HLW management – distrust, if effectively channelled, may stimulate actions that lead to more acceptable solutions – for example, by means of more systematic enquiry, and the creation of opportunities for building social relationships, organization and negotiating power.

In one of his last publications, the wise and gifted anthropologist Roy Rappaport (1996) noted that the human environmental focus of traditional risk analysis has been largely instrumental, relying on quantifiable demographic, economic, physical and social properties and activities. Beyond these, he suggested, lie other 'more general and, from the point of view of the actors, more fundamental' considerations: conceptions of morality, equity, justice and honour; religious doctrine; ideas concerning sovereignty, property, and rights and duties; aesthetic values about what constitutes quality of life; and distinctive understandings concerning nature and the place of humans within it, proper behaviour with respect to it, and equitable distribution of its fruits, its costs and its dangers.[15] At yet deeper levels, he suggested, lie assumptions about the nature of reality: what is given, what requires demonstration, what constitutes evidence, how knowledge is gained. Such loosely structured bodies of understandings and the conventions and practices they inform are what anthropologists call 'cultures' and what lay people probably mean by such phrases as 'way of life' or 'tradition' (Rappaport, 1996, pp65–66).[16]

Cultures, and the most fundamental and important values that they embody, Rappaport noted, tend to be 'low in specificity' and difficult if not impossible to evaluate quantitatively – such as in monetary terms. Given the high stakes such fundamental values hold, the most common vulnerability-reducing strategy – 'mitigation' – is, therefore, unlikely to be acceptable.

A second vulnerability-reducing strategy – 'spreading vulnerability over a series of trustees' (Heimer, 2001, p57) or over a collection of the insured, as is done with insurance policies – is also problematic. Indeed, the spread of some forms of vulnerability over multiple actors does not result in greater resiliency, but in even greater vulnerability. Traditional cultures often have been destroyed by conquest and as a result of the introduction of new diseases. A more subtle process occurs when traditional ways of life are undermined by the introduction of new technologies and their by-products (see, for example, Erikson, 1994). Although often initially welcomed, new technologies inevitably alter existing ways of life. Many traditional cultures have been destroyed in this way, leaving in their wake victims who were unaware of the stakes at issue. Accompanying the globalization of technologies, 'man-made disasters' have increased in modern and developing societies, as well, disrupting cultural patterns in many ways (Turner, 1978; Shrivastava, 1991; Capek, 1999).

Spreading vulnerability among different trustees, via insurance or government guarantees, is a common recourse in such matters and may, in some instances, be acceptable *ex post facto*, if only for the lack of an alternative. In the case of technologies such as nuclear waste, however, given the depth of the dreaded imagery associated with the word 'nuclear', such a strategy is unlikely to be successful (Weart, 1988).

Fairness, justice and equity

Scholars who have studied risk acceptability place great stress on the general value of fairness (see, for example, Rayner and Cantor, 1987; Sjöberg, 2000; Sjöberg and Drottz-Sjöberg, 2001) and on the importance of recognizing, and taking into account, local communities' conceptions of justice and equity. Ignoring these opens the way for the escalation of disagreements into principled conflict that tends to polarize issues, hindering effective communication and negotiation of the rules by which risks are to be characterized and managed.

Control

The trust/distrust puzzle is informed by research conducted on both individual and organizational levels. Surveys and case studies alike suggest that people place a high value on their ability to exercise control over risks (Slovic, 1987; Zeiss and Atwater, 1991). Asked to rate the trust relevance of hypothetical news stories about a large nuclear power plant in their community, for example, college students rated as the most trust-increasing event the creation of an advisory board of local citizens and environmentalists with authority to monitor the plant and legal authority to shut the plant down if they believed it to be unsafe (Slovic, 1993). Although the nature of this study limits its ability to generalize, the finding is consistent with survey data indicating that people tend to especially fear risks over which they have little control.

Recognizing that direct control by non-expert stakeholders over technologically complex operations is not always feasible, case studies of corporate and government agency response to stakeholder concerns suggest, nevertheless, that mutually satisfactory outcomes are possible (see Chess, et al, 1994; Leiss, 1996; Stern and Fineberg, 1996; Chess, 2001). Efforts are also underway to develop the structures and procedures for effective deliberation among contesting stakeholders (Stern and Feinberg, 1996). In the historical absence of such procedures, effective organizational responses were not given freely; rather, they typically followed threats and pressures from stakeholders, often through the political process.

The relationship between trust, values and preferences is, of course, complex. Few values rival in importance concerns over health and human survival; and these are closely tied to environmental values. Health concerns are increasingly linked to technologies that either create environmental hazards or are associated with their remediation – for example, the production and use of toxic chemicals, nuclear power and weapons, and the disposal of high- and lower-level nuclear wastes. Despite global environmental awareness (Dunlap et al, 1993) and a high level of consensus concerning environmental values, Kempton and his colleagues noted that the only utilitarian value that was held with 'real emotional force' was 'that the Earth should be preserved for our children and subsequent descendants' (Kempton et al, 1995, p223). The most deeply held values are durable and resilient, as well as low in specificity, and the manner in which they relate to policy preferences is often diffuse and varies a great deal; hence, they do not translate simply or straightforwardly into agreed-upon policies. A congruence of values does not ensure a congruence of policy preferences because the most serious disagreements – the 'devil', in common parlance – often 'is in the details'.

The debate concerning values and trust is joined by James March (1992), who suggests that society today is more and more driven by strategy, rather than by values, as attempts are made by governments and corporations to bypass or finesse the values that lie at the heart of concerns of affected publics. As a result, trust becomes a mere commodity to be employed for strategic purposes rather than a fundament of social life, as the glue for societal coordination and consensus. This appears clearly to be the case with disposal of HLW. No mechanisms have yet been devised to unravel the mutual distrust that exists among interested parties and to create trust and effective collaboration among those parties.

Legitimation and the Review Function

Returning to the Yucca Mountain Project and the state of Nevada and Clark County, both the TRC and the PRC served a legitimating function for the research and monitoring programmes of the state and the county. This was entirely proper, consistent with the spirit of the 1982 and 1987 Nuclear Waste Policy Acts, and much to the benefit of the programmes. However, mandates were ill defined, and their execution depended heavily upon offices in the state and county that were responsible for nuclear affairs. Clark County, in particular, spent a good deal of DOE money on functions that did not come within the purview of the PRC. It was unclear, for example, what the role of the committee was with respect to how funds were budgeted, and how functions that were not reviewed were carried out. Increasingly, Clark County DOE funds were spent for staff and coordinating activities with other county and municipal agencies. Although the PRC chair met occasionally with representatives of those agencies, the committee was not called upon to review such activities. Importantly, PRC members were not well versed in the 'realpolitik' of county political organization and conflict.

Throughout the existence of the PRC, political concerns within Clark County slowed and, ultimately, prevented the development of the programme of socio-cultural studies that was envisioned – and that would have met the first condition of proper implementation of the waste policy acts. Of critical importance in these studies was a special type of ethnography that Roy Rappaport called 'chronicling,' a method designed to ensure that events and reactions to them are noted in order that important perceptions and behaviors are not lost to history and enquiry. Without such data, even the most careful and comprehensive data systems may miss information that may eventually prove to be critical to emergency response, as well as official and citizen understanding and action. Often such information is known but not recorded in the course of building and maintaining databases. Yet, such shared cultural knowledge and meaning may prove crucial at some future time. At an early PRC meeting, for example, one of the contractors in attendance replied to a question about a particular agency, 'Oh, we know where all the bodies are!' One doubts, however, that the location – let alone the nature – of all the relevant 'bodies' are ever systematically recorded in databases; and perhaps they cannot be. Yet, we must be sensitive to information that, while not part of routine data collection and management, may be of critical importance when crises occur in projects of the magnitude of the YMP.

Conclusion

The urgent need for understanding the contexts within which siting controversies are engaged derives from the rapidity with which social change, driven by science and technology, creates problems that are technologically and politically intransigent. Many of these problems pose threats that extend far beyond international boundaries, some assuming global proportions. Problems deriving from unanticipated or untoward consequences of technologies seem to stretch beyond human capacities for knowing; and achieving effective and acceptable solutions present unprecedented challenges to all forms of human organization and endeavour. Even when they are technically brilliant and imaginative, scientifically based solutions often fail to gain the support of communities, governments and powerful organizational and institutional interests. Gaining such support by democratic means often seems all but impossible; yet, except under the most draconian and dystopian scenarios, democratically arrived at solutions may be the necessary condition for success. Dissension in these matters is common, not only among policy-makers, scholars and lay publics, but among scientists, as well. The issue addressed in this chapter – disposal of high-level nuclear waste (HLW) – is regarded by many as the paradigm case of low probability, high consequence and dreaded risks. As such, it provides lessons for managing risky technologies that go far beyond the particular case.

The failure to reach consensus regarding the issue of HLW disposal should come as no surprise. It has long been known that public acceptance of nuclear power and the management of its by-products, such as nuclear waste, are the sine qua non of nuclear's success as a viable technology (Freudenburg and Rosa, 1984; Dunlap et al, 1993). Numerous studies of public perceptions, attitudes and policy preferences about various facets of nuclear energy abound. The overwhelming focus of these studies has been on individual citizens – their demographic and socio-economic characteristics. Cumulatively, this body of evidence has provided a clearer picture of citizen perceptions and concerns, and its framing obviated serious examination of other units of analysis – in particular, larger social organizational and institutional processes. Virtually neglected in this literature are the institutionalized actions of affected publics via social movement activities, and the actions – or reactions – of established political and other institutions.

Our key point is that if we are ever to fully understand the emergence of gridlocked decisions over a wide variety of siting decisions, if we wish to know about the panoply of forces impinging upon the siting of nuclear waste facilities, and if we wish to inform public policies about these technological challenges, we need to better understand the processes of decision-making and implementation and the larger contexts in which they are embedded. The focus of social scientific work needs a wider lens, a conclusion sustained in a follow-up report on HLW by the National Academy of Sciences (National Research Council, 2001, p84):

> Only with a dedicated and sustained effort will social science research become a fully functioning support to the nuclear waste management process. Targets for this research should include not only public perceptions and concerns, but also the *design of improved organizations, institutions and the deliberative processes.*

Social science must broaden its purview to capture these pivotal, but largely neglected, elements of technological policy discussed in this chapter. We have attempted to illustrate the deeper purchase offered by this wider lens through examination of the actions and reactions of several key stakeholders (most notably the nuclear energy industry, the state of Nevada and Clark County), as well as powerful institutional actors (including the US Congress and the Department of Energy). Decision-making and actions by these actors, it should be clear, were instrumental forces as the implementation of the US Nuclear Waste Policy Act evolved. The stakeholders remain active. The controversy continues. And we still have much to learn about these dynamics.

2 Where Does It Go? Siting Methods and Social Representations of Radioactive Waste Management in France

Claire Mays

INTRODUCTION

A report published by the Board on Radioactive Waste Management of the US National Research Council (NRC, 2001) explored, on an international level, the continuing societal and technical challenges in the disposition of high-level radioactive waste and spent nuclear fuel. Among the principal findings were that:

> Today's growing inventory of high-level waste requires attention by national decision-makers. The feasible options now are monitored storage on or near the earth surface and geological disposition[1]; geological disposal[2] remains the only long-term solution available. Whether, when and how to move toward geological disposal are societal decisions for each country, and a stepwise process is appropriate for decision-making under technical and social uncertainty. Successful decision-making is open, transparent and broadly participatory (NRC, 2001, pp2–4).

The attempt to site facilities for the disposition of nuclear waste is often the first encounter between publics and the technical project and its proponents. Scientific uncertainties are joined abruptly by other types of uncertainty until then excluded from the paradigm (Mays and Poumadère, 1996). Siting attempts trigger or reveal controversy over the choices, implicit and explicit, that lie behind waste production and management. Finding that the biggest challenges in the management of high-level nuclear waste today appear not so much technical as societal, the NRC committee wrote that:

> Difficulties in achieving public support [for national waste disposition programmes] have been seriously underestimated in the past, and opportunities to increase public involvement and gain public trust have been missed. Most countries have made major changes in their approach to waste disposition to address the recognized societal challenges. Such changes include initiating decision processes that maintain

> choice and that are open, transparent and collaborative with independent scientists, critics and the public (NRC, 2001, pp29–30).

This chapter recalls France's response to lack of public support for plans to dispose of high-level nuclear waste (HLW) from nuclear energy production. France, in late 1991, indeed introduced a decision-making framework that officially keeps choices open and lays the basis for collaborative deliberation. However, the opportunity to involve the public, this chapter argues, has been neither fully utilized, nor even fully conceived.

This chapter recounts how France's framework law came to be, and the effects of its application. Notably, it gives the first detailed description in English of the most recent HLW facility-siting events (1999–2000). The chapter outlines civil society reactions to those events, and then places those reactions in context by reporting an interview study of general public views of radioactive waste and its management. From these juxtaposed descriptions, the chapter reflects on the role of public participation in waste management governance and offers recommendations.

The first part of this chapter describes three successive waves in siting an underground laboratory to study the feasibility of deep disposal in various geological media. Each wave used a distinct approach to gain local cooperation and acceptance.

The first wave, conducted during the late 1980s by France's Atomic Energy Commissariat (CEA) in a top-down manner, ended in public protest and failure. The legislative branch responded with a new stepwise and open-ended framework. The law voted in 1991 reorganized institutions, set milestones, created an independent review body, and provided for local consultation, dialogue and monitoring of the overall waste management process.

The second laboratory siting wave was launched by government (the prime minister and cabinet) in 1993 and was conducted by Member of Parliament (MP) Christian Bataille. This mediator relied on volunteerism and sought a 'sustainable consensus' among social and political partners in the region that would accept a lab. The five-year outcome of this bottom-up approach was one licensed site. As the law called for more than a single laboratory, however, the site search had to be renewed.

In 1999, the French government launched a third siting attempt, stipulating that the second lab would be sited in outcropping granite. Desk studies produced a map of potential host regions. The 'Granite Mission' created to implement the required public consultation had not yet contacted the regions when the map was leaked in early 2000. The revelation sparked refusal by local political actors to envision the siting, empowerment of an anti-nuclear network, and a certain paralysis of the process sketched by law. It also triggered the expression of what local civil society saw to be the risks associated with waste facilities.

The second part of this chapter characterizes general public response to radioactive waste management (RWM) issues. We present data from a qualitative study among 40 urban residents of France. We asked focus groups and individuals to 'tell us about long-lived radioactive waste'. They answered with images of radioactive waste being unmanaged, abandoned or on the road with no resting place. Interviewees consider that underground laboratories share the high risks attributed to an actual repository; that is represented as falling into disrepair within 100 years and posing a serious threat to unaware future generations. Images of industry and government or scientific authority show them to be untrustworthy.

Such views among the public may be seen as severely handicapping future siting efforts and radioactive waste management, in general. This chapter suggests that these views may, in fact, be an outcome of the role in waste management decision-making that today is offered to members of the general public. Changes in procedures are therefore necessary in order to involve stakeholders in dialogue about radioactive waste management choices, unconstrained by pressure to deliver a site.

History of high-level radioactive waste facility siting in France

France is the nation most reliant on nuclear energy. More than 75 per cent of its electricity derives from nuclear power. General de Gaulle's vision of France as a strong and independent nation in both the defence and energy supply spheres framed the creation of the CEA in 1945. The oil crisis of the 1970s sealed the decision to go 'all nuclear' and draw energy from France's domestic uranium resources. Over the years, the French government confirmed the dominance of nuclear power in national supply plans. A strong state-owned nuclear industry seeks to remain on the forefront of technological innovation, and sees progress in waste management as vital to securing approval for the development of a new generation of reactors.

Public utility Electricity of France (EdF) operates 58 nuclear reactors in France, grouped in 19 sites (see Figure 2.1). National doctrine holds that the producers are responsible for waste management up until its evacuation to an authorized installation. Each year, 1000 to 1200 tonnes of spent nuclear fuel are discharged from the EdF reactors (after about three years of furnishing energy). The spent fuel cools in water for two years at the plant site and then travels by rail to a facility operated by national nuclear fuel company COGEMA at La Hague on France's north coast. After about six more years in wet storage, the spent fuel is reprocessed to recover the plutonium and enriched uranium with remaining fuel potential (producing mixed oxide or MOX fuel, used by 20 EdF reactors). The high-level and long-lived radioactive residues from this process are vitrified. They are temporarily stored at the La Hague installation while waiting for a final storage solution.[3] Currently, some 4500 cubic metres are stored in this way (1998 figures, in Le Bars, 2000).[4] Such waste represents almost 99.5 per cent of the radioactivity resulting from all industrial, defence and medical waste sources throughout France, while representing less than 10 per cent of total annual volume (DGEMP, 2003).

The long-term management of high-level and long-lived nuclear waste is framed by France's law 91-1381 of 30 December 1991. The following section describes how this law came to be.

First phase of efforts to site an underground research laboratory

France has long had a tradition of technocracy in which a highly trained scientific elite has held responsibility both for formulating technological solutions and for implementing many decisions; the CEA is a prime example of this tradition (Jasper, 1990). This scientific elite participated in forming the international judgement by the early 1980s that the most desirable long-term management solution for HLW is permanent disposal in deep geological layers (OECD NEA, 1985).

A top-down, linear decision-making model was applied to identify a geological repository site in France. As early as 1979 France's Bureau of Geological and Mining Research (BRGM) sampled granite, schist, clay and salt deposits in a variety of locations; in 1983 the Ministry of Industry drew up a 'secret' list of potential sites. In 1987 the RWM agency Andra, formed in 1979 as a small section of the CEA, began prospecting in four western localities identified with BRGM data. The technically best-suited site would host an underground laboratory. If studies confirmed its feasibility, a final deep repository would then be built.

Andra technologists carried out an information effort meant to reassure the elected officials and inhabitants of these four localities by minimizing the question of risk, explaining the importance of the repository project (portrayed as the only possible management solution from both technical and scientific perspectives) and highlighting its value for the nation (Barthe, 2000). However, the apparent suddenness of Andra's arrival, with neither prior warning nor prior negotiation and dialogue, raised vocal objection in each locality.

Citizens' collectives were formed. In 1988, 400 armed riot police were called out to quell protest in Bourg-l'Iré, Maine-et-Loire. Large demonstrations (one gathering 15,000 individuals, according to organizers) took place in Brittany in 1989–1990. Civilian injuries occurred in confrontation with police. Recognizing a 'grave disorder', in February 1990 the prime minister declared a one-year moratorium upon RWM siting activities, during which time a range of stakeholder representatives would be consulted. He asked the Parliamentary Office of Evaluation of Scientific and Technological Choices (OPECST)[5] to gather views and then to make proposals for framing the 'conditions under which dialogue could be restored' (OPECST, 1990). After conducting hearings, MP Christian Bataille handed a report (OPECST, 1990) to government. Over the course of the next year, a RWM law was written and deliberated; it stands out as a political innovation.

Law of 30 December 1991 relating to research on the management of high-level, long-lived radioactive waste

The law of 30 December 1991 relating to research on the management of high-level, long-lived radioactive waste was the first major vote of French parliament in the nuclear domain. It marks a transition from a purely scientific and technical approach, relying upon an authoritarian decision model, to the legitimization of HLW solutions through a socially responsive decision model (Mays and Poumadère, 1996). The law shifts emphasis from evaluating designated sites to creating a 'responsible, democratic and transparent' management process (Bataille, 1994) under legislative control. The RWM agency Andra was recreated as a public enterprise, overseen by the environment, research and industry ministries and independent from waste producers. A stepwise process sketches three research paths to be conducted in parallel over a 15-year period. Andra is directed by the law to investigate 'reversible or irreversible' geological disposal by constructing at least two underground research laboratories (URLs). No waste can be placed in the laboratory. The CEA's tasks are to investigate partitioning and transmutation (advanced techniques to reduce waste volumes), and packaging and long-term interim surface (or subsurface) storage techniques.[6]

A National Scientific Evaluation Committee (CNE), including two foreign experts, performs independent annual reviews of the work by Andra and CEA. The safety regulator is the Autorité de Sûreté Nucléaire (ASN, supported by a Permanent Expert Group for Wastes and by the Institute of Radiation Protection and Nuclear Safety, or IRSN). Government (the prime minister and delegated ministers) makes interim policy decisions to spur the research process, and also issues national siting authorizations and various decrees of application. In 2006, on the basis of reports by the research partners and the CNE, the French government is to present recommended management solutions to parliament, which deliberates with input from OPECST. The national legislature will decide whether to authorize deep disposal among the alternatives studied, or (the most likely hypothesis at the time of writing) to set up further milestones.

The process framed by the 1991 law does not map out public involvement in policy-making beyond the strong role given to the national legislature. However, it does incorporate a series of guarantees meant to restore a workable relationship and foundation for trust between the implementer Andra and affected populations – or, in fact, their representatives. Two articles of the law outline mechanisms for public information and consultation.

Article 14 creates another major programme actor, the local information and monitoring committee (CLIS) set up for each URL. These committees (similar to those required since 1981 in France for all large industrial facilities) are convened by the regional prefect (state administrator). Membership is stipulated to include elected officials (including two MPs from both the national assembly and the senate), representatives of environmental protection organizations, chambers of agriculture and of labour organizations (including site worker unions) and the URL implementer. At least half of the CLIS members must be drawn from the regional and local elected bodies normally consulted in a public licensing inquiry. The CLIS is to meet at least twice a year (in practice, a smaller executive bureau meets more often) to receive progress reports; it is consulted on all URL works with incidence on the environment or the locality. Its mission typically might include monitoring URL progress through hearings with Andra personnel and other experts (the CLIS can command funds to obtain full counter-expertise and can also seize the CNE); collecting or compiling baseline environmental and public health data; competence-building through scientific lectures and visits to foreign URL sites; and providing information to local residents and the press through open meetings, printed and internet documents, and reading rooms.[7]

Article 6 of the law specifies: 'Any underground laboratory siting project must include, before any [geological prospecting], consultation of elected officials and the populations of the sites concerned, in a manner to be set by governmental decree.' The principle of consultation and dialogue was thus highlighted, but no required method was set. Furthermore, the timing of this consultation, and its precise role in decision-making, were left open – leaving two alternatives in view. Are local actors to be consulted solely after a technically driven pre-selection of potential sites? Or is dialogue to be an integral part of the pre-selection procedure itself, its results thereby shaping site-selection criteria?[8] Indeed, the two URL siting efforts conducted in France after the promulgation of the 1991 law varied on that point.

The following section describes the 1993–1998 URL siting effort (resulting in a licensed site) and the 1999–2000 attempt (resulting in crystallized opposition). The first effort relied on volunteerism and dialogue to develop firm site candidatures. The second attempt planned for local consultation only after sites had been pre-selected on 'scientific' grounds. This approach left the dialogue and deliberation process extremely vulnerable to the resentment sparked when the map of potential sites was leaked.

A new siting approach targeting socio-political feasibility: Bataille Mission

In August 1993, the French government named C Bataille, MP, OPECST member and the author of the HLW management law, as mediator for the URL site pre-selection process. He stated in an interview with *Le Monde* (14 January 1993): 'I propose to verify the geological feasibility of the projects that will be volunteered by interested regions, and not, as was done before, attempt to convince populations of the sites [pre-]selected for their geological qualities' (quoted in Bathe, 2000).

The bottom-up process organized by the Bataille Mediation Mission advertised for volunteer sites in the gazette distributed nationally to elected officials. Some 30 expressions of interest were received, not least because the project carried significant economic incentives. These included yearly funds of 5 million francs to candidate regions and the promise of 60 million francs yearly during construction and laboratory lifetime, plus infrastructure jobs and a purpose-built university technopolis. The BRGM performed a desk study to screen general geological features and narrowed the 30 pre-candidates to eight *départements*.[9] The mission conducted two-day visits to these *départements* to meet with elected officials and representatives of local unions, chambers and civil society organizations and to hear arguments for and against a URL (Bataille, 1994; see also Mays and Poumadère, 1996). These hearings were announced and given wide coverage in the local and regional press. Although any individual or group who wished could obtain an invitation to participate, and all participants saw their input recorded, the meetings were not public in the sense that any citizen might walk in off the street.

In December 1993 the mediator reported to government (Bataille, 1994) stressing the importance of regional political consensus – moreover, a 'sustainable consensus' – to make the URL project viable. Some candidates, indeed, withdrew after the mediator's local visit. On Bataille's recommendation, four candidate *départements* moved into the geological prospecting phase. The sought-for political consensus had been achieved here: the regional council presidents saw the URL project as economic manna and had rallied a significant number of local officials.[10]

Andra finally conducted surface-based geological investigations on three sites in all. The 'Vienne' site, in the *département* of the same name, was located at La Chapelle-Bâton, 50 kilometres (km) south of the city of Poitiers in central western France. The 'Gard' site at Chuslan is 40km north of Nîmes, in the south-east of France. Significantly, this site is just 7km east of Marcoule, the 'cradle' of nuclear power in France, and still home to one military and four civil installations, of which two are concerned with nuclear waste. The 'eastern' site at the village of Bure, situated on the border between two candidate *départements* (each of which benefited from the same promised funding) is located 60km south-west of Nancy. The location of these sites (along with the location of nuclear power plants, for reference) is seen in Figure 2.1.

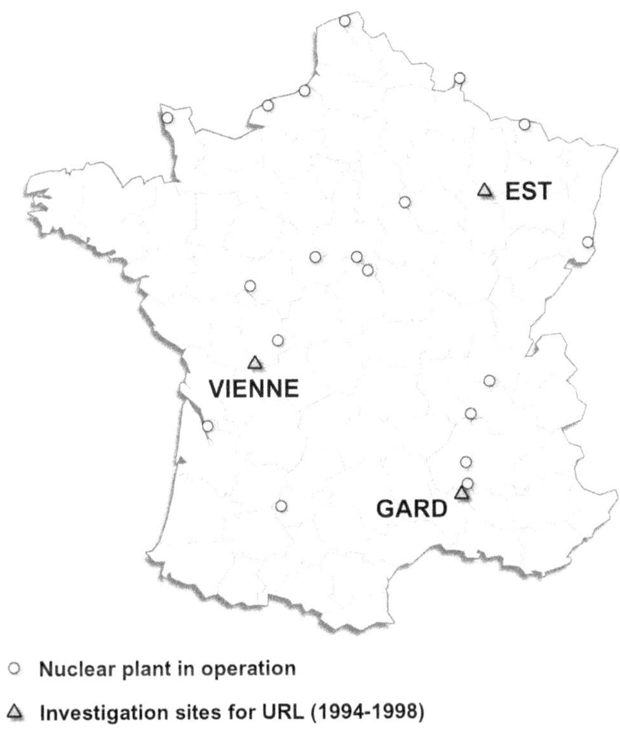

Note: dotted lines indicate *département* borders.

Source: Thierry Merceron, Andra

Figure 2.1 *Location in France of the three potential URL sites investigated by Andra (1994–1997); location of Electricity of France electronuclear production site*

Although the law calls for local information and monitoring committees to be created in association with actual URLs, the mediator recommended that CLIS – as part of the 'continuous democratic control' over the research process – be set up earlier (that is, on the three candidate sites themselves).

This first siting process framed by the 1991 law resulted in governmental authorization in December 1998 to construct a laboratory in the thick sedimentary clay formation in Bure. The two other sites were eliminated: the government rejected the Vienne site on grounds that the CNE had questioned the quality of its granite. The Gard site was also rejected, ostensibly on scientific grounds; but observers attribute its elimination to the strong opposition mounted by regional winegrowers. These feared that media focus on a waste facility would place stigma on their commercial product (Barthe and Mays, 2001[11]; NRC, 2001). The political consensus sought by Bataille had proved unsustainable here.

Transition to a new site search: Pre-selection on 'indisputable scientific bases'

The law calls for at least two URLS to deliver comparative study results to parliament. After authorizing Bure in 1998, the French government was thus obliged to launch yet another site search. Note that the socialist prime minister, in office under a conservative president, had ridden to power 18 months earlier thanks to a coalition with the Green party whose leader was now environment minister. Although her party generally was opposed to all things nuclear, and she took action to weaken the nuclear establishment, the Green minister could gracefully acquiesce to the new URL search because the law required it. It will be seen, however, that her associates were not in uniform agreement with her on this point.

In June 1999, the government asked Andra to identify potential URL sites in outcropping granite (this medium is much studied in other countries and would, ostensibly, provide contrast with the clay site at Bure). A licensable site had been found for the first URL at the price of a five-year, frankly political, process involving three regions, of which two were left disappointed: in the Gard the longtime equilibrium between wine and nuclear interests had been upset, and careful consensus-building and bargaining in the Vienne had gone to waste. Government specified that the new pre-selection must rest upon '*indisputable scientific bases*' (Merceron, 2000) in the apparent desire to create a process perceived as more efficient and less messy. This directive sparked a top-down pre-selection process, swinging back to a geological criterion to replace the socio-political feasibility and volunteerism favoured in 1993 by Bataille.

Andra used data from the BRGM and other expert input to identify areas in France theoretically appropriate for a second laboratory. Their report, including a map, was handed to the CNE in autumn 1999. It identified 15 extensive zones in granite deposits, involving a total of 16 *départements* located mainly in Brittany and central France.

Granite Mission: A doomed attempt to perform more inclusive public consultation

Even an irrefutably 'scientific' selection process could not avoid seeking local deliberation and agreement. A government decree in August 1999 created a mission to establish contact with the pre-identified regions. Andra, the decree stipulated, could not undertake the geological assessment of pre-identified sites until after the 'Granite Mission' had tendered its report to government. Three high civil servants, with experience in stakeholder dialogue but no prior service in the nuclear sector, were named to the mission in November 1999.

The plans for consultation developed by the Granite Mission took into account two criticisms earlier voiced in regard to the Bataille Mission. These concerned the role of economic incentives (seen as placing undue pressure upon poorer regions to accept siting) and Bataille's principled emphasis upon representative democracy to the exclusion of direct citizen participation.

In order to avoid any objection of 'corruption' – an accusation that had been levelled against Bataille, and later against Andra concerning local sponsorship activities[12] – the Granite Mission did not plan to discuss economic incentives or compensations. The only money spoken of was 1 million francs (approximately 150,000 euro) made available by the environment ministry to any region wishing to make a formal assessment of potential laboratory impacts.

The Granite Mission plans drew a contrast, as well, with Bataille's almost exclusive focus upon accord-making with elected representatives and civil society organizations. This focus had been criticized earlier in the context of a 1997 suit brought to the Conseil d'Etat, France's high administrative court for conflicts between citizens and the state. Some residents of the Bure URL candidate region claimed in the suit that the Bataille Mission had not performed public consultation as intended by the 1991 law. In particular, they charged, ordinary members of the public had not been sufficiently informed or involved. Minority court opinion agreed that institutions should respect what is implied when a law mandates the consultation of affected populations. Press articles and written input to the Bure 1997 licensing inquiry were cited, showing that residents interpreted the absence of the expected grassroots consultation as a 'manoeuvre and a cheat'. The local feeling was that 'the state, both government and parliament, had lied'. The minority opinion described the failure to carry out meaningful local dialogue as a sure way to 'slowly bankrupt' the credibility of state commitments (Conseil d'Etat, 1997, pp14–15).

The high court majority refused to invalidate the Bataille consultation. Nonetheless, the Granite Mission was attentive to the strong statement of the responsibilities implied by promised consultation. The ambition of the mission was to 'inform and listen', and to 'approach the population by [developing], from the beginning, the means to reach the ordinary citizen' (Granite Mission, 2000, pp10–11). The mission worked through mid February 2000 to prepare a set of explanatory materials to facilitate dialogue with laypersons about the URL and its place in RWM. It planned not only presentations to regional and local elected officials and civil society, but also to hold 'open house' appointments in town halls and local public debate meetings. The dates were to be worked out after sending to elected officials a letter including the section of the Andra map relevant to their region – annotated to explain that the map had been drawn up by geologists on purely technical criteria, and that the traditional place names attached to the granite formations did not signify that any town carrying the same name was pre-identified to receive a laboratory.

The letter and map excerpts were to be the mission's first contact with local representatives, and also the first notice to regions that they were pre-selected on geological criteria. The mission planned to send this material to the local decision-makers on 14 February 2000 before a national press conference scheduled for 21 February. However, on 27 January, these careful efforts were sabotaged: the full map was leaked by members of the environment minister's cabinet to be posted on the internet and given to the press by Sortir du Nucléaire, a national federation of local associations opposed to nuclear power.[13] The mission immediately triggered the actions they had planned for two weeks later;[14] but the letter and information materials came to local officials already aware of the map and antagonized by what appeared to be secret governmental siting manoeuvres (Granite Mission, 2000, p12; NRC, 2001, p137). Local objections and resentment were high. This sequence of events illustrates the weight of site-specific information when wielded as a scandalous revelation; moreover, it highlights the sense of outrage felt by local actors when decisions bearing on even broadly defined sites are taken without their being consulted.

The political leaders of the Vienne region, which had reached the very final stages of evaluation in the Bataille process, still entertained interest in hosting a URL despite the 1998 decision against the Vienne site. The dramatic explosion onto the public scene of the granite map, however, made it difficult for even potentially interested bodies to respond positively. High-profile political figures such as the national secretary of the Socialist party – vice-president of the Limousin regional council and a candidate for upcoming European elections – made public declarations vowing that they would never host a nuclear 'dump'. Concerned citizens formed local associations against siting a URL or a repository. Some publicly argued (for example, on internet home pages) that nuclear waste should not be buried in anyone's back yard, and that nuclear energy itself therefore should be rejected. The Sortir du Nucléaire federation, including some member associations created at the time of the very first URL siting attempts of the 1980s, found itself reinforced and empowered, interlocutor of township and regional deliberative bodies. One after another, town and regional councils passed resolutions forbidding the storage of radioactive waste on their territory (the text of these resolutions, often nearly identical, was provided by the pro-phase-out federation).

In March 2000, the Granite Mission attempted to carry out its regional visits but was met by protest and disorder. Local open-house appointments were disrupted by opponents beating on oil drums, effectively rendering all dialogue impossible. Public protest meetings, petitions and marches, supported by elected officials of both the right and left wings, mobilized up to 8000 individuals. Finally, the mission arrived at one meeting scheduled with the leaders of local environmental organizations and was informed that, as the associations' members objected to such contact, they would 'expel' the Mission from the *département* (Granite Mission, 2000, p40). The civil servants were escorted at a snail's pace over an eight-hour period by up to 3000 people lined along the road and banging upon the sides of their vehicle.[15]

Activists believed that it was important to refuse all contact and discussion with the mission so that elected people in a depressed region would not become tempted by the economic opportunity of a big infrastructure project. Despite the fact that the mission specifically excluded economic discussions from their remit, opponents met them in one place holding a 1 metre long 'wooden check' meant to represent the hollow economic promise of a laboratory. Physical risks were warned against in dramatic statements by the Green party's national spokesperson – a nuclear physicist and board president of France's national Institute for the Industrial Environment and Risks (INERIS). She toured the *départements* and reportedly described the danger of an underground repository as equivalent to '180 Chernobyls' (based on a simple comparison of the total quantities of radioactivity to be confined in a future repository, on the one hand, or released in that catastrophe, on the other hand, without consideration of the different physics relevant to the two situations).

The mission was able to spend a total of just six days visiting three regions before putting an end to its field expeditions. It attempted to continue the consultation from Paris, soliciting public comment by email or via a response card posted to local residents, holding press conferences and information sessions when invited by elected bodies. On 31 May 2000, the government decided to terminate the Granite Mission in a move called by national daily *Le Monde* a 'disavowal'.

The Granite Mission report, tendered in June 2000, surveys the concerns expressed by regional representatives. Many of the targeted regions base their development strategies on so-called 'green tourism', relying upon the rural attractions of unspoiled countryside, protected parkland, traditional customs and gustatory experiences. Up to 20,000 seasonal jobs may be found in each *département*. It was feared that the URL and possible repository would alter regional identity and image, tainting them with radiation stigma, and thus pose a direct threat to economic health. Elsewhere, objections were related more specifically to agricultural product image. In light of the recent European experience with BSE (Bovine Spongiform Encephalopathy or mad cow disease), regional officials stated, great care must be taken to avoid linking a food product (such as cheese or Cognac) with any risk of contamination.

The Granite Mission found itself perceived locally as 'selling' a preconceived decision to build a final repository. The URL siting process, and its role in a stepwise RWM research programme, received no perceptible support by government and other actors. During the period when the Mission was restricted to consulting from Paris, only opposing voices were heard in the field. The mission's report decries the 'total silence' from other actors, and the fact that 'neither [senators], nor institutions, administrations, research organizations, major [industrial actors] or scientists took the floor to deny or correct [opponents'] declarations, to complement or to illuminate the discussion: discussion [in fact] did not take place, or only exceptionally' (Granite Mission, 2000, p41). The mission condemned the silence of the national partners as destructive of the waste management programme. As well, it saw the absence of discourse explaining and supporting the programme as a disservice to citizens. The members of the public who did engage in dialogue during the local visits, and the associations and elected bodies who requested an exchange of information, bear witness, according to the mission, to the public's 'great need for knowledge and understanding' of HLW, its risks and its management in France and abroad (Granite Mission, 2000, p57).

Cleavages in Radioactive Waste Management Policy and Implementation

The URL siting efforts seen in France after the 1991 law on the management of HLW are revealing. After a bottom-up volunteer approach delivered one licensed site, the government reverted to 'scientific' siting criteria for a new search. As we will discuss below, decrees in both cases sharply restricted the scope of local consultation. These events suggest that national decision-makers at heart consider public participation and deliberation as mere accessories. This attitude results in – or is symptomatic of – a cleaved process, whereas an integrative program was sought.

The 1993 Bataille Mission experimented with an apparently open-ended process to identify candidate sites. A call for volunteers was published; the mediator had *carte blanche* to consider any region and any geological milieu in France. Only after a first set of regions had expressed interest – attracted by significant economic benefits – was any technical filter applied to selection. The subsequent process relied heavily on the mediator's political savvy. His task became to identify and develop candidatures firmly backed by a network of regional political heavyweights capable of persuading their peers. The Bataille consultation was not just the symbolic encounter between a mediator presenting a national technological project and representatives of the localities vital to its accomplishment. It was as much a move to spark conference and agreement among those actors.

The 1999–2000 effort to site a second URL was conducted in a different manner. In 1998 the government found itself at the end of an intensive five-year, three-candidate process, with only one licensed site. Another URL was needed more quickly in order to deliver comparative results to parliament before the legislated *rendez-vous* of December 2007. In the government's analysis, it may have seemed that the approach chosen by Bataille was too uncertain and inefficient. Paradoxically, the approach's strong points were its very weak points. Creating political consensus around an important socio-technical project was absolutely necessary in democracy, but had proved to be unstable or insufficient in the face of local lobbying (Gard site) or scientific uncertainty (Vienne site). The economic advantages linked to the URL project had acted as strong, attractive incentives, and yet were criticized as corrupting the decision process. The reliance upon interactions with only elected or economic representatives was both judicious (building a firewall around a hot topic) and destructive (credibility was lost with a disillusioned public).

The compromise reached by a government highly divided on nuclear issues was to call upon Science to decide. Avoiding any unpleasant suggestion of political deal-making, the pre-selection of potential candidate sites would be made on 'indisputable' scientific bases. The apparent thought was that such incontestable bases would, indeed, do away with contestation; the new URL siting process would be off to a reassuringly brisk and rational start. Securing the necessary local support would come in a second stage. The former mediator Bataille, considering that his efforts and those of regional elected officials had gone to waste, had declined to start over. It would be a relatively simple matter to ask three neutral civil servants to step in and honour the legal obligation to consult the population.

This set of arrangements indicates that government overestimated the success attained, to date, in creating a trustworthy, robust waste-management decision process. It betrays either a belief that there was sufficient social capital in the process to go forward, or a failure to recognize that social capital is built over time and must be maintained. Professing confidence in science, the government conjured the risks of a complex project nonetheless composed of scientific, technical and socio-political elements. Neglecting to carefully negotiate an agreement among the cabinet factions, and to prepare a strong public statement of the need for a second URL to manage France's energy wastes, the government sent the Granite Mission out on a wing and a prayer to attack the societal front. Sabotaged by political actors who could not accept the process, the mission crashed.

The decrees promulgated to honour the public information and consultation commitments of the 1991 law directed Bataille and the Granite Mission alike to:

> perform all useful consultation of elected officials, associations and affected populations...present the economics of the overall [URL] project...the objectives of the [laboratory] research programme, its integration into radioactive waste management policy, *the potential harmful impacts of the preliminary works prior to [URL] construction* [emphasis added] and the mitigating measures taken.

It is interesting to note how the language of decree tightly scopes the 'potential harmful impacts' submitted to consultation at this early stage of local site deliberation. This scope is limited to the simple *intrusion* of the laboratory project upon the local context. The decree limits consideration to 'preliminary works' – that is, the surface-based geological feasibility evaluations that would be undertaken at candidate sites, if agreed, by Andra. Although the Granite Mission, in particular, chose to enlarge the discussion, the decree in effect excludes the impacts of an actual URL – and of a potential future deep repository – from the scope of local dialogue. This may be seen as appropriate in that early dialogue with mediators cannot replace a future formal public inquiry, held if and when a permit application is made to construct a URL. However, with this language, the government effectively limited the *legitimacy* of local publics' concerns about the URL project, HLW management or even energy policy itself – that is, anything beyond the simple arrival of geological teams and the drilling of a few boreholes. The decree thus restricted the consultation promised by law to the most superficial level of local impact implied by the siting project.

This tight scope may be interpreted as a prudent governmental measure to prevent local dialogue from becoming the theater of discussion about RWM or energy policy overall, national issues that transcend the local scene. However, consider it in context. The required consultation appears to be tacked on to the end of what government planned in 1999 to be a 'scientific' selection process. In this light, the tight scope placed on the consultation suggests that French institutions of government, despite the landmark nature of the 1991 law, conceive of public involvement in HLW policy deliberation as neither useful nor desirable. The tight scope demonstrates that French institutions consider the local impact of policy implementation – facility siting – to be relatively minor.

The 1991 law had many qualities. It addressed the perceived need to involve a wider range of stakeholders in French RWM. It aimed for a more transparent programme and introduced stepwise decision features. Three research paths were set up to guarantee that legislators could wisely evaluate management solutions. The construction of at least two URLs would guarantee that a community, when accepting to host a lab, did not *de facto* accept to host a future repository. Provisions were made for public dialogue and consultation. The legislative branch showed confidence that these measures would succeed in bringing the programme forward (the state budget voted for Andra in 1997, indeed, reflected the assumption that *three* laboratories would be constructed). Despite the value of the law, an overview of the French experience suggests that URL siting became split off or cleaved from what was supposed to be an integrative programme.

In practice, the URL siting task was isolated from discussion of national energy policy, tacitly transformed into a predominantly economic and regional issue, and never seized as an opportunity for collective reflection on the haunting specter of environmental risk. It is perhaps because these cleavages were not recognized and addressed that France is still unable to deliver that important guarantee to the citizens and neighbours of Bure: a second URL.[16] The national need for a RWM facility has been transformed into a 'ball and chain' for a region and a headache for legislators.

Social representations of radioactive waste

After the second siting wave, the mediator's report highlighted the widespread concern that the presence of a lab could deal a heavy blow to regional tourism and commercial image. It called for a 'serious study serving as a reference' to determine the extent of any stigmatizing potential (Bataille, 1994). This reading of the situation is supported by findings in other contexts and countries: 'stigma happens' (Slovic et al, 1994; Flynn et al, 2001) and is commonly anticipated by professionals and local authorities confronted by the perspective of hosting a radioactive waste facility (see, for example, Avolahti, 1999). During the third siting wave, elected and civil society representatives also justified their rejection of a URL with this economic argument, easily read by public institutions as appropriate and legitimate. These actors argued that an underground laboratory (and a fortiori a nuclear waste repository) was incompatible with regional economic development (Granite Mission, 2000). They feared that an association between radioactive waste and a place or product would automatically discourage consumers. In making this argument, they assumed that members of the public have a strong negative reaction to radioactive waste. In this way, these actors rely upon an implicit theory of social representations.

Social representations (Moscovici, 1976, 1988) are understood as a widely shared set of beliefs and values, which function in society as a systematic and generally tacit framework for explaining events and evaluating them. Individuals and groups build such shared meanings through normal social communication. In objecting that a URL would stigmatize their region, officials and civil society organizations gave an indirect reading of social representations of radioactive waste. Their argument amounted to expressing a set of negative representations, and contributed – whether or not intentionally – to confirming and reinforcing them.

Negative social representations of HLW and management facilities have been amply demonstrated in many cultural contexts (see a review in NRC, 2001, p69). A 1993 comparative survey of representative US–French samples showed that French respondents ranked nuclear waste highest in a list of technological, natural and lifestyle risks that might affect themselves and their family, as well as the general public (Poumadère et al, 1994; Slovic et al, 2000). As in the US, waste was ranked by survey respondents as more hazardous than nuclear power plants themselves. The IRSN barometer of public perception of risks and safety finds 93 per cent of French residents as stating that they would not accept living near a radioactive waste repository site, a figure unchanged for the past ten years. Only chemical waste installations are represented in a less desirable (but closely comparable) light (Charron et al, 2002).

One way of studying social representations is to elicit discourse in interviews in the most non-directive way possible – asking individuals and groups to talk about a subject without putting words into their mouths – and then to analyse their discourse in a structured way. The rest of this section reports an in-depth qualitative study of individual and social representations of long-lived radioactive waste (Mays and Charron, 2000, 2002). Sixty-two people were interviewed in France in focus groups or individually between December 2000 and March 2001.[17] Interviews were initiated with the open question: 'Tell us about long-lived radioactive waste.' The findings reported here reflect the urban samples' representation of where and how radioactive waste may be managed. This account of *where does it go?* is drawn strictly from the representations communicated by interviewees, their views and interpretations. It is presented in order to gauge the societal context of URL siting efforts.

Our findings confirm the observation reported by the Granite Mission: HLW and the management programme set up by law in France are little known to the general public. Waste forms, packaging, transport, and the destination and destiny of long-lived wastes were all evoked by interviewees. In general, though, the life cycle of nuclear materials, and the back end of the nuclear cycle in particular, did not appear to be highly articulated in participants' minds. Few described wastes as possibly differing in their level of radioactivity or period of decay; there was little notion that varying levels of protection may be needed to handle different types of waste. Indeed, 'radioactive waste' for our interviewees appears to be an undifferentiated term for a class of industrial products synonymous with danger. In contrast, participants easily described what is done with this material: long-lived radioactive waste, according to their expressed representation, in France is managed principally through *abandonment*. As it is difficult to find and secure a storage site, they suggested, radioactive waste is constantly on the road, in transit. While interviewees cited a range of technical management methods and options, this variety itself was interpreted as confirming that no good working solution has been found.

Just as striking as their pessimistic evaluation is the fact that most interviewees were unaware of the existence of waste management institutions. France's nuclear power plants or other ill-defined 'private' enterprises are seen as the source of waste. Our interviewees reasoned that since large sums of money must be involved, the state must play a role in waste management (through regulating a lucrative services market or providing partial payment for these services). Engineers and scientists are cited as the expert parties to waste management. The La Hague reprocessing plant is cited relatively often. However, any other agency or government entity directly involved in radioactive waste management, research or regulation appears to be essentially unknown to this public. No participant had heard of the Granite Mission or the protest marches of spring 2000, less than one year earlier.

Interviewees affirmed that *abandonment* is today's most widespread method of managing long-lived radioactive wastes. This is a dominant representation, indeed, as measured by the frequency and the dramatic conviction with which it is voiced. It appears to be built upon stories – recounted locally or gleaned from the media – of radioactive or toxic wastes regularly discovered in out-of-the-way sites:

> It's hidden here and there... It's probably to be found all over [France]... They found some buried in drums, near a residential zone.
>
> [Radioactive waste] is to be found everywhere, everywhere. We realize it when they go through dumps and find radioactive things that have been put there – stuff that comes from hospitals, anywhere. It's frightening.
>
> I think it's on our doorstep and maybe it's in [our city]; it may be that there are a barrel or two of radioactive waste and we don't even know about it. There's no traceability. No one knows where they put it, how they put it, who transports it.

The view that *no solution exists* for managing radioactive wastes is well anchored and expressed in myriad ways. The diversity of methods that can be cited by interviewees only highlights the fact that managers 'don't know what to do with it':

> There is no management. They're looking for a solution and if they don't find it, we're stuck... There is no solution!

> They make a hole; they vitrify the stuff.
> It may just be that we'll give our old drums of waste to poor countries... The fuel goes to La Hague; it's stored in pools... It's poured into concrete... And then into the bottom of the ocean... Stored in old mine shafts.

The *transport* of radioactive waste, nationally and internationally, is seen as another sign of inability to manage waste or even incompetence. The fact that interviewees 'often hear of waste transport'[18] is taken as proof that managers 'don't really know where to put it':

> I'm talking about the waste that is transported from one place to another and that nobody knows what to do with.

Numerous images were cited of waste 'wandering around just about anywhere' or 'drifting over the sea':

> All in all we're tossing it back and forth to one another and we still don't have a solution.

The name of La Hague, COGEMA's nuclear fuel *reprocessing* plant and the interim surface storage site is well known thanks to frequent television documentaries. Reprocessing or 'recycling' nuclear materials, the sole 'reassuring' method discussed, is seen to diminish the chances that waste will end up 'out in the wild' or under the sea. Reprocessing and transmutation are represented in a combined solution that would lead to the total elimination of wastes (and any need for storage).

The *underground laboratory* and its role in a stepwise decision process are very little known to our interviewees. When discussed, a laboratory is represented as experimenting with actual loads of waste. Risk is seen for both laboratory personnel and for neighbouring populations, who would find themselves exposed to radioactive emanations from ventilation openings:

> Whether it's in a laboratory or anywhere else, there's no such thing as zero risk!

Since apparently no system of confinement is imaginable, the laboratory should be sited, according to participants, in an uninhabited area – for example, the polar tundra. The very nature of the experimentation would make it impossible to ethically site a URL, much less find residents who are willing to host one:

> It's unthinkable to propose to someone to put a bomb in his garden, to say to him that you're going to wait and see, that you're going to test when it might explode; it's impossible!

Deep geological disposal is identified as a management method; but the interviewees did not know whether underground repositories exist at this time. Some believed that former mines in the east of France are being reconverted for the purpose. Interviewees believed that a disposal site would become a 'banished', forbidden and rejected region.

Earthquakes, labelled as a significant risk apt to grow over time, are seen as the major obstacle to the deep disposal method. A variety of depths for geological disposal are cited, starting at 40 to 50 metres to seclude waste from terrorist access:[19]

> 40 metres of concrete above and below, and guarded by soldiers.

Other participants cited depths of 150 to 400 metres necessary to protect the environment from the inevitable 'rise' of radioactive emanations. Trees, animals and farmed foods are seen as the primary potential targets of radioactive contamination (groundwater or drinking supplies were very little mentioned).

An underground repository (like a URL) is represented as potentially explosive:

> The day it blows, it blows.

The concept of waste *retrievability* has gained prominence in disposal programmes worldwide in response to pressure by concerned publics (cf NRC, 2001, p129; OECD NEA, 2000). Participants in our study, however, discussed retrievability only as an absolutely impracticable option. They represented waste containers as completely degraded and therefore irretrievable after 10 to 100 years.

Interviewees rather frequently suggested the use of *rockets to fire waste* 'light years into space', onto uninhabited planets, the moon or the sun. Generally, this option is seen favourably; some participants foresaw regular transport toward the moon:

> It's true that not many people live up there, neither your relatives nor mine.

However, apprehension is expressed in equal measure that the waste will 'fall back down'. The metaphysical value of our satellite rules out this option for a minority:

> I'm not really attached to the moon; but even if the moon is useless, I don't want us to send waste there.

Discussion

The arguments by elected officials and by local associations against siting a URL, as reported by mediators, centre on economic and land-use planning issues and on the need to protect regional or product image. These arguments are perfectly appropriate to these actors' role and perimeter of action. The local actors responded in a symmetrical way to what they understood to be the role of the mediating missions, and couched their arguments in terms that could be read by the governmental institution. Some stipulated to the Granite Mission that national energy policy had to be discussed before looking at how to handle waste; this demand could be read, but it could not be received, and therefore brought dialogue to impasse (Mays et al, 2001).

By extension, we may hypothesize that the persons we interviewed for our qualitative study also formulated appropriate representations: perfectly adequate to their role, to their level of reflection, and to what they understood we could hear, receive and process. We called together sets of urban residents unknown to each other and asked them to talk, with very little framing aside from the words 'environment' and 'long-lived radioactive waste'. These groups responded to our demand by working up a rich, dramatic image of lack of control, extreme danger, untrustworthy managing actors (seen as motivated primarily by financial gain) and the ethical impropriety of playing the sorcerer's apprentice (Mays and Charron, 2002; Mays et al, 2003). We approached these interviewees as members of the general population – the public – and this was the expression they offered. These representations expressed in a group discussion flesh out the results often found in opinion surveys, and confirm the assumptions made by local actors who warned against stigma effects. Representations of radioactive waste as unmanageable and waste managers as untrustworthy are widespread and deeply rooted.

'Where does it go?' The interviewees told us that radioactive waste is all over the place. Abandoned or in transit, there is no 'right' place for it. Anthropologist Alf Hornborg (2001) linked these striking images of radioactive waste circulating on land or sea to that of the ship of fools set afloat by medieval society, unable to manage its alienated members within the usual confines of terrestrial social space.[20] This image is reflected in the recent garbage barges of urban New York, which floated for weeks seeking a harbour, a host site for disposal. Both images portray the societal solution of *expulsion* of that which has no place, and for which no place shall be created.

The social representations of radioactive waste bear witness to the rightness in our culture of such a solution: of all the possible accounts that could be chosen, the one that most satisfied our interviewees was this representation of radioactive waste in transit. Elsewhere, we have interpreted the Finnish parliament's decision-in-principle, which designates underground disposal as being in the good of society, as an expulsion of spent fuel deep into the Earth when it could no longer be expelled more simply to the Soviet Union (Mays, 2002). The interest expressed by members of the public for firing radioactive waste into the stratosphere reflects their understanding that this dangerous material must be expelled from the biosphere; they simply diverge with technologists who favour expulsion into the geosphere (Le Bars, 2002).

In such a context, how should a place be created for long-lived radioactive waste? Under what conditions will it become culturally right to represent waste as having or capable of finding a site, and not criminally abandoned or monstrously and uncontrollably polluting its environment? How and when can a representation develop of waste as manageable and managed?

Danger, abandonment and transit are similar, perhaps, to the representations that were encountered by Bataille and the Granite Mission in their interactions with members of the general public. These mediators, grounded in their role as legislators or public servants, representatives of public authority, diagnosed such representations as symptoms of ignorance. They voiced calls for information to adjust or 'demythologize' the social representations of radioactive waste; the Granite Mission, indeed, convened representatives of non-governmental and civil society organizations to consider how to educate and inform fellow citizens.

Before accepting 'ignorance' as a universal diagnosis and gearing up to apply only the (perhaps salutary) therapeutic of information, however, we would suggest an exploration of the role and status of the individuals who constructed and communicated such representations.

The 1991 law, it may be argued, created a status for a new set of participants in the management of radioactive waste. Decisions no longer excluded all but an elite sphere. The Bataille Mission gave a temporary new status to regional elected officials. As potential lab hosts, their role was to inform and deliberate. Other groups such as wine growers in the Gard had to forge for themselves a role as vocally objecting lobbyists.

The legal requirement for public consultation and dialogue before siting a URL offered an opportunity to involve members of the affected population. Nevertheless, the man in the street still had no official role here at all, for MP Bataille was attached to the principles of representative democracy. As mediator, he introduced the perspective of hosting a URL by clothing it in incentive, casting it as an economic project attractive to regional decision-makers, creating desire and facilitating the opening of a deliberation process. The context he constructed, however, could not see the process through to agreement in each case.

The members of the Granite Mission were sensitive to the expectation that affected publics should be involved directly in dialogue. The mission attempted to set up a context for this. Their action was received, however, not as an opportunity for deliberation but as a requirement to adapt to a foregone siting decision. The actors who adapted most quickly and responded most energetically were members of associations in favour of nuclear phase-out: individuals, we suggest, who have already worked out their representation of radioactive waste and view it as the product of an unacceptably dangerous energy source.

What role and adaptation were seen in other groups in society? What about other segments of the public who, today, when asked, express negative representations of waste – for instance, survey subjects, interviewees in focus groups or citizens inhabiting geologically appropriate regions? The persons consulted in these contexts appear to have little role or status in the RWM arena. They are 'only' voters, consumers of nuclear electricity and of mass media, and residents of France. They have no closer connection to RWM than the connection created when they are called upon suddenly by researchers or by a governmental mission to emit an opinion.

Our abrupt question to interviewees might be compared to the internet posting of the granite map in 2000, or to the arrival in French communities of Andra assaying teams during the late 1980s. The opinion voiced by our interviewees – waste is unmanaged and unmanageable – is perhaps typical, and perhaps comparable to the opinion of residents suddenly solicited to host a URL (with the difference that home place and lifestyle in the latter case are more directly placed at issue). In such a situation, one is not surprised by the adoption of a polarized, defensive, rejecting position, justified by images of unacceptable physical and social risk. Such social representations, we suggest, are at least in part a product of the RWM role consented to members of the public.

Sociologists have long studied collective representations and suggest that these symbolize the way in which a social group conceives of itself in its relationship with the objects and things that affect it (Durkheim, 1982, originally 1895). We learned from our interviews that radioactive waste is dangerous and out of control, that it belongs to unmonitored private corporations and that managers are untrustworthy in myriad ways (Mays et al, 2003). These representations might then reveal a perceived societal relationship in which the public has no control and is excluded from dialogue, learning and deciding how to control the waste.

When our interviewees talk to us about unmanageable wastes, they may be telling us about the lack of opportunity for them to assume a management role. When they state their conviction that waste is produced and managed by private corporations, they may be telling us that this activity is situated beyond their ability to intervene. When they recount scandal and outrage, they may be giving us their evaluation – how they feel about this state of affairs. When they talk to us about untrustworthy managers, they may be telling us about the absence of contexts in which they can come to view managers in any other way.

The frequency and variety of contexts in which such representations are heard (opinion surveys, in-depth interviews, local consultations) suggest that they correspond to the 'right' thing to think in our culture. Can a radically different set of relationships between RWM and the public be conceived in order to build up a new set of collective representations? Can radioactive waste lose its negative image and its potential to stigmatize? Can RWM become the object of societal cooperation? Our interviewees told us about an uncontrolled process. We suggest that getting together and talking about how to control waste might itself become a basis for building a new social relationship among participants in such a dialogue.

Change in widespread and deeply ingrained perceptions rejecting HLW management options is likely to require a process of societal discussion over many years (see Rosa et al, 1993). Up to now, however, we observe that little thought appears to have been given in France to how a broad-based discussion might take place. Public consultation and dialogue are restricted in the 1991 law to a tightly scoped phase in the overall stepwise process. In practice, there has been heavy reliance on representative bodies. The Granite Mission's attempt to involve the ordinary citizen in dialogue was sabotaged. The societal discussion sparked by that site search found no support or participation from knowledgeable national actors, experts or proponents, but raged locally among the most dramatically opposed. Deliberation is treated as the prerogative of the national parliament, and representative democracy is enshrined. Yet *being represented* in debate or deliberation is not at all the same thing as forming one's own representations, and that, this chapter argues, is key.

Callon et al (2001) explore what they call hybrid forums, the new formal or informal deliberations that today are seen to bring together social actors from many horizons to assess and manage the uncertainties associated with our technologies. They characterize the activity of these forums as generating representations of possible worlds, and choosing among them. Today, we observe that the possible worlds that have come into view during the French URL site searches do not contain representations of a shared management of the wastes of our energy consumption.

As of today, ordinary citizens in France have been invited to participate in thinking about RWM only under the pressure of accepting or rejecting a local facility. If citizens are to reconsider the view that wastes are unmanaged and unmanageable and rally to the idea of managing them, and if decisions are to be taken in concert rather than in adversity, then this set of actors may need to involve themselves at the highest level of formulating the problem – rather than considering the issues only in the pressured context of accepting a solution.

France appears to have missed the opportunity to involve publics – to spark a process of forming new societal views on what to do about HLW – despite the opening constructed with the 1991 law. This chapter's analysis of siting approaches suggests that there may have been overconfidence in the existing, top-heavy decision structure.

In 2003, the French government launched a national energy debate meant to cover the spectrum of issues. Each of seven themes was addressed using a day-long expert colloquium (open to the public and each in a different major French city) with internet reporting and access. Among the seven themes was 'Nuclear: Energy for the future or false solution?' Concerning RWM, in particular, a live 'chat' allowed citizens to pose questions to Andra directors. As in the web-based forum devoted to the general nuclear theme, interveners seemed to be well versed in their subject and the exchange relied on a technical vocabulary. The general nuclear forum, while boasting 2500 messages, came to resemble a jousting match for a very small set of radically pro- and anti-nuclear discussants.[21]

While legitimate in institutional terms, such arrangements for national debate[22] cannot be considered to spark or sustain dialogue and deliberation among a broad range of citizens. Participation in the 'debate', although theoretically open, in practice becomes restricted to persons interested and able to attend colloquia, or to read or compose and send electronic messages in an exchange rapidly dominated by technical considerations. The actual impact upon policy decision in each case is not transparent. Like media reporting or other information events, such an exercise may affect social representations about RWM. It may, in fact, reinforce the social representation that decisions are taken independently of the professed intention to consult and involve the public.

Citizens will need time to reformulate their views, and time to learn to respond to the opportunities that may be offered to deliberate. Elected representatives and policy designers themselves will need time to create and adjust to a more broadly participative model, and to accept that the outcomes of deliberation are not always those foreseen at the start. There can be more confidence in a management system that uses stakeholder discussion as an asset to build safety (Fluëler, 2003). A stepwise decision process is driven by the need to manage HLW safely and securely; but its greatest value lies in offering opportunities to create a new shared view of what that management will be in context:

> Rather than being viewed as a handicap or a threat to current progress, the structural time lapse implied for learning, for institutional revamping, and for developing the capacity to choose among uncertainties can be viewed as a valuable opportunity to build both the scientific and the societal knowledge needed to successfully manage HLW (NRC, 2001, p84).

ACKNOWLEDGEMENTS

This chapter is based on a presentation at 'New Perspectives on Siting Controversy', a seminar organized by the University of Göteborg in Glumslöv, Sweden, 17–20 May 2001. The author thanks the organizers for their invitation. The first part of the chapter draws on interviews conducted for Numark Associates Inc in 2001 with Pierre Boisson (Granite Mission), Thierry Merceron (Andra) and Rémi Portal (CNE), to whom thanks are offered. Thierry Merceron also kindly provided the map for Figure 2.1. The qualitative study reported in the second part of the chapter was performed in January 2000 with Sylvie Charron and funded by the IRSN (France's Institute of Radiation Protection and Nuclear Safety; complementary funding was obtained from the French environment ministry). All analyses are the sole responsibility of the author.

3 Institutional Thinking in Siting Conflicts: The Case of Stripa Mine

Ylva Uggla

Introduction

This chapter explores the issue of siting conflicts related to environmentally harmful activities. The analysis uses a theoretical perspective emphasizing the social origin of cognition and the significance of the institutional setting for how people perceive, experience and create knowledge of certain phenomena. The chapter focuses on how we can understand and explain the deadlocks that arise in many siting conflicts. The analysis is based on a case study of a conflict over a plan to carry out deep disposal of mercury in a community in Sweden. Both parties involved in the conflict advocate the idea of reasoning things through, and they are both frustrated by the failure to do so in this case. The analysis reveals an uncompromising conflict between two institutions based on incompatible core ideas of safety versus risk connected to epistemological concerns – that is, whether or not it is possible to predict the long-term safety of the project. The case study concludes that the institutional influence is a contributing factor in understanding the impasse of a conflict.

Modern society confronts us with complex issues involving various kinds of competence and experience. Political decisions must often be based on partially fallible knowledge, where the consequences of the decision are difficult to predict. When discussing such issues, a number of claims will be put forward, emphasizing different fields of knowledge and perspectives. As a consequence, we can observe a large number of siting conflicts involving a wide range of enterprises. The aim of this chapter is to enquire into the frequent impasse in, and severity of, some of these conflicts. These are conflicts over establishments with incalculable consequences and where the issue of environmental risk and safety is at the core.

Within risk research and risk communication, the main actors have often been conceptualized as 'lay people', on the one hand, and 'experts' on the other. Emphasis is placed on how to improve communication between these groups (see, for example, Sandman, 1989; Gutteling and Wiegman, 1996, pp6–13; Renn, 1998). Risk perception of experts and lay people, then, has been considered to be divided by objective versus subjective risk perception (see Sandman, 1989, p45; Gutteling and Wiegman, 1996, p90). From this perspective, experts' risk assessments are associated with rationality and objective criteria forecasting potential harm, while lay people's risk assessments are associated with, for example, familiarity, fairness and dread – that is, subjective and emotional aspects. The different groups' (experts' and lay-people's) perceptions or understanding of a phenomenon, then, are explained in different ways. Experts' understandings, considered to be objective risk assessments, are explained with reference to their correspondence with reality, while the understandings of lay people, or the public, are explained with reference to psychological factors or social influence. When local acceptance has not been obtained, blame has been put on public ignorance. Especially within earlier risk research and risk communication, this has led to a 'top-down' perspective, involving a desire to create a better-informed citizenry (cf Douglas, 1992, pp30–31; Irwin, 1995, pp10–14; Gutteling and Wiegman, 1996, p12; Löfstedt, 2000, p34). This static and biased account of knowledge has been criticized by others (see, for example, Irwin, 1995; Jasanoff and Wynne, 1998; Irwin et al, 1999). Instead, the attention ought to be directed towards sense-making processes and the social origin of perception and cognition.

The area of risk research which concerns social trust, public participation and communication involves, to a large extent, considerations about how to improve communication in the siting process. An underlying idea is that different options and their consequences should be comprehensively evaluated through dialogue between the parties involved. This, in turn, rests upon a view similar to Habermas's notion of the ideal situation of communication, where opinions may be modified in dialogue and where discussion will be completed by the force of the better argument (Habermas, 1996). This perspective, however, overlooks the conditions of communication. The deficient elaboration of context in this perspective ignores the importance of prior agreement on criteria for evaluation and consensus on ends. It neglects the fact that human rationality, goal-setting and interests depend upon the institutional setting (Douglas, 1987; Schwarz and Thompson, 1990, p57; cf Simon, 1997, pp92–94).

This chapter emphasizes the social origin of cognition and the importance of the institutional setting for rationality, criteria of evaluation and goal-setting. Emphasis is placed on the underlying and sometimes unseen core ideas and assumptions behind definitions brought to the issue by the respective actors. How can we understand and explain the deadlocks that arise in many siting conflicts? What are the underlying premises for actors' understandings of each other and the project, and what are the consequences? These questions will be approached using a case study of a Swedish community where there is a conflict concerning a planned deep disposal of mercury: the case of Stripa mine. This case study describes how the argumentation of the opposing parties is founded upon underlying classifications, which are upheld by different and incompatible core ideas of risk versus safety.

The following section outlines the theoretical perspective and concepts used in the analysis. The third section discusses the representation of final disposal of mercury at the national level as put forward by the Swedish Environmental Protection Agency (EPA). The Swedish EPA is the major voice expressing the national representation of final disposal of mercury in Sweden today, and its report *Final Disposal of Mercury* reveals an ambiguity in the discussion of risk and safety connected to the project (Swedish Environmental Protection Agency, 1997). The fourth section provides a short introduction to the case of Stripa. The fifth and sixth sections focus on the case study, analysing the core ideas and classifications of the parties involved in the conflict. The chapter ends with some concluding remarks.

THEORETICAL PERSPECTIVE

In *How Institutions Think* (1987), Mary Douglas draws on the work of Émile Durkheim and Ludwik Fleck to examine the social control of cognition. Douglas's theoretical project is not to find out which party is right and which is wrong in a conflict, but to ask why neither party is able to convince the other using reasoned arguments. The theoretical approach suggests an understanding of the 'selective deafness in which neither of two parties to a debate can hear what the other is saying' (Douglas, 1987, p3). The main point is to stress the social origin of individual thoughts and feelings, entailing a sense of a priori rightness of some ideas. In most case, this a priori sense of rightness, in turn, rests upon unconscious classification. Classification involves drawing boundaries between things and placing them in order of precedence. Furthermore, classification is tied to institutions that bestow sameness and identity (Douglas, 1987; Chapter 5) – that is, institutions 'in the sense of legitimized social groupings' (Douglas, 1987, p46). Douglas (1987, pp112) also refers to Durkheim's notion of sacred objects as a way of understanding how the social edifice is secured by making certain principles sacred. These sacred principles or core ideas must not be abandoned, and any attack on them will rouse emotions of defense.

Douglas (1987, p63) suggests that socially based analogies assign disparate items to classes, which, in turn, are loaded with moral and political content. One way of approaching this underlying classification is through the self-definition of the interest groups – for example, the actors involved in a conflict. A self-definition also entails a definition of others; to recognize a class of things is to polarize, exclude and draw boundaries. These classifications are often unconscious and hidden; but they nevertheless guide our thoughts, feelings and actions (Douglas, 1987; Chapter 5).

Douglas's enquiry into institutional thinking is a functional analysis that explains how certain processes reproduce, or fail to reproduce, a social whole, how solidarity and cooperation is possible, and how the institutional setting influences the individual mind. A functionalist explanation points at the necessary conditions of existence of a social whole. Such a functionalist theoretical approach is useful as long as we do not turn conditions of existence into causes and exclude the possibility of action and change (Mouzelis, 1995, p158).

This chapter focuses on how it is possible that people remain firm in their convictions in a way that obstructs attempts to generate dialogue and communication. The functional explanation of how institutions work provides an understanding of the causal power of institutions (Eriksson, 2001, p3) – that is, how an institution may influence people under certain conditions, and therefore why they act the way they do in certain situations. The causal power of the institution might be regarded as a causal mechanism that may or may not be realized, depending upon the circumstances in the specific situation (Ekström, 1993, p36). The explanation of how institutions work can contribute to an explanation of the impasse of a conflict. However, the constancy of the institution and the institutional grip upon the individual mind may vary depending upon context.

Before analysing the core ideas and classifications of the different actors involved in the conflict in Stripa, the next section describes the national representation of the suggested final disposal of mercury as promoted by the Swedish EPA (Swedish Environmental Protection Agency, 1997). In this description, emphasis is placed on the discussion of risk and safety.

Mercury disposal as a national risk discourse

In Sweden, mercury is considered one of the most harmful toxic substances to the environment (Swedish EPA, 1997, and Directive 1999, no 104) and it has recently been subject to far-reaching regulations. The current objective is to phase out the use of mercury and to ensure that it is not be recycled or exported (Swedish Code of Statutes, 1998, no 944). As a result, there is a requirement for a domestic disposal of mercury. The disposal is also critical to governmental environmental policy, which aims to achieve sustainable development and to carry out responsible handling of hazardous materials with regard to future generations (Directive 1999, no 104).

It is the responsibility of the waste owners to achieve final disposal of mercury. However, to proceed with the process, legislation compelling the mercury waste owners to carry out disposal deep in the bedrock will probably be needed (SOU, 2001, no 58, pp77). Today, the Swedish EPA, through its report *Final Disposal of Mercury* (Swedish EPA, 1997), is the major voice expressing the national representation of the meaning and consequences of the suggested mercury policy. In its report, the Swedish EPA emphasizes open dialogue, local acceptance and democratic anchorage as decisive for accomplishing the disposal of mercury deep in the bedrock (Swedish EPA, 1997, p126).

The idea of the proposed mercury waste management strategy is to detoxify the community area and establish a disposal deep in the bedrock, where nature itself provides a solid barrier (Swedish EPA, 1997, p19). As a complement a clay buffer will be used to partition off the mercury from the surroundings. 'This alternative is in harmony with nature – that is, nature itself is used as barrier and buffer; but for the sake of safety it is complemented by technical solutions to compensate our ignorance about the long-term processes that regulate the diffusion of mercury' (Swedish EPA, 1997, p49). The bedrock is supposed to provide stable surroundings for the future and function as barrier to both emissions and trespassing (Swedish EPA, 1997, pp44, 71).

Another important aspect of the proposed final disposal is to bring mercury back to a form similar to the one that occurs naturally in the bedrock. 'This, one can say, is a way of bringing mercury back to the cycle of geochemistry and to establish the final disposal in harmony with nature which will provide ground for considerable long-term safety' (Swedish EPA, 1997, p72). According to the Swedish EPA (1997, pp77–78), this conception of mercury waste management is supported by studies of natural analogies.

In the report's concluding environmental assessment, the Swedish EPA (1997, pp91–96) states that disposal deep in the bedrock – in comparison, for example, with surface disposal or the zero-alternative (doing nothing about today's situation) – is the best alternative for the environment.

One problem with deep disposal is that potential leakage cannot be controlled or properly measured. The Swedish EPA (1997, p36) states that estimates based on model calculations can indicate effects of leakage in broad outline. It is not possible to model an ecosystem over a span of 10,000 years. However, the Swedish EPA states that 'final disposal ought to be accomplished in a way that guarantees that the leakage is minor under the estimated circumstances' (Swedish EPA, 1997, p93). Likewise, the suggested deep disposal is presumed to meet the rigorous security criteria, such as limited discharge and environmental security. The former criteria imply that any discharges of mercury must not exceed the acceptable load on the surroundings, either in the short or long term. The latter criteria imply that the disposal must be sustainable even in the face of unforeseen events, including unintentional trespass (Swedish EPA, 1997, p27).

In its report, the Swedish EPA tries to convey and reconcile two inconsistent standpoints. On the one hand, the Swedish EPA expresses awareness of the problems of predicting and estimating the consequences of deep disposal of mercury. On the other hand, the proposed disposal deep in the bedrock is supposed to be safe, meeting severe long-term security requirements (10,000 years).

This ambiguity is implicit in and colours the discussion in a local community, which has been proposed by a company to be a feasible place for final disposal of mercury.

Conflict over a potential siting[1]

Stripa is a closed mine located in Storå-Guldsmedshyttan, in the Swedish municipality of Lindesberg. It is located in an old mining area, and the community has historically been linked to the ironworks, the mine and the church. The mine and ironworks probably go back to the Middle Ages. Today, the locality has approximately 2500 inhabitants, and the housing consists mainly of owner-occupied houses. During the 1970s, mining came to an end and during the period of 1977–1991, research related to final disposal of radioactive waste was carried out in Stripa mine by Svensk Kärnbränslehantering AB (SKB, Swedish Nuclear Fuel and Waste Management Company) in international cooperation.

During the early 1990s, a plan was formulated to severely limit and phase out the use of mercury in Sweden (Governmental Bill 1990–1991, no 90; Official Letter from the Swedish Parliament 1990–1991, no 338). On basis of the report *Phase Out of Our Hidden Mercury Depots* (Swedish EPA, 1993, no 4177), the Swedish government presented *Better Control over Hazardous Waste*, with proposals for further actions in the field (Governmental Bill 1993–94, no 110). This induced the owner of the closed mine Stripa Mine Service AB (the company)[2] to inform the working committee of the municipal executive board about its intention to apply to the Swedish National Franchise Board for Environmental Protection for licence to store hazardous waste in the closed mine.[3]

The plans were made known through the local press, and two weeks later, expressions of local protest appeared (*Bergslagsposten*, 2 April 1994). Since April 1994, there has been conflict between the local opposition and the company, articulated primarily in mass media through articles, letters to the local press and broadcasts on local radio. In October 1995, the local opposition formed an organization, Storå-Guldsmedshyttans miljöförening. The single aim of this group is to 'oppose and put an end to the plans of hazardous waste dumping in Stripa' (Regulations, 19 October 1995).

Incompatible core ideas: safety versus risk

In Stripa, both parties to the conflict – the company and the local environmental organization – are dedicated to their cause. Company representatives are convinced that they have such a good project that they have to carry on. For them the only legitimate reason to stop would be if the application were not authorized, while the local environmental organization has as its single aim to stop mercury disposal in Stripa. The local representative for the company stated: 'They will not give in... and we think we are right; no one will yield' (Interview, 7 February 2001), while a representative for the local environmental organization emphasized: 'There is nothing that can make me change my mind... this is some kind of instinct for self-preservation' (Interview, 23 February 2001).

The conflict in Stripa is an example of an uncompromising conflict between institutions, based on incompatible principles. These principles or core ideas must not be abandoned, and any attack on them will rouse emotions of defence.

For the company, the core idea that generates defensive feelings is the safety of the project at hand. This position is based partly on investigations using data from SKB's research period in Stripa: 'We are convinced that this is a safe and innocuous handling' (*Bergslagsposten*, 14 September 1995). The local representative (a former mining engineer and production manager) also referred to his long experience of mining: 'I know rock, and I know what the mine is like... how it is to work in a mine and how it is to do things in a mine' (Interview, 7 February 2001). Any criticism or questioning of the safety of the project arouses resistance by the company representatives, and the appropriateness of the suggested deep disposal is defended partly by a dismissal of the alternative of surface disposal.

For the local environmental organization, the core idea is the risk connected to the project, and that Stripa mine, under any circumstances, is unsuitable for deep disposal of hazardous waste. Information about a technique to stabilize mercury induced the local environmental organization to advocate a deposit close to the surface: 'Selenide [a stable form of selenium and mercury] is so stable that it can only be dissolved in aqua regia. With such a stable compound, there will be no need for disposal deep in the bedrock, as, for example, Stripa mine' (*Bergslagsposten*, 19 September 1996). The reporter then asks: if this is the case, it must be harmless to store the mercury in Stripa mine? The response from the local environmental organization is clear: even if the new technique is used, one can never be sure about the safety.

The core ideas of the company and the local environmental organization – safety versus risk – are connected to epistemological concerns, whether it is possible to predict the long-term safety of the project or not. Between institutions that refer to the same principles and core ideas, common criteria for evaluation and goals may be agreed upon through reasoning and communication (however, this must not necessarily lead to consensus). Between institutions with differing core ideas we find divergence between different rationalities; as a result, communication will generally fail. What seems reasonable to one party will seem irrational or irrelevant to the other.

For an institution to be stable, people need to acknowledge its legitimacy (Douglas, 1987, pp111). Therefore, for the institution to persist, the core ideas of safety and risk must be maintained to uphold the ideological edifice that the classifications provide. Accordingly, these core ideas are indispensable if the parties are to be dedicated to their cause. If the core ideas appear unfounded, it would be hard to sustain the classifications connected to the parties' self-definition and definition of the other party in the debate. The classifications, as is shown in the following section, include attribution of certain qualities to oneself and to the other party in the debate.

Classifications: self-definition and definition of the opposing party

Classification helps to make the world reliable, intelligible and predictable to live in, but the presumed equivalence of things cannot be recognized in the things themselves. Institutions are founded upon sameness, and they bestow sameness using socially based analogies by which disparate items are assigned to classes. The moral and political implications of those analogies lead to hierarchical dichotomies. Since one cannot be both superior and inferior within the same context, these classifications also accord priority to different qualities and abilities, while others are dismissed or deprecated.

In the debate over the potential mercury disposal in Stripa, the parties' conflict expresses underlying classifications connected to their self-definition. Likewise, these classifications give precedence to one side and deprecate the other. As a result, boundaries are drawn between what are considered to be legitimate or irrelevant aspects of the issue.

The company

Through debate, company representatives are revealed as experts, capable of dealing with and comprehending complicated matters, technology and scientific investigations, while the opposing party in the conflict, the local environmental organization, is defined as comprising lay people, ignorant of relevant aspects of the issue and without sufficient experience.

The classification connected to the self-definition of the company representatives and their definition of the opposing party in the conflict is depicted in Table 3.1.

Table 3.1 *Classification connected to the company representatives' self-definition as experts and their definition of the opposing party in the conflict as lay people*

Experts	*Lay people*
Knowledge and experience	Fallacies and ignorance
Try to reason and use matter-of-fact discussion	Irrational and emotional
Responsible	Disloyal
Follow authorities and legislation	Act on the basis of self-interest

In the debate in Stripa, company representatives express understanding of the local inhabitants' anxiety about potential mercury disposal in the mine; but this does not affect their confidence in the project or their determination to proceed with the process. According to company representatives, deep disposal of mercury is a difficult matter to understand, and the tendency to perceive things as hazardous reflects ignorance and fallacies: 'I think there is also simply ignorance... there arise some fallacies on the subject; yes, of course, it is ignorance' (Interview, 7 February 2001). The local representative also refers to the fact that some people have moved into the community: 'New people with no tradition whatsoever of mining, instead they see everything as more or less dangerous' (Interview, 7 February 2001).

Company representatives state that their aim is to be open with information and to achieve a dialogue with the local citizens. However, 'a discussion with someone who has already made up his mind cannot be meaningful' (Information meeting, 25 May 1994). The key priority for the company is to demonstrate the safety of the project, and it advocates what it calls an objective, matter-of-fact discussion. For company representatives, matters of fact mean facts that are related to the technical and scientific aspects of the discussion. The company representatives are convinced that once these facts are understood, there will be no doubt about the appropriateness of the project: 'Yes, I can understand that one feels anxious... but I think that if one familiarizes oneself with the available investigations and matters of fact, I think it will be discovered that there will be no need to feel anxious' ('Straight to the Point' Radio Örebro broadcast, 14 September 1995).

At an information meeting (25 May 1994) a company representative stated that if all matters of fact – defined as chemical, mathematical and geological facts – indicate safe conditions and someone still argues against the project, that person takes on a great responsibility (in other words, the responsibility of not embracing solutions to serious environmental problems). The company's standpoint is that it is trying to come up with solutions to difficult problems on the basis of fact and under existing legislation. In this, company representatives define themselves as reasonable and responsible, while the opposing party is defined as disloyal, acting on the basis of self-interest.

The perspective of the company representatives reveals a modernistic and science-centered view that entails a certain understanding of the relations between science, technology and the wider public, expressing a desire to create a better-informed citizenry. Therefore, aspects relevant to the local inhabitants, such as the sense of place and future representation of place, are dismissed. This entails a refusal to listen to reason outside a rather narrowly defined field, where only subjects related to technology and science count as matters of fact.

The local environmental organization

Through its position in the debate, the local environmental organization defines itself as being exploited, and as acting on the basis of its domiciliary rights and the interests of a majority, while the opposing party in the conflict, the company, is defined as the exploiter, acting strategically upon self-interest.

The classification connected to the self-definition of the representatives of the local environmental organization and their definition of the opposing party in the conflict is depicted in Table 3.2.

Table 3.2 *Classification connected to the representatives of the local environmental organization's self-definition as exploited and their definition of the opposing party in the conflict as exploiter*

Exploited	*Exploiter*
Try to reason	Act strategically
Use reasonable arguments	Not trustworthy
Domiciliary rights	Greedy
Act on the basis of the interests of a majority	Act on the basis of self-interest

Representatives of the local environmental organization agree that disposal of mercury deep in the bedrock might be the most appropriate action. However, for several reasons (for example, cracks in the rock shelter and the populated area), they find Stripa mine inexpedient for the purpose: 'It does not matter how safe they say it is. There will always be an uneasiness living on top of a refuse dump' (*Bergslagsposten*, 2 April 1994). Representatives of the local environmental organization insist that they have a good cause and are supported by a majority of people in the region: 'We got great support from the beginning…after a short while we had 1200 members' (Interview, 23 February 2001).

Like the company representatives, the representatives of the local opposition advocate dialogue and want to reason things through. However, they state that the company representatives never show up (with the exception of two information meetings in May 1994 and September 1995). The earlier expectations that the company would listen to reason have been dashed: 'The company is still determined that Stripa mine will be a waste disposal facility and has by no means adjusted to the will of the majority' (*Annual Report 1995/1996*). In this regard, the representatives of the local environmental organization express distrust of the company. They express doubt about the investigations and findings referred to by the company. Representatives of the local environmental organization also question the intentions of the company, and stress that it is a business enterprise. This contributes to doubts about how safety and environmental issues will be evaluated when it comes to adjusting to the economical aspects: 'They are very businesslike... they have also invested a lot of money in this' (Interview, 23 February 2001). The local environmental organization has also been encouraged by Miljöcentrum (a private environmental research foundation) to express its view in the mass media and 'not be confident that everything takes place in public' (Storå-Guldsmedshyttans Miljöförening Record, 4 March 1996). In the view of the local environmental organization, the company's invitation to dialogue and consultation is cosmetic, and the self-definition and the connected classification reveal a view where the company suffers from *a priori* guilt by association – that is, the objective of industry is to make a profit and this may influence all of its actions.

Representatives of the local environmental organization define themselves and the local inhabitants as objects of strategic action by an actor who cannot be trusted. This accords with research findings where people subjected to toxic risks or catastrophes defined themselves as victims and experienced mistrust of authorities, industry and subsequent fact-finding (Irwin et al, 1999; Lidskog, 2000; Ferreira et al, 2001). This view also accords with studies showing how the company and the authorities involved in a conflict were blamed for being greedy and untrustworthy (Löfstedt and Renn, 1997). This leads to an *a priori* suspicion of acts and arguments from the company in a way that obstructs dialogue.

CONCLUSION

In the Stripa conflict, both parties advocate the idea of reasoning things through, and both are sincerely annoyed over the failure to do so. However, when speaking of reasoning things through, the underlying aspiration is that the opposite party in the conflict must listen and adjust. Both parties stress that they use reasonable arguments, and both are disappointed and troubled over the fact that the other does not seem to want to listen to reason. This is a conflict between two parties with divergent classifications and core ideas; arguments appealing to reason, which are compelling to one party, will not convince or even make sense to the other party. In this course of action, company representatives draw boundaries between what ought to be considered legitimate issues in the debate and, accordingly, who is going to have a say. Representatives of the local environmental organization cast suspicion on the company representatives and their actions. They therefore draw boundaries between who is going to be considered reliable and, hence, worth listening to. The parties' classifications result in boundary-making and the connections to self-definition and definition of the opposing party in the conflict entail a clear distinction between 'us' and 'them'. This distinction implicitly summons up separate identities, such as local pride and a sense of community for local people and disembedded rationality for the company representatives (cf Irwin et al, 1999, p1321).

As mentioned, institutions do not have a deterministic or imperative force upon the individual. The explanation of how institutions work can help to explain the impasse of a conflict. However, the constancy of the institution and the institution's grip upon the individual mind may vary according to the context. The core ideas and classifications that guide the individual's thoughts, feelings and actions may be almost intact in a conflict with no new input or external imperative to go on with the process. In the case of Stripa, the situation of a pending decision might have contributed to the institutional grip upon the parties involved in the conflict and the stagnation of the debate, where the parties restate the same arguments over and over again. During the years that the conflict has lasted, there has been no external change calling for institutional adaptation to new circumstances. Furthermore, the actors involved in the conflict have clear objectives to accomplish or to halt a suggested project. As a result, the core ideas that legitimate the institutions cannot possibly be abandoned – if so, the institution would lose its purpose and justification.

The case of Stripa is an example of a conflict over an issue where the ultimate responsibility belongs to other actors than those immediately involved in the conflict – namely, the waste owners and, in the last resort, the government. These actors have so far been absent from the debate. The external contribution to the issue has come from the Swedish EPA, through its report on final disposal of mercury. However, this report does not seem to affect or challenge the core ideas and classifications of the parties involved in the conflict. The main issue and crucial point in the conflict is safety versus risk, and associated epistemological concerns – whether it is possible to predict the long-term safety of the project or not. Therefore, the local conflict seems to echo the tension between safety demands and uncertainties in calculations and management connected to proposals of final disposal of mercury at the national level, a tension manifest in the ambiguity that the Swedish EPA reveals and tries to allay in its report on final disposal of mercury. In the case of mercury disposal, the Swedish EPA advocates local acceptance as an important factor. This corresponds to the line adopted by the nuclear industry concerning final disposal of radioactive waste. By emphasizing this, decisive power is transferred from elected representatives to the local citizens and to actors such as local opposition groups. The local opponents disapprove of the imposed burden of having to deal with a national problem, which is fully possible to pass on to other actors (other sites in other municipalities that might just as well be taken under consideration).

For the moment, the issue of mercury disposal is located among actors considered to be non-political – primarily the waste owners. It is likely, however, that this political issue of mercury disposal by local opposition eventually will resurrect on the political agenda. This, in turn, may contribute to a widening of the debate and an opening for the discussion of political issues, such as how to set priorities between the conflicting values and interests that are inevitably part of the siting of a mercury waste deposit.

4 Siting Conflicts in Renewable Energy Projects: A Biogas Case Study

Jamil Khan

INTRODUCTION

Conflicts sometimes arise over the siting of renewable energy facilities. This chapter starts with a discussion on the differences and similarities in comparison with conflicts over other controversial issues, such as nuclear power plants, chemical factories and the construction of roads. The main part of the chapter is concerned with the results from a case study of a failed attempt to site a biogas plant in southern Sweden. The results show that a lack of public participation in the early stages of planning and the local residents' negative perceptions of the developer and of their ability to influence the decision contributed to opposition to the project and polarization of the conflict. The role of planning legislation in shaping processes that mitigate or accentuate conflicts is also discussed. The chapter concludes with the observation that the biogas case showed similarities to both traditional siting conflicts and other conflicts concerned with renewable energy.

Governments, industry, environmental groups and the public, in general, are all very positive in their response to the increased exploitation of renewable energy sources, which are seen as a crucial element in developing a sustainable energy system (Government bill, 2001/2002:143; Holmberg, 2000; Government bill, 1996/1997:84). At the local level, however, specific renewable energy projects can be controversial. Previous research on environmental siting conflicts has primarily dealt with technologies that have a clear negative impact on the local area and few environmental benefits, such as hazardous waste facilities, chemical factories, waste incinerators and the development of infrastructure (Lidskog, 1994; Rabe, 1994; Dorshimer, 1996; Leiss, 1996; Löfstedt, 1997).[1] The increasing exploitation of renewable energy sources calls for research into the conflicts generated by the siting of renewable energy facilities and into the ways in which such conflicts can be handled. This chapter seeks to contribute to this body of research.

This first section provides an introduction to different types of renewable energy and a discussion on differences between, and similarities to, other siting conflicts. The aim of the discussion is to outline an agenda for further empirical and theoretical research on the characteristics of siting conflicts involving renewable energy facilities. Empirical research in the form of case studies of specific renewable energy projects that have led to conflict is needed. The main part of the chapter presents the results from one such case study – that of a failed attempt to site a biogas plant in southern Sweden. The second section provides an introduction to the case, while the third and fourth sections discuss the main results. The final section presents concluding comments about the case and about its relation to other siting conflicts.

Renewable energy is the umbrella term for a heterogeneous group of energy sources (mainly bio-energy, wind power, hydro power, solar power and solar heating), which have in common the fact that they are not consumed once they are exploited, but can be replenished. They contribute little or nothing to the emission of greenhouse gases, such as carbon dioxide (CO_2), which means that switching from fossil fuels to renewable energy sources reduces the problem of global warming.

A central question concerning the siting of renewable energy facilities is whether such facilities are associated with new problems in comparison with traditional siting conflicts. First of all, it should be acknowledged that renewable energy projects are very heterogeneous and can mean anything, from the installation of a solar heating system in a single-family house to the siting of a large wind park of several megawatts. Renewable energy projects differ regarding aspects such as the scale of the facility, the risks they imply in the local area, the uncertainties in those risks, the type of ownership and the actors involved in the planning of the facility. Despite these differences, renewable energy facilities have many characteristics in common that distinguish them from the siting of other facilities, and it is useful to discuss them in general terms. Renewable energy tends to be strongly supported by public opinion, while activities such as the use of nuclear and fossil energy, the burning of waste, chemical factories and the construction of roads are often met with resistance. This has implications for the nature of local siting conflicts.

While conflicts over other facilities are often connected to the agendas and activities of established environmental organizations (Lidskog, 1994; Rootes et al, 2000; Jiménez, 2001), local opposition to renewable energy facilities is typically organized by ad hoc interest groups, consisting of neighbours and other people in the community who feel that their local environment is being threatened. The major environmental organizations have a positive attitude towards renewable energy and see it as a key factor in the development towards sustainable energy. This means that environmental organizations working at the local level are faced with a dilemma since they, in principle, support renewable energy, but, at the same time, are confronted with the worries and opposition of local communities. This dilemma was evident in a study based on interviews with representatives of local environmental organizations in different municipalities on the Swedish west coast about their views on wind power development (Böhler, 1998). All of the organizations involved wanted to see an increase in wind power in their local area; but none of them were actively working to promote it. Furthermore, they were sceptical of the large-scale exploitation of wind power. While established local environmental organizations are hesitant, new networks, as in the case of wind power, are being established that unite people who have had bad experiences in their local area and who are against the implementation of renewable energy facilities in their own areas.[2]

Since the literature on siting conflicts is primarily concerned with facilities characterized by high uncertainties and risks, work has focused on the development of appropriate methods for assessing and communicating risks. It can be argued that such a focus might be somewhat misplaced in the case of many renewable energy projects, where the uncertainties are not so pronounced and where the risks are less dramatic. For wind power, the main cause of conflict is the visual impact on the landscape, something that does not cause much uncertainty. For bio-energy and biogas plants, the uncertainties in the risks are higher, even though they cannot be compared, for example, to radioactive waste or a chemical factory. This suggests that for many projects in renewable energy generation, there would be less need to use the more elaborate and sophisticated methods of risk analysis and communication developed within the field of risk research.[3] Considering the relatively small scale of many renewable energy projects, such a strategy would often prove impossible because of the limitations on time and resources. However, we can still learn a great deal through comparisons with other siting conflicts, since some of the reasons for the development of local opposition are essentially the same and stem from worries about the effects of the facility, lack of trust in the developer and the lack of opportunity for citizens to influence the outcome of the project (Kasperson et al, 1992; Leiss, 1996). A closer look at renewable energy siting conflicts shows that, in most cases, people are genuinely worried about the possible effects of the facility and tend not to perceive the project as environmentally friendly. Regarding wind power, the visual impact on the landscape might be the most important environmental question for people who have lived for a long time in an area with an unspoiled landscape. From such a perspective, a large company wanting to build several wind turbines is not necessarily viewed as environmentally friendly and certainly not as working for the good of the local area.

The opposition against a specific project is often connected to local residents having a negative perception of the developer and of the limited opportunity they have to influence the planning process. In the discussion on the biogas case study (see 'Lessons to be learned from the case'), this chapter argues that an expert-oriented planning process which excluded public participation contributed to the development of opposition to the biogas plant and to the highly polarized conflict between the developer and the opposition group. The same observation has been made in relation to wind power projects (Wolsink, 1990; van Erp, 1996; Hammarlund, 1997). The fact that a project is concerned with renewable energy does not mean that it will be automatically welcomed by everybody, and the lessons concerning inclusive planning processes are as important here as in the siting of other facilities. The people who oppose a facility are not usually negative towards renewable energy per se, even if they are critical of the location chosen and the way in which it has been selected.[4] Bad experience with specific projects can, however, lead to a more sceptical attitude towards the technology itself. The fact that renewable energy projects tend to be small scale and are often initiated by actors at the local level increases the possibility for the economic involvement of people from the local community, which can help to create a feeling of ownership in projects and thus increase the likelihood of acceptance. The development of wind power in Denmark is a good example of the potentials of economic involvement (Brunt and Spooner, 1998; Tooke and Elliot, 2000). Even without economic involvement, the small scale of the projects may make it easier for the local population to become involved in the planning processes and to influence the decisions about the siting of a new facility.

The above discussion has touched upon some of the issues concerning renewable energy facility-siting conflicts. Further empirical research is needed to obtain a more complete picture of this matter and to answer the question of whether renewable energy constitutes a special case in siting conflicts. The remainder of this chapter is devoted to a discussion of the results from a case study, which deals with a failed attempt to site a biogas plant in southern Sweden. The findings are, of course, specific to this case and cannot form the basis of general conclusions regarding renewable energy facility-siting conflicts. They can, however, indicate interesting questions for further research.

Biogas in Lund: An introduction to the case study

In January 2000, a political majority in the municipality of Lund in southern Sweden decided to abort plans for a biogas plant outside the village of Dalby – a decision that put a stop to a planning process that had been in progress for more than four years, and that had been met by heavy local public opposition and much political hesitation. The overall purpose of this case study is to reconstruct the planning process and the interactions of the actors involved in order to understand why the siting of the facility failed. One of the main areas of interest in the study is why opposition to the project developed, and this is discussed in relation to the form of the planning process and the lack of public participation. The importance of the local residents' perceptions of the planning process and of the developer is given particular attention. The discussion also covers other aspects, such as different interpretations of the planning process and the role of relevant legislation in shaping constructive or destructive planning processes.

The empirical material for the case study consists of written documentation and interviews. The *written documentation* has been collected from various sources, such as the developer, the authorities, the opposition group and newspapers. Since the case study focused on the interaction between the key actors and on how they interpreted the planning process and the actions of other actors, interviews have been the most important source of empirical information. Eleven semi-structured interviews were carried out with different key individuals, such as representatives of the developer, members of the opposition group, municipal politicians and civil servants.

Case background

Biogas is a form of bio-energy that is derived from the digestion of organic matter, such as manure and animal and vegetable residues. The main purpose of a biogas plant is to make use of such organic waste instead of depositing it on landfills or burning it. The biogas process produces two end products:

1 biogas, which can be used to produce heat or as a substitute for natural gas in pipelines and vehicles; and
2 the digested product, which can be returned to the land and used as a fertilizer.

Biogas plants typically create concern among local communities regarding the risk of unpleasant odours.

This case study followed a failed attempt to site a biogas plant in southern Sweden. The facility was planned to be located in the municipality of Lund, 2.5 kilometres (km) away from the village of Dalby, which has around 7000 inhabitants. The planning and application process extended from 1995 to the beginning of 2000 and involved a variety of different actors. The key actors were the developer, the municipality of Lund and the local opposition group. *The developer* was the regional waste management company. The company is jointly owned by nine municipalities in south-western Skåne (the southernmost county in Sweden) and is in charge of waste disposal and recycling in the area. The developer was in charge of the planning process and made the formal application to build the biogas plant. The municipality of Lund was a central actor throughout the process and its role was rather complex. Politicians and civil servants played different roles, and the municipality's role, as a whole, varied in the different stages of the planning and application process. In short, the municipality initially worked actively to site the biogas plant in Lund, but later distanced itself from the plans and acted more as a critical authority in the application phase. At the end of the process, a political majority within the municipality voted against the project. The *opposition group* consisted of neighbouring residents, who worked actively to oppose the plans. Other significant actors were the county administration, which administered the environmental permit for the biogas plant, and the population of Dalby, where strong public opinion against the plant developed.

The key issue in the conflict was the specific location of the biogas plant and the perceived negative impact it would have on the local environment and on the people living there. The main concerns were unpleasant odour, increased traffic, adverse effects on the landscape and the fact that the use of water might affect an environmentally protected pond and the groundwater level (Letters from the public, comments by the authorities and interviews with members of the opposition group). It is difficult to judge who was right and who was wrong in the debate about environmental impact, since further studies on the suitability of the plant were blocked by a political decision. Such a judgement is beyond the scope of this chapter and would demand a detailed analysis of the different arguments and of the environmental impact assessment. However, it is possible to make a few comments.

In a study of siting conflicts, Carlman (1992) distinguishes between genuine and false conflicts of interest. *Genuine conflicts* are those where the parties agree about the actual effects of a facility but disagree about how to handle them and how serious they should be considered, while *false conflicts* occur when one of the parties has a mistaken idea about the effects of the facility. False conflicts should be possible to resolve through more information while genuine conflicts have to be resolved by other means, such as a legal decision, compensation or compromise. The picture becomes more complicated, however, when there is uncertainty associated with the effects, which allows for different interpretations and makes it unclear whether a conflict is genuine or false. Furthermore, distrust of the developer can mean that information which could potentially solve a false conflict is viewed as unreliable. The main issues of conflict in the biogas case were either genuine or fraught with uncertainty. This was also the view of the authorities involved, who called repeatedly for supplementary information before considering themselves ready to make a decision. However, several false conflicts also existed and the opposition group used some arguments that were clearly wrong or exaggerated and brought up issues that had nothing to do with the environmental impact of the facility, simply in order to discredit the project.[5]

Two phases of the planning process

The planning process for the biogas plant can be divided into two distinct phases, the early planning phase and the application phase. The *early planning phase* started in 1995 and continued until June 1998, when the first consultation meeting was held with neighbours of the chosen site. The early planning phase began as two parallel processes, where both the developer and the municipality started planning for a biogas plant. In 1996 the developer completed the first location report in which six locations in its geographical region of activity were studied. One of the alternatives was the location 2.5km outside Dalby (hereafter called the Dalby location). The report did not state whether any of the locations was better than any other and it concluded that more research was necessary to determine this (16 September 1996, Lloyd). Since politicians in the municipality of Lund were very positive towards a biogas plant, it became natural for the developer to focus on Lund in the continued planning.

The final part of the early planning was carried out as a joint planning project between the developer and the municipality and was characterized by close cooperation between the two parties. The planning was done in working groups covering issues such as the location of the plant, technology and market, the use of the biogas and cooperation with farmers (30 January 1997–1 September 1997, Memoranda from the developer). Civil servants from several of the municipal departments were involved in the working groups and the most active politicians took part in the steering group that supervised the planning process. The early planning also involved other actors who had an active interest in the project, such as farmers' organizations and the local energy company.[6] However, a striking feature of the early planning phase is that it only involved stakeholders who would benefit from the project, and therefore had a positive interest in it.

Table 4.1 *Chronology of the planning and application process*

The Early Planning Phase	
1995	Political discussions about the construction of a biogas plant start in Lund. The regional waste management company develops plans for a biogas plant somewhere within its region of activity
October 1996	The first location report is completed by the developer
1997	Joint planning between the developer, the municipality and other stakeholders occurs
Autumn 1997	The second location report is completed by the developer
The Application Phase	
June 1998	Consultation meeting with the neighbours of the site takes place
July 1998	The application is submitted. Protests start from neighbours
September 1998	An opposition group consisting of neighbours to the site and residents of Dalby is formed
November 1998	Two public meetings are held in Dalby. There is strong opposition to the project
January 1999	The authorities ask the developer for supplementary information
October 1999	The developer supplies the supplementary information
Autumn 1999	The opposition group continues its activities to stop the project, including personal lobbying of politicians
January 2000	A political majority of the planning committee decides not to allow detailed planning to take place. The project is stopped

The planning dealt primarily with technical aspects of the project and did not include a broader political discussion on issues that could be controversial, such as environmental aspects and the location of the facility. There was, for example, no working group that dealt exclusively with environmental aspects, and planning did not involve local environmental organizations. Likewise, the working group on location involved only civil servants and did not include consultations with the public or the local political representatives of the areas in which possible locations had been identified. The purpose of the working groups was not to reach a consensus that all parties would accept, although they partly served as a means of spreading information and gaining support for the project among the major stakeholders. Instead, their principle purpose was to make the planning process more efficient by including experts with different types of experience and knowledge (Interviews: 5 September 2000, Ekwall, and 27 June 2000, Tufvesson). Although the working groups involved different parties, the developer was in charge of the planning process and made the final decisions about, for example, the location of the facility. One possible reason why nothing was done to involve the public in the early planning phase, or to encourage a broad political discussion, is that the project was not seen as controversial since all political parties were positive in their response to biogas. The feeling of strong political support was expressed by the representative of the developer several times during the interview (Interview: 5 September 2000, Ekwall). At the end of 1997, the developer completed a report in which the Dalby location was declared as the chosen location and this later served as the basis for the legal application (13 October 1997, Ekwall and Lloyd).

The *application phase* started in June 1998 with the first public consultation meeting and ended in January 2000 with the political decision that put an end to the project. The biogas plant needed a permit according to the Environmental Protection Act,[7] and this application was sent to the county administration in July 1998 (16 September 1998, Sysav AB). A building permit was also needed under the Planning and Building Act and this was handled by the planning office in Lund. While the early planning phase was characterized by an atmosphere of cooperation between the developer and the municipality, the application phase was marked by a polarized conflict between the developer and the local residents.

Project developers can use different approaches towards the public when they want to site facilities that imply risks to the local area. Leiss (1996) has distinguished between three main approaches: the expert, the market and the participatory approach. In the *expert approach*, risk management and project planning are seen as strictly technical tasks, which are best carried out by experts. Public worries are considered to be due to a lack of knowledge, implying that the best way to avoid opposition is objective research and relevant and sufficient information. This approach is furthermore characterized by a disregard for public and local knowledge, which are considered irrelevant. In the *market approach*, the developer is more aware of the importance of good communication and borrows communication methods from the marketing sector. However, the underlying view is still that planning is best carried out by experts alone, which means that the public is not invited to take part in the decision-making process. The market approach, therefore, does not address the fundamental gap between the technical risk assessment of experts and the views and worries of the public. In both the above approaches, public participation is limited to information from the developer and to legally prescribed consultation, which tends to be interpreted in a restrictive way. The *participatory approach* recognizes that public trust in the developer and in the project is fundamental for public acceptance and that trust can only be based on a planning strategy that takes into account the views of the public and allows them to influence the outcome of the project. This approach is characterized by the use of deliberative methods to involve the public in planning, and often strives to go beyond what is legally prescribed.

The siting approach of the developer in the biogas project was a typical example of an expert approach. The public was not involved at all in the early planning phase, and in the application phase the only forms of public participation organized by the developer were an information meeting and legally prescribed consultation. According to the Environmental Protection Act, the developer is obliged to hold a consultation meeting before the application is submitted, with those members of the public who will be affected by the facility. The consultation meeting was held with neighbours in June 1998 and this was the first time they had any notice whatsoever of the plans. People living in the nearby village of Dalby were not invited. The meeting was held one month before the application was submitted to the county administration, and at this point the technical description, as well as the environmental impact assessment, had already been completed. The meeting was strictly informational, and although the neighbours had many questions and comments there was no possibility for these to be included in the application since it had already been completed. During the first meeting people wondered whether there would be further meetings, and the developer answered that no other informational activities had been planned (Interviews: 30 May 2000 and 6 June 2000, neighbours). Shortly after the consultation meeting, some neighbours started writing letters to the local authorities in which they criticized the plans, and when the application was submitted people in Dalby also started to raise similar questions. Soon, an opposition group with ten core members had formed, consisting of both neighbours to the site and residents of Dalby.

The members of the opposition group formed a homogeneous group of middle-class, well-educated, middle-aged or older (mostly) men (Interviews with members of the opposition group). The members of the group were very active and opposed the plans both by mobilizing public opposition and by influencing decision-makers. They wrote letters to the local newspapers, as well as formal petitions to the county administration and the municipality. They had door-to-door discussions with people in Dalby, spread flyers criticizing the biogas plant, collected signatures for a petition and organized public meetings. In response to the negative public opinion and as an effort to counter the intense informational activities of the opposition group, the developer organized an information meeting in November 1998 to which the residents of Dalby were invited. By that time, however, there was already strong public opinion against the biogas plant, which could not be swayed. The county administration was of the opinion that there was not enough information in the application to determine the environmental impact of the plant and requested supplementary information, which was submitted by the developer in autumn 1999 (1998–2000, County Administration; 30 September 1999, Sysav AB). Meanwhile, civil servants in the planning office came to the conclusion that it was necessary to make a detailed plan of the site before a decision could be made about whether to grant a building permit according to the Planning and Building Act (Interviews: 20 July 2000, Aronsson; 15 November 2000, Källqvist).[8] It was then up to the politicians in the planning committee to decide whether they would allow a detailed plan to go ahead. These developments in the application process meant that the activities of the opposition group went into a new intensive phase at the end of 1999, with more letters to the editor, formal petitions to the authorities, the attending of official meetings and personal phone calls to politicians in the environmental and planning committees. The county administration decided to call for a final consultation meeting concerning the suitability of the plant, which was to be held at the beginning of 2000. The meeting never took place, however, since a political majority of the planning committee decided, in January 2000, that they would not allow a detailed plan to be made (1998–2000, Planning Office and Planning Committee, Municipality of Lund, minutes; Interviews: 16 January 2001, Brinck; 11 January 2001, Jönsson; 1 December 2001, Wadenbäck). This meant that the project was stopped on political grounds and that the decision was not the outcome of a full legislative process.

Perceptions of the developer and the planning process

One of the important aims of the case study was to explore the reasons why opposition developed to the project and the following section provides a discussion of this issue. It is, of course, very difficult to give a full account of all the reasons behind a siting conflict and the development of opposition, and any attempt will have to focus on certain aspects and disregard others. This study focused on how people's perceptions of the developer, the planning process and their ability to influence the outcome of the project contributed to the development of opposition. Before discussing this, this section briefly discusses people's perceptions of the possible environmental impact of the facility and the risks it implied to the local community, since such perceptions played a significant role in the development of opposition.

The numerous letters to the newspapers and the authorities, and interviews with members of the opposition group, indicate that the environmental impact was at the heart of the conflict (1998–2000, Letters from the public; Interviews with members of the opposition group). Regardless of whether the criticism from the public corresponded accurately to the actual risks and possible impact of the facility, it did reflect an authentic worry, and the main issues were genuinely perceived as potential threats to the local environment and the local population. From the perspective of the activists themselves, the environmental impact was the single most important reason for their opposition. In contrast to this view, it can be noted that other biogas plants in Sweden have not created such opposition, and in comparison with some of these, the plant near Dalby would not have been in a particularly bad location. There were four farms closer than the recommended safety distance of 500 metres, and the distance to Dalby was 2.5km. Some existing plants are located much closer to residential areas. Furthermore, within the municipality of Lund, this was one of the best locations considering proximity to housing. Even though the perceived impact of the plant played an important role, there was no obvious reason why it should be seen as an unsuitable project and the chosen location was not necessarily destined to face such fierce opposition.

In the literature on risk communication and the siting of controversial facilities, the concept of trust is given a very important position, and lack of trust is stated as one of the key factors in public opposition and a major reason why it is often difficult to reach a solution that is acceptable to all parties (Kasperson et al, 1992; Löfstedt, 1999). There is a general consensus among risk researchers today that in order to gain the trust of the public regarding a project, it is important that planning processes are open and that they allow for early and substantial public participation. In this case study, we have, instead, a situation of an expert-oriented planning process with very little room for public participation and the underlying question in the following discussion is to what extent this had a negative effect on trust and thus contributed to the emergence of public opposition.

It is, of course, very difficult to determine a direct causal link between people's perceptions of the developer and the planning process, and their opposition to the project. Such a link can hardly be identified from the direct answers of respondents, and, as mentioned above, the members of the opposition group said that the only real reason for their opposition was that they were of the opinion that the plant would be harmful to the local environment. The negative perception of the developer and the planning process was not seen by them as a crucial factor in their opposition. However, when people look back on their role in a process they tend to seek logical explanations of their own behaviour which, in this case, would mean opposing the project based strictly on objective motives, and they might play down, both to themselves and to others, the significance of negative perceptions held by the developer and the planning process. The task of the researcher then becomes to try to read between the lines and interpret whether the views of developer and the planning process is of any significance, even if no causal explanation is evident. Because of these methodological complications, no attempt was made to weigh the importance of any perceived environmental impact in relation to the outlook of the developer and the planning process. Instead, it is argued that these two factors are likely to reinforce each other, which means that in a siting case where potential conflicts may arise, it becomes even more important to use planning procedures that do not exacerbate conflicts and undermine public trust.

When the neighbours were called to the first consultation meeting they did not know anything about the plans, and during the meeting there was no outright opposition to the project even when the atmosphere was tense and suspicious. The suspicion turned into a clearly negative attitude after the meeting had been held, and this change had a lot to do with the neighbours' negative perception of the developer and the way in which the project was being handled. There was a perception that the developer wanted to carry out the application process with as little public contact as possible, and that the information given was neither comprehensive nor objective:

> They told us rather clearly that they had arranged this consultation meeting in order to fulfil the requirements of the law. We asked if they planned a further information meeting in Dalby and they said no, and that they had fulfilled the requirements placed on them. The purpose of the meeting was not to inform us or to hold a consultation with neighbours or those who saw themselves as being affected; it was that such a meeting had to be held. So they did (Interview: 30 May 2000, neighbour).

The impression of skewed information continued throughout the whole process. Both the opposition group and the authorities asked for supplementary information on several issues, which fed people's suspicions that the developer could be holding back information or did not itself have the required knowledge to begin with.

Apart from dissatisfaction with the information, there was an impression at the first meeting that the developer's representatives had difficulties in answering questions about the project and, in particular, that they did not have good knowledge of the local conditions of the site – for example, how the facility would affect the groundwater and a nearby environmentally protected pond (Interviews: 30 May 2000 and 6 June 2000, neighbours). The perception that the developer did not have enough knowledge about the specific conditions at the site was especially important since the crucial controversy was over the location itself. It may well have reinforced the impression of a big company 'from outside' building a facility in the local area without knowing or caring about how it might affect the people living there. The members of the opposition group acknowledged that their view of the developer's competence improved as the process went on, and they also expressed respect for the competence and professionalism of the consultant appointed by the developer, who had written the technical and environmental report. However, the work of the consultant was, ultimately, seen as depending upon the motives of the developer, and their respect for his competence could not compensate for the lack of trust in the developer.

Another important perception that affected the attitude towards the project was that the developer acted as if the real decision had already been made and that there was no point in trying to do anything about it:

> At the consultation meeting they presented completed plans and they even said when building was going to start and when the plant would be ready, before the application had been sent to the authorities. So the fact that it was going through the county administration and the environmental committee was really just a formality (Interview: 30 May 2000, neighbour).

The main conflict was about the specific location of the biogas plant, and one issue that greatly affected public trust in the developer was how the decision regarding the site's location had been made. There was suspicion among the opposition members that the site was chosen simply because the developer had found a farm property for sale, that the location report was basically made after the site had been chosen, and that the report was manipulated in order to show that the selected site was ideal. A closer scrutiny of the planning process shows that this suspicion was unfounded and it is clear that the location decision was based on a great deal of prior analysis.[9] However, a few critical issues regarding the location decision fuelled people's suspicions. First, there was some confusion about the alternative locations that had been investigated in the first location study, but which were not presented in the application to the county administration. The alternative locations had advantages concerning economy and local environmental impact, but had the major disadvantage that it would be necessary to use sewage sludge, making it difficult to return the end product to the land (16 September 1996, Lloyd). The reason why the developer did not present these alternatives in the application was that they were located in the municipality of Malmö, while the plan was to locate a biogas plant in Lund. However, the developer later presented the two alternatives after the authorities asked for supplementary information on other possible locations. The opposition group interpreted this as fear on the part of the developer that it would be obvious that the locations in Malmö were more suitable (Interviews with members of the opposition group). Second, it was clear that political pressure from the municipality had influenced the decision to find a location in Lund, and this was interpreted by members of the opposition group as doubt as to whether it was suitable to site a biogas plant in Lund. Third, after the developer had made the decision regarding the location, it focused completely on showing that the chosen site was ideal and it was no longer interested in discussing alternatives. This inflexibility on the part of the developer made it easier to believe that it wanted to avoid a discussion, knowing that this was, perhaps, not the best location. This case study demonstrates the importance of an open and transparent planning process in order to avoid misunderstandings and to counteract the spreading of rumours.

On the whole, the interviews with members of the opposition group show that trust in the developer was minimal and that this originated from the way in which the project had been presented and from a perception of the developer as arrogant and uninterested in the views of the public. This lack of trust meant that the negative attitudes towards the project, and particularly towards the specific location, were exacerbated, and the main objective of the opposition group early on became to stop the facility from being built at the chosen location. Since it was not possible to discuss any alternative locations, they focused on trying to stop the project entirely. If this was not successful, their second aim was to implement strict environmental conditions on the facility. This meant that they were not interested in a dialogue with the developer since they perceived that their objectives and those of the developer were impossible to reconcile (Interviews with members of the opposition group).

Lessons to be learned from the case

An underlying question regarding a siting conflict such as this is whether it is an example of a sound project that has been stopped because of the influence of a small group of individuals guarding their selfish interests, or if it is an example of a bad project that has been avoided thanks to a working local democracy and active citizens. This question is very difficult to answer since it depends upon different interpretations of the possible effects of the facility. The different actors had diverging and, sometimes, contradictory perceptions of the planning process and it is impossible to say that one way of looking at it is more legitimate than the other. Instead, it is better to realize that the present case demonstrates a situation where all of the key actors, to some extent, have lost something and that this could have been avoided. The members of the *opposition group* felt ignored and were worried that the project would be carried out without them being able to influence the situation, which made them expend considerable time and effort throughout the application process on opposing the plans. The municipality lost the chance to build a biogas plant within its area, something that all political parties favoured, and it seems that the chance will not return for many years. The *developer* had long been seeking a suitable place to locate a biogas plant and had invested a great deal of time and money in the Dalby location, which can be considered as largely wasted. The most serious loss resulting from this case is that of trust. The public lost trust in the developer, who will find it even harder to site facilities in the future. Biogas technology might also have been affected by the loss of trust, making biogas appear more like a controversial technology and less like something that is beneficial for the environment. Regarding such a perspective, it is more appropriate to ask what we can learn from this case about how to avoid planning processes that are perceived as negative by all parties involved, and how we can achieve processes that are both democratic and effective at the same time. In relation to this question, the following section discusses two themes that have been significant in this biogas facility planning process and that might be of interest regarding siting conflicts, in general.

Different interpretations of the planning process

An interesting result of the case study is that the actors involved show very different interpretations of the planning process, which are derived from their own positions and from what they have been able to observe. It is noteworthy that the developer interpreted the planning process as being open and inclusive, while the opposition group perceived it as a typical example of a closed process, where the aim was to hurry through the project in secret. The lack of communication between the actors involved fostered misunderstanding and misinterpretation and enabled them to create images of each other's motives and actions that did not correspond with reality. This was most obvious in the relationship between the developer and the opposition group, which was, from the very start, marked by mutual distrust. The developer saw the conflict as a typical NIMBY (not in my back yard) phenomenon, where local people, out of purely selfish motives, manage to stop a project, which they would otherwise regard as positive since it benefits society as a whole, as well as the environment. This view was reinforced since the opposition group was not interested in a discussion with the developer and organized public meetings without inviting the developer. Public opinion in Dalby was seen as being largely created by the opposition group through the use of aggressive propaganda and information that manipulated the truth. The opposition group, on the other hand, was deeply suspicious of the motives of the developer and perceived the information coming from that source as being modified in order to show that the chosen site was the best. This negative view was based on the first meeting, when the developer's representatives had difficulty in answering some of the questions and when it became clear that they had not planned any further informational activities. The view was reinforced by the fact that the developer was not willing to contemplate any other locations. Distrust made it possible to question how the site had been chosen and even made people suspect that it was more or less a random decision. As we have seen, both views were highly exaggerated, although they contained some elements of truth.

These findings are similar to those of an earlier study from the mid 1980s concerning conflicts surrounding the siting of energy facilities in Sweden (Sjöström, 1985). From a psychological perspective, the author illustrated the processes in which the actors created and reinforced the negative images of their counterpart in order to maintain the image of themselves as fighting for a just cause. As in this case, the main reason why these images could be sustained was a complete lack of communication between the opposing parties. The solution that was advocated in the report was to strive for more democratic and participatory planning processes, where the different perspectives could meet, which would counteract decisions being based either on the influence of experts or on single-question opposition groups. In a later study from the early 1990s, which included case studies of several energy projects, the same conclusions about the importance of more participatory planning processes was reached (Carlman, 1993). And almost a decade later, in this study, the same conclusions have once again arisen.

Open and closed planning processes

One of the most striking features of the decision-making process in the biogas project is the sharp contrast between the level of public involvement in the different phases of the process. The developer, the municipality and the direct stakeholders were the only ones involved in the initial planning of the project, which completely excluded any form of citizen involvement. When the developer had decided upon a location and the application was ready to be submitted, the neighbours of the site were still unaware of what was being planned in their vicinity. However, when the application entered the legal system, citizen involvement became very pronounced and took the form of active opposition to the project. The legal system allows for a certain influence from members of the public when a project with potential environmental impact is proposed and, for instance, gives people the right to submit official comments and opinions about an application, which the authorities must take into consideration. When official channels are combined with other ways of influencing the decision, as in this case study, active citizens have considerable opportunity to affect decisions and even to call a halt to a project. Thus, we have a situation in which there is normally little incentive for project developers to involve the public in the planning of projects, while there are many opportunities for people to become involved in the legal process and to influence whether the project is approved or not. As this case study has shown, this tends to lead to polarized conflicts between the different parties involved and points to a shortcoming in the legal system, since it guarantees public involvement only during the later stages of the process and may thus contribute to confrontation, rather than serving as an instrument to deal with conflict and to mediate between different parties.

In Sweden, this problem has partly been addressed in the new 1999 Environmental Code, which stresses the importance of early consultation with the public and states that alternative locations should also be proposed when a new facility is to be built. It is, however, still unclear how much the new law can actually contribute to shaping planning processes and to encouraging meaningful public participation since the regulations concerning the type and aims of consultation are vague. Case studies of planning and application processes which follow the 1999 Environmental Code are necessary in order to gain empirical knowledge about the possibility of increasing public participation and avoiding polarized conflicts.

CONCLUSION

This case study is one example of the conflicts that may arise regarding the siting of a renewable energy facility, and we can find similarities with other renewable energy siting conflicts and with traditional siting conflicts. Regarding the nature of the opposition and the role of the local environmental organizations, there were clear parallels to other renewable energy siting conflicts. The opposition was organized by an ad hoc interest group whose members did not have ties to the environmental movement. The local environmental organizations remained passive throughout the planning and application process. They did not object to a biogas plant somewhere in Lund, but were unofficially critical of the specific site and the way in which the planning process was handled by the developer. Although they were critical of the same things as the opposition group, they did not voice this openly since it would contradict their support for biogas.

In other ways, the case resembled traditional siting conflicts: the facility was fairly large scale, there was no economic involvement of the local community and there were unresolved uncertainties concerning the impact of the facility. Most strikingly, it showed how a project developer failed to involve the public in the crucial early stages of the planning process and the role this played in turning differences of opinion between the parties into a polarized conflict. This result is in line with earlier research, and the case study serves as yet another reminder to project developers that the public can have a decisive influence on the outcome of a project, originating both from their legal rights and from the fact that people today are more aware of environmental matters and better able to fight for their case (Rabe, 1994; Dorshimer, 1996; Leiss, 1996; Löfstedt, 1997). Planning strategies with the aim of hurrying projects with a minimum of information and dialogue will be more and more difficult to pursue, and developers will face the risk of being discredited.

The reaction of the local population and their genuine concern about their local environment were also similar to other siting conflicts. The fact that biogas production is both an environmentally sound way of dealing with organic waste and a substitute for fossil fuels did not mean that the local population saw the project as good for the environment. To some extent, this might be explained by a lack of information and awareness about the nature of a biogas plant. However, some members of the opposition group were environmentally aware and were not against biogas, in general, but still felt that the negative impact of the specific siting in the local environment would outweigh the positive outcomes. In this way, the conflict can be viewed as a variant of the well-known dilemma, where the local community bears the burden while society, in general, reaps the benefit. From this perspective, it is not surprising that it became difficult for the developer to make people listen to arguments affirming that the biogas plant was an environmentally friendly facility. Since these arguments were not followed up by a clear effort to mitigate the negative effects of the facility or a willingness to discuss the possibilities of compensation to the local community, they were not viewed as relevant or trustworthy by the opposition group.

5 The Smell of Money: Minor Risks and Olfactory Sensibilities (Anatomy of a Protest)

Simone Abram

Introduction

Much risk research is concerned with redefining risk and its perceptions. The 'technicization' of risk analysis, and its consequent distance from popular perceptions of danger and safety, are familiar phenomena in the arguments about the relativity of defining risks in situations of conflict over large-scale infrastructure or biotechnologies. Minor discomforts have, perhaps understandably, not received so much attention in the debate; but the risks of changing what might appear to be small details in the environment can lead to major conflicts in the lives of those involved and give rise to considerable discomfort and unhappiness. This chapter examines the furore surrounding the siting of a factory on a semi-industrial site, and anatomizes the debate over the potential environmental consequences.

The key element to this particular conflict relates to the smell of a place. A great deal of attention has been given to the look of places, not least with the help of Foucault's analysis of the constructed way in which we 'gaze' on sites (see Abram, 2003, for a summary), in line with what Jay calls a preoccupation with the ocular peculiar to modernity (Jay, 1993). Our 'faith in visual evidence' (Jay, 1986, p182), for example, is reflected in a wealth of means by which we can record visual properties and define forms of visual 'pollution'. Similarly, our ability to measure and analyse sound reflects our concern with aural experience. Whether it is the lack of emphasis on the sense of smell that accounts for the difficulty of measuring and analysing it, or vice versa, we certainly do have few reliable measures of smells, and our ability to record smells is correspondingly poor. Equally under-documented is the extent to which the 'smell of a place' is constitutive of what we loosely refer to as 'identity'. If we can extend our imagination to include hearing as a 'way of dwelling' (Soneryd, 2002, p123–148), perhaps we ought also to reflect on smelling as a way of dwelling in the world.

The significance of smell is heightened in certain environments, and among the most regulated of environments in the UK are the rural stretches of the

Home Counties (those bordering Greater London). These 'rural retreats' (Lowe et al, 1995) represent a carefully constructed environment that fulfils a number of key desires in the imagination of a 'good life' for its residents. The way in which residents reconstruct rural settlements both physically and socially to conform to an image of the English rural idyll is well documented (see Newby, 1980, 1988; Abram, 2003); but little is recorded about the centrality of environmental smells to a sense of 'belonging' (Cohen, 1982). Changing the smell of a place may seem a rather minor affair compared with the introduction of life-threatening fumes; but its potential to damage elements considered essential to quality of life can arouse real anger and grief. The relative importance of smell to other 'goods', economic or otherwise, is played out in the conflict described below, giving us an indication of the complexity of the construction of collective senses of 'place', class formation in English rural settlements, the relative rationalities of argumentation and the sometimes crude political realities of decision-making. In what follows, therefore, just as in the case presented, these different elements weave in and out of each other, bobbing up at different times like the apples in a water barrel at a country fair.

Settings

The description presented here is derived from ethnographic research based in a village in the south-east of England. The research did not focus on one particular social group, but on a set of issues and all of those with interests in them. In particular, research focused on the creation of a local plan, parallel to the debate about employment land discussed here. The account is therefore based around participant observation of public meetings, private interviews and general participant observation of what one might loosely call 'village life'. The different settings presented here suggest the multiplicity of perspectives on the issue of siting, and this chapter has attempted to account for the very different perceptions of the site held by some of the main actors in the case study. The intention is to show that an innocent description of the 'context' of the siting controversy described is not possible since context defines argument (and sometimes vice versa).

Setting 1: The factory

McCormick is an American-owned transnational corporation. Amongst its products are several ranges of spices, including Schwartz spices and products marketed under the names of McCormick and Nash. The company represents itself as follows:

> McCormick is the global leader in the manufacture, marketing and distribution of spices, seasonings and flavours to the entire food industry. Customers range from retail outlets and food service providers to food processing businesses. Founded in 1889, McCormick has approximately 8000 employees (www.cpd.mccormick.com, June 2004).

During the mid 1990s, McCormick began to implement a restructuring plan, aiming to close one of its main processing factories that was located in Ellesmere Port, an economically depressed industrial town in north-west England, where there had been long-standing unresolved environmental health problems. That is, the factory had encountered significant local protest against odours and dust pollution emitted from its factory into the area and had been subject to inquiry by the local environmental health authorities. The company planned to consolidate its operations near its headquarters in High Wycombe (within 24km of the village) and near its most effective factory, which was located in Thame, a small market town about 5km from the village.

In this chapter, the company's view is not represented directly from interview material, but is interpreted through the presentations that company representatives gave in public arenas, their own marketing and publicity material, and through stories that circulated within the village. In this way, an explanation of why the relocation of the factory was so strongly contested from both within and without the village is presented. The story of the relocation will be 'reconstructed' through accounts gained during ethnographic fieldwork based in the village.[1] Details about the firm itself were obtained at a public tour of the factory organized by the factory directors in 1997 for the benefit of the village society and at public meetings held within the village.

Setting 2: The village

The village lies about 64km north-west of London, north of the Chilterns Area of Outstanding Natural Beauty (AONB).[2] It is known that there has been a village here since at least Saxon times, strung along the banks of a stream in fertile farmland (Clarke, 1854). The name of the village, Haddenham, is thought either to refer to the name of a Saxon lord, Hadda, given to the hamlet or to be derived from the name 'home among the heaths (or heathens)'. The village was passed to Archbishop Lanfranc by William the Conqueror during the late 11th century and then passed into the hands of the Church. Lanfranc's manor still stands, and the barns behind the church are built on medieval timber frames. There are still some archaeological remains of the early village and of the medieval cloisters that once stood near the village church; but most of the early wooden houses were destroyed in a succession of fires, including a particularly destructive event in 1701. Around this time, people began to build houses out of a mixture of mud and straw known locally as Witchert, with thatched and, later, tiled roofs.

The village population declined dramatically after the agricultural crisis of the late 19th century, but began to expand again with the building of a railway through the village and the opening of a station. The railway was closed again after World War II for economic reasons. The wartime airfield was partly converted into an industrial site and a number of factories opened, including aircraft wing manufacturers, hose makers and other forms of light industry. From the 1960s, larger housing estates were built up in and around the village, and the reopening of the railway in 1988 marked a major step in its transformation from a rural village to a commuter dormitory.

The history of the village can also be told in other ways (as most histories can – see Hastrup, 1992). It was centrally located during the English Civil War, and its yeoman farmers bought their way out of manorial ownership. The spirit of rebellion lives on through action groups, although their membership tends to include many people who have moved into the village from all over the country from other rural areas and other cities, as well as from London (see Abram and Waldren, 1998). When changes are mooted in the village, villagers pay attention and stand up against potentially malign influences. Many villagers have been involved in protest actions, mostly peaceful, from a regional campaign against the siting of a third London airport nearby during the 1960s, to another regional campaign against an east–west motorway (see, also, North, 1998, on styles of protest against the 'Motorway by Stealth' affair). Plans for the latter were abandoned by the government in the early 1990s under a general 'cutback' on road spending, although protests over a national-scale railway construction rumble on.

It is impossible to characterize wholly a population of around 5000; but it is fair to say that during the 1990s the village was home to a high proportion of professionals and 'service-sector' employees, entrepreneurs and highly qualified individuals. At the same time, the village also had a manual labour force, some of whom worked in a stationery factory in the middle of the village, and a number of other people were unemployed since the closure of a mechanical parts factory and the relocation of another manufacturing company away from the area. Public meetings on issues of future development often aroused significant local interest, with large turnouts to public meetings and, as one villager stated, an 'expert' for every occasion: 'Whatever the issue you're talking about at these meetings, someone always pops up as an expert.'

Within this context during the mid 1990s appeared a planning application to build a spice-processing factory.

'Non-setting' 3: The closing factory

As part of its restructuring plan, McCormick planned to close down a plant in Ellesmere Port. Ellesmere Port lies across the River Mersey from Liverpool, on the Wirral peninsula. The whole borough has a population of around 80,000. The town's location at the meeting point between the Manchester Ship Canal, the Shropshire Union Canal and on the banks of the River Mersey made it a good location for 19th- and 20th-century industry, and it has been developed for petrol production, chemical plants and vehicle manufacture. While the borough also includes more rural areas, it is dominated by chemical and manufacturing industries.

The spice factory had been a site of conflict for some years, due to the odours and dust that were released into the surrounding neighbourhood. After a string of complaints, the local environmental health authority began to press the company for environmental improvement, but the results had been poor. After an economic downturn during the 1980s, the region had suffered severe unemployment problems (with male unemployment running at around 15 per cent in 1991; see www.irdss.wirral.gov.uk), and although local people objected strongly to the smells of the factory, they hoped to force the company to clean up the factory, while still retaining the employment it offered. In other words, they were campaigning for better working practices, but not for the closure of the factory. News of the company's plans to close down and move out of the area into what appeared to be the rich, over-employed south of England came as very bad news, and the local council offered the company better-located sites within the borough, further from residential areas, where there would be less risk of causing nuisance smells. However, the company was determined to move out of the area altogether. A villager was told by a company employee that they considered the work force in Thame to be 'better' (further references to company tactics will be found within the chapter). Ellesmere Port employees spoke to concerned village residents who went 'to see for themselves' what their conditions were like. The old factory therefore had a role in the dispute in the village, although its location was over 240km away.

THE MEETINGS

The first public meeting

In 1995 a planning application from McCormick to build a new factory on the village's business site was made public within the village. As with any application for planning permission, potentially affected residents must be consulted, and the list of statutory consultees includes both the parish council (the most local level of statutory government in England) and a long-standing voluntary group called the Haddenham Village Society. The village's parish council held a public meeting in late March to inform residents about the application. At this first of many meetings, some residents expressed concern about potential smells from such a factory, so close to the centre of the village. The audiences at these village meetings tend to include highly educated people, often with extensive knowledge of business and manufacturing. Such individuals pride themselves on not allowing the wool to be pulled over their eyes. Typically, one resident, a retired Air Force engineer who had also run his own manufacturing business, commented:

> They said the smells would be minimal; but when someone says that it will be a minimum, I want to know what that minimum is, where are the figures, how will it be measured and who will monitor it? I think we need it in writing beforehand that if it goes above a certain level, then the factory will be shut down.

He also queried where employees relocated from the existing factory would be housed, given the housing shortages within the village, and how much new traffic would be generated. His scepticism and criticism were not unusual among those who had been present at the meeting.

Very soon after the first meeting, a group of people organized themselves into a campaigning group to ensure that full details of the application would be made public, and to fight for the views of villagers to be taken into account. This small group of agitators called themselves a ginger group. This is, in fact, an established term for groups of agitators who aim to raise awareness of issues in the hope of making it impossible for powerful agents to simply walk over people by withholding facts and using propaganda. These people were not about to let the district council take a decision about the factory without local people being made aware of the potential environmental consequences. This was not the first ginger group to be established in the village. A similar group had been established to lead a fight against a proposal to upgrade the country road nearby into an eight-lane motorway (North, op cit). In the earlier protest, the village group joined a regional campaign, which was orchestrated by a man living in a village about 8km away (who complained of secret-service surveillance and threats to his 'personal safety').

The second public meeting

The parish council held another public meeting on 3 April, where the response to the planning application was both well researched and vociferous. The village hall was full to overflowing, the parish council chairwoman was present wearing her mayoral chains,[3] and a 'team' from the spice company sat at her side. Representatives of an environmental engineering firm were also present. A letter from the manufacturers about the potential odours that might be created, and the processes they were going to install to prevent odours from escaping into the atmosphere, was discussed. There was talk of the Atomic Energy Authority (AEA) and of a process called 'Purafil'. However, rather than scientific and technical references intimidating local participants or parish councillors, the responses were wide ranging:

- A ginger group member suggests that, after reading all the AEA appraisals, there was clearly a risk that the Purafil process may not be totally effective. He calls for a further AEA study to find better solutions, but acknowledges that McCormick have been helpful in providing a reasonable level of information.
- A local resident asks: 'Why should we accept any smell where there is no smell now?'
- Another resident, who says he has been to visit the site at Ellesmere Port to investigate, reports that the company has been less than open about the difficulties of containing odours from its factories. He spoke to local residents who said they have to keep their windows closed on summer days, and to employees who have to keep their work clothes in separate wardrobes to avoid making all their other clothes smell. They insisted that any new factory should be built well away from housing to reduce the risk of pollution. In addition, he says the noise level from grinding nutmegs is 36 decibels (dB).
- A resident asks why the company wants to move to Haddenham; is it because it has a smaller population than Ellesmere Port who might complain less? 'We can't be intimated.'
- Another resident says that 36dB is the background noise level and asks what the peak level is. The noise from heavy goods vehicles averages 75dB, and

the resident demands to know how many heavy goods vehicles (HGVs) would service the site and when.
- The company representatives specify 50 lorries a day from 7 am to 7 pm.
- The local police officer demands a written report about the changes in local traffic and expresses concern over the danger from heavy lorries to adults and children who walk or cycle along lanes with restricted footpaths.

It is clear that the company employed a classic tactic of attempting to 'blind with science'. It began the meeting with a discussion of technical processes, heavily referring to legitimization through the AEA, a high-tech national scientific organization. However, the tactic was not wholly successful on two accounts. First, there were villagers present who were more knowledgeable on technical issues. Their technical questions were answered, but not satisfactorily, and the technicization of the discussion on noise and smell was not reassuring; indeed, the opposite was the case, revealing the extent of the potential problems. Second, the argument shifted from technical grounds to issues of rights and conditions – particularly local issues of traffic, noise and smell.

As if to accentuate this point, the meeting moved on to the issue of local employment, which the district councillor and parish mayor had used to raise support for the location of the factory in the village. The company suggested approximately 100 new jobs would be created, but were immediately challenged on how many of these would be available to local people. At this point, a split among the residents present became more explicit. It was clear to villagers that this split ran partly along class lines, but also partly along lines of village identities – between so-called 'old villagers' and 'incomers'. The meeting started to take on the character of a performance, with 'local yokels' (see below) standing mainly around the back of the hall, and 'commuters' and other wealthy 'incomers' seated in front of the councillors. Among the range of social groupings within the village, this particular configuration proved powerful in mobilizing dissent, particularly in this instance where potential employment was at stake.[4]

The comments began to take on a different flavour, aimed less at attacking the company, and more at undermining the attackers:

- There's nothing wrong with the smell of herbs; it smells better than traffic!
- There has been an industrial site in the village for 50 years, and it is the livelihood of the village. We're not all peasants; we need jobs!
- A local man, well known amongst 'old villagers', complains that the village is full of incomers and commuters, and says, 'I'm going to tell you something now; I'm going to educate you' about the village being a working place, not just a picturesque landscape.

The use of words in anger about 'educating' wealthy incomers demonstrates the level of resentment among some 'old villagers' against incomers whom they perceive as feeling superior by dint of their education, income or career. However, long-standing villagers, themselves a very diverse group (including internationally jet-setting sales executives, wealthy farmers and entrepreneurs, as well as manual labourers) included a group who responded to others' formal education by asserting their local knowledge, gleaned through contact with previous generations. 'Educating you' therefore indicates a crack through which we can glimpse profound social histories of both oppression of the rural peasantry by absent and present landlords, to alienation of lower-income residents under late 20th-century counter-urbanization (see Boyle and Halfacree, 1998). It does not indicate, however, any formal or static division between social groups in the village. As Strathern showed some years ago, notions of 'authentic belonging' in English villages are very much imagined rather than definable (Strathern, 1981). While some 'old villagers' can be defined through centuries-old kinship connections with village families, the precise features of these 'roots' vary greatly. What is being described here is, rather, symbolic boundaries that are evoked by such naming practices as 'I'm just a local yokel', or 'bloomin' commuters' in order to effect a particular type of social alliance (Cohen, 1986). In other words, social groupings do not simply 'exist', waiting to be mentioned in certain circumstances, but are invoked in order to lend weight to the sides of conflicts. This was particularly obvious by the radical regroupings of villagers under previous and later conflicts (Murdoch and Abram, 2002). While, in the dramatic situation of the meeting, the villager can call upon his historical and genealogical links with the village, and his associations with other 'old villagers', outside the meeting, it was clear that other 'old villagers' did not all agree with him.

There are meanings that are implicit in the comment, however. The angry response, while arousing amusement in some of the audience, may also be interpreted as a reaction to the technical discourse that had begun to dominate the meeting. We might understand these references to village knowledge as a counterpart to the references to scientific practices used by the company to legitimize (or disguise?) their intentions. Instead of being silenced by this detailed technical language, the villager tried to shift the ground of authoritative knowledge away from science to 'local knowledge', again seizing the legitimate ground for argument over the planning application.

Pre-public, private meetings

Here, we should perhaps note that the parish council at that time was not actually elected. That is, no election was held to appoint councillors because, for 11 places on the council, only 10 candidates came forward, and therefore one had to be co-opted to make up a full council. As the statutory representative body for village opinion to the planning authority, candidates were perceived as being vulnerable to being 'wooed' by a multinational company. Of this they were duly accused. Other villagers noted that the parish council had been 'entertained' by the company, that it had accepted gifts (albeit relatively low-value gifts of spice racks) from the company, and some members of the parish council had appeared annoyed that members of the village society had been present at an early meeting with the company, which they had considered a 'private' fact-finding meeting. Notions of transparency in local government are limited in the UK, and private meetings with potential developers are accepted as necessary by local councils. Villagers, on the other hand, felt that such meetings indicated that the company had 'bought' the parish council without giving proper assurances of the appropriateness of building on that particular site.

The third public meeting

After the second meeting, the ginger group that emerged demanded further public meetings and better information from McCormick. They were angry that the parish council appeared to have approved the application without full knowledge of what was being applied for, and without any technical review of the application. Calls for a public meeting at which McCormick could be questioned directly were intercepted by the parish council, who organized a meeting – of the Parish Council – where company representatives would be 'given the opportunity' to present their case for planning approval to villagers. This meeting was held on 27 April in the village hall's largest room, which was again overflowing 20 minutes before the meeting was due to start at 8 pm, with several hundred people crowding in through the main doors. Those present included all ages of people, including children, and residents from all parts of the village. Representatives from the company sat on a stage across the front of the hall, alongside parish councillors and the area planning office and environmental health officer. Other company representatives sat amongst the audience.

The chair of the parish council introduced the company representatives as having 'kindly agreed' to come to the meeting. The representatives then presented themselves as the world's largest producers of spices and as a household name, with a reputation for good relations. They insisted that they hoped the village would become their UK or European Union (EU) headquarters and centre for manufacturing 'dry' products (not sauces). They explained that they already had a warehouse at a nearby town, and said they required a site for a new factory which their present sites could not house. They had looked at other sites, they said, but the village site fitted their purposes best (no further details of specific sites were given). Furthermore, they claimed that they would be a 'responsible tenant', building a brand new, state-of-the-art factory with improved noise and smell controls, fully landscaped and with a new access road. Describing 'road improvements' that would keep heavy traffic out of the village, members of the audience began to shout out 'rubbish' and were swiftly asked by the chair of the parish council to 'leave any questions to the end of the presentation'.

After further presentations about the company's intentions to be a 'responsible neighbour' by sponsoring community activities, the representatives began to be more technical and defensive against accusations about pollution. There was no evidence that the odours could affect asthma; traffic would be restricted to one main road in and out of the site; they would invest in noise reduction; a number of dust-removal systems would be built into the new factory. They also said that their nearby factory had the 'best work force', and that this had encouraged them to consolidate here. They would contribute to 'regenerating the local economy' and would share 'your concerns'. They added that they were still investigating the causes of problems at Ellesmere Port (to cries of 'unsuccessfully').

The representatives' comments were supported by the officers of the district council present, who reinforced arguments about control of odours, measures to calm traffic and so on. One could argue that they used the same discourse, calling on authenticating powers of science and technology to assert the legitimacy of their proposal:

> We have used consultants from Salford University to advise us on noise levels. You can't compare the new plant to that at Ellesmere Port, which produces wet goods. We will use a heat exchanger which removes 90 per cent of particulates and cools from 100° Celsius to 50° Celsius, which condenses the oils and the particles. We tested three systems with the Atomic Energy Authority and the best was 'Purafil', and we will continue with testing this and other systems.

However, these comments were met with like responses, since powerful discourses only dominate those who cannot engage with them. Had the audience not been scientifically, politically or financially educated, then they may have been intimidated by such assertions. However, many of them were rather more knowledgeable and fluent in these discourses and epistemologies than the representatives on the podium. One member, perhaps the most active (who had previously been highly involved in an anti-road protest) pointed this out vigorously. He, however, was regarded by some other villagers as self-seeking, concerned mostly about his property value. This was discernable in the following exchange:

> *Villager:* The only point of this meeting is to put questions to McCormicks, so we need to hear facts from McCormicks. Houses near their Ellesmere Port factory are on the market at 30 per cent below the market value.
>
> *McCormick*: I have no idea about that. This is an industrial area near a major road.
>
> *Villager:* They have also been offered another factory site there.
>
> *McCormick:* No, that offer was not made until after the closure was announced.
>
> *Villager:* We are dealing with a business where expert opinion is being presented as fact – do not simply accept these but ask for warranties in case these so-called facts turn out to be untrue. If you believe there will be no adverse effects, then you should guarantee compensation in case there are.
>
> *Another villager:* If your property values went up after the factory was built, would you give the profit back (general laughter; cries of 'as if')?!
>
> *McCormick:* We are working with the district council and the county council.
>
> *District council environmental health officer:* We are concerned about the dust, smoke and noise issues. We have carried out investigations and the company is using the best available equipment. However, they cannot guarantee that there will be no odour.

A detailed discussion about potential increases in traffic followed where the roads authority, the county council, appeared to support McCormick's application. The debate then turned again to odour issues, and to the technical details of cleansing processes, this time in relation to the land-use class (zoning criteria) of the site. The ginger group had identified that the 'business park' was classed as a B8 site – that is, a site appropriate for business use that causes no significant noise, pollution or other impacts on surrounding residents. The part of the site in question backed directly onto housing and gardens, including some housing which was very newly built, and some much older properties. A factory 10 metres high would cause significant shadows, quite apart from other impacts. Lorries turning and loading would be very close to people's back gardens, and very close to the middle of the village. The ginger group calculated, therefore, that they could prevent the approval of the planning application on the grounds that it did not fulfil the criteria for use-class B8, and pressed the issues of heavy-goods traffic and odour control to show that the company could not guarantee that these use-class restrictions could be met.

During the course of the meeting, villagers made other comments. One young man said: 'Any noise or smell is worth the jobs' to loud applause from the back of the room. Another said: 'I'm a local peasant from Okely, and I think the stench from [the village] pond is awful; so I don't know why you are worried about a few spices' to much laughter.

The meeting ended late, and people tumbled out of the village hall and began to make their way back to their homes in different parts of the village, some driving, most walking (the furthest distance could only be under 1km within the village). One relatively new incomer to the village commented: 'If you live in the countryside, you expect farm smells; if you live in the town, you expect noise and smells.' Another said: 'It's terrible that they allowed new houses to be built right alongside the proposed factory, when they knew it could be a factory site as long ago as 1988.' But at this stage, village protesters were confident that the application would have to be rejected on technical grounds of inappropriate land-use class.

Given the difficulties for the proposed factory of meeting the restrictions on use-class B8, however, the district council proceeded to vote a change in the use class to mixed use-classes B1, B2 and B8 to include 'heavy industrial' use. This conveniently side-stepped all technical objections to the proposed factory and opened the business park to any type of heavy industrial use, despite its being immediately adjacent to existing housing, contrary to the spirit of planning law.

The action of the district council, however, shocked local protesters. Ginger group members, while not perhaps totally surprised, were still disgusted that the district council could simply change the rules. What, they argued, was the point in having use classes at all if they could simply be changed if they proved inconvenient? This point was made by a ginger group supporter, who was himself a trained planner (from field notes):

> When he was at planning school, they were taught that the whole point of business classifications was to separate residential areas from industrial areas because they are incompatible. So what the hell were [the district council] doing putting the factory right there in the first place?

This action, indeed, contributed to a general cynicism and denigration of public-sector planning and local authority planners. Villagers were equally sceptical of 'planning gains' offered almost in mitigation, where McCormick would be obliged to fund traffic calming along the main road through the village as a condition of planning permission. However, many villagers felt that this was a ruse to distract them from the main issue of potential smells from the factory: put crudely, to buy them off.

The loss of faith in even the technicalities of the planning system, quite apart from the skills of the individual planners at the district council (which many in the village questioned already), had significant consequences later on. When the council proposed an expansion of housing at the village, a year after the events described here, members of the original ginger group were joined by many 'old villagers' and public-housing tenants in fighting an organized campaign against the district plan, which went right through an ongoing public inquiry. This later campaign also illustrates the momentary nature of the groupings described during this episode, since the 'old villagers' were no longer pitted against 'incomers' in the same way, but in many cases allied themselves and presented a much more unified front towards the council.

Unspoken elements

Throughout the events described above, there were a number of themes which were not discussed openly, but were alluded to. These warrant some consideration. One or two people did comment that the problem with the factory was that it would smell of spices. Despite the radical transformation of the British countryside, and particularly the collapse of small-scale agriculture, many residents in the village still associated rural life with mythical or nostalgic pre-industrial farmyards. One working farm within the village produced poultry; but village residents had complained about the heavy lorry that regularly came to collect the packaged meat from the farm. Much of the recent housing development in the village could only be described as 'suburban' in style, and a number of residents said that they had moved to the village as an alternative to the extreme overpricing of housing in the more fashionable suburbs of London. Therefore, even modern farming was not easily tolerated by some. However, one might speculate whether the imposition of 'foreign' smells was part of the difficulty. The village population was predominantly white. To my knowledge, there was one family of East Asian ethnicity (who ran a restaurant) and one of Asian (who ran a grocery store), one former Ugandan Asian (married to a Welsh woman) and two African children (adopted). As already mentioned, there were no formal complaints about smells from the local chip shop (although people did sometimes complain that it could be smelled some distance away). Nor, for that matter, were there objections to the Chinese restaurant. However, all of these smells were localized. There was, effectively, no explicit discourse about ethnicity within the village. Village social life was dominated by church groups, of which there were several, including three established churches. As Lowe et al (1995) have indicated, there is an association of rural England with implicitly nationalist nostalgia. Rural Britain still remains predominantly white in contrast to urban Britain, and the picturesque rural village remains symbolically significant to certain forms of 'Englishness'. The ever-present scent of roasting spices simply did not fit with the aspirations of many of those who had consciously made the move to live in the English countryside. The irony that 'Jim', a 'local', constantly pointed out was that few of these objectors were concerned about the smell of their petrol and diesel exhausts, equally 'foreign' to the countryside, as far as he was concerned.

Given the efforts made by villagers to intensify the 'picturesque' nature of the village – for example, through maintenance of the village pond, cleaning of pathways and cutting of lawns – one can assert that these efforts were associated with emphasizing the 'Englishness' of the village. This was not limited to visual changes, however. Groups of villagers continued to perform traditional activities, such as Morris dancing (a tradition revived and transformed during the late 19th century), and country-style Mayday celebrations: not a celebration of Labour day, but another Romantic revival of the celebration of the coming of spring. The celebrations usually comprise elements such as a procession through the village with decorated 'floats', and children dancing round a maypole, weaving patterns with ribbons, supposed partly to signify fertility. The village Morris dancers also perform, and there are often a few market-style stalls on the village green. It is not hard to see how pervasive smells of roasting spices might seem to be a distraction, or a counteracting tendency, to energetic efforts to establish a particularly nostalgic version of 'Englishness'. They could signify the intrusion of that other, less agreeable, side of imperialism. The problem with the factory was not that such a factory should exist, but that it would be 'inappropriate' – that is, out of place. As well as potentially bringing heavy goods transport, which people associated with larger towns, particularly with industrial areas and with motorways around larger cities, it would also bring a type of smell that would not enhance the village's symbolic 'English' identity. In addition, by undermining both the 'rural' and English aspects of the village, it would threaten not merely the 'quality of life' within the village but also villagers' ability to move to other locations more in line with these values through property-pricing mechanisms.

What happened?

As predicted by ginger group members, the factory was built during 1996–1997, after receiving planning permission in 1995 contingent upon the change of use class, and the construction of a 'new landscaped access road' (Aylesbury Vale District Council, 1997). Local objections were considered 'not material' to the granting of planning permission. A group of employees from Ellesmere Port were brought to the new factory as the core of its new labour force, and also to train new workers. Of the 100 jobs mentioned during the early meetings, less than 20 went to local workers. There were immediate and enduring problems with odour control, despite the company's efforts to introduce the most up-to-date technology and investing a great deal of money in the factory. It might be claimed that objections to the smells of spices roasting were a form of displaced racism, since spicy aromas were thought to be 'out of place' in a village trying to be quintessentially English. That is, while non-white people may be accepted for as long as they either behaved as 'English' people, or played expected roles in domestic food supplies, if the nature of the village was changed radically by altering its smell to one considered 'foreign', this acceptance would not be so forthcoming. It is not possible to ascertain the validity of such a suggestion conclusively (by definition, since it would be covert). However, the odours emitted from the factory were not those of gently roasting herbs and spices, such as might emanate from a domestic kitchen, but the much more sickly burning smells of an industrial manufacturing plant. Therefore, rather than dismiss local objections as some kind of disguised racism, it is important to highlight the overwhelming odours that confronted people at unpredictable times. Village reactions included anger, disillusion and dismay, although the chair of the parish council remarked that she knew one or two people who had gained jobs at the factory and were delighted with the outcome.

McCormick began to publish a 'neighbourhood newsletter' with information about its attempts to control the 'emissions' from the plant. It invited members of the village society on a guided tour of the factory, and sponsored some village events. These activities were received with some scepticism by many villagers. For instance, the first Christmas after the factory opened, McCormick donated a Christmas tree to the village, which was erected outside the village hall. For some time, the village had been suffering problems with vandalism. Racist graffiti on the village hall was considered shameful by many villagers, although it took the parish council more than six months to arrange to cover it with anti-graffiti paint. Still, complaints were markedly muted when 'vandals' pulled down the Christmas tree. Some villagers also remarked that the company's sponsorship of a village drama event smacked of paternalism, as the company's efforts to be a 'good neighbour' by sponsoring village groups soured in the smell of concentrated roasting cumin that wafted over village houses during the spring and summer months.

As soon as the factory opened, villagers began to note down the appearance of heavy goods lorries travelling into the village from the east on restricted roads. The chair of the parish council was seen racing through the village trying to mark down the registration number of vehicles turning through narrow lanes. Villagers also began keeping 'smell diaries' of when and where odours from the factory were perceptible, and correlating these with weather patterns. Eventually, some support was offered by the district council environmental health department, although villagers complained that on the days when the environmental health officer came to the village, smells somehow disappeared.

One of the ginger group members looked back on developments during 1997 as follows, in a conversation held over coffee in his beautifully tended garden:

> There's a tremendous fear, really, and concern and anger certainly on this side of the village that these smells are very pungent. And almost daily... It's not like housing – you can shut your gates to housing; it might even be good for the village, you can't actually tell. But one thing's for certain; if you want to sit out here and have coffee and you've got a pungent smell coming in, that's just not acceptable and that affects everybody, whether you're gardening or sitting outside or opening your window or whatever.
>
> Plus the fact that if it continues, not only will people's way of life be affected, but it could create an absolute crisis in property disposals and values. I mean, if [the village] became known as the village of smells...one of my nieces has actually been

> looking at houses [here], and I"ve been saying to her, well, if you want this side of the village you'd better wait and see if the smells clear themselves before you buy something and find it's not saleable. So that's a very bad situation, and I think [it] is an absolute dereliction of duty by the planners and the various offices, not in allowing it, perhaps, but allowing it so close.

After five years, the problem of smells from the factory had diminished; yet it took this long before the factory was fitted with double doors to cut down on emissions during deliveries. Simultaneously, however, the company changed their operations again and the factory was to be used for 'wet' processes rather than 'dry' ones, although the exact details of the processes were not available at the time of writing.

Conclusion

While much theoretical commentary about siting controversies has concentrated on the clash of interests between private/local and national, in this case, no national interest appeared to be at stake. Instead, it was a much more clear-cut conflict between commercial interests and private interests. Indeed, one could characterize it as a competition between the private interests of householders (property values) and of the company and its potential employees. At this level, the decision of the council to permit the factory was based on old-fashioned economic politics (indeed, the Liberal Democrat leader of the council believed – quite wrongly – that objectors were simply 'the Tory party'). On the broader scale, there were more environmentally appropriate sites elsewhere (locally), and a good national economic argument for keeping the employment in a deprived area (Ellesmere Port). These larger questions, however, on whether it should be a government's task to guide economic activities into areas that were in need – which would, in effect, stem the flow of labour to the economically overheated areas – were never seriously discussed.

What is curious about this case is that in contrast to many studies of risk, our assumptions about who constitutes the 'lay public' are undermined by the realization that many of the local residents in this instance were more 'expert' than the 'experts'. We cannot, for example, simply categorize the participants in this case study into 'risk bearers' or 'risk managers'. We can, however, see that local protesters attempted to transfer the risk back to the responsibility of the company. Early calls for any planning permission to include a clause that would force the factory to shut down if pollution were to materialize can be understood from the awareness amongst different parties of who would suffer the consequences of such pollution. This was clearly demonstrated during public meetings in exchanges such as the following:

> *Questioner:* The best you can offer us is a reduction of emissions by 96.5 per cent; but 96.5 per cent of what? How can the council guarantee that the site will comply with the land-use class?
>
> *Environmental health officer:* We will not advise the planning committee that the factory can achieve 100 per cent emission control.

> *Questioner:* So how can you comply with the use class? B2 use is not allowed in a residential area!

This even balance of 'expert knowledge' indicates that no amount of dialogue would have altered local perceptions of risk since the risks were, in fact, clear right from the beginning of the story despite the company's (and the planners', if not the environmental health officer's) attempts to disguise them. What villagers were not able to achieve was to force the company to take responsibility for ensuring that emissions would not be allowed to continue. The main reason they were not able to do this was because the local district council withdrew from its responsibility under the planning act to ensure that manufacturing processes that incorporated known risks of pollution should not be sited adjacent to residential areas. One could argue that the 'decide, announce, defend' style of government[5] has supposedly lost support, and no longer appears legitimate; but the above case illustrates that it is still adopted and that when it is, local residents, however well resourced or qualified, are unable to destabilize it. That this should happen where there is no overriding 'public interest' in choosing a difficult site over a more appropriate (technically, economically and/or socially) is particularly worrying. In this instance, we see technical planning solutions, so often the scourge of environmental campaigns, brushed aside in a cavalier fashion to fit with a predetermined political choice about siting development. What is more, this implies that the responsibilities for industrial risks are being transferred into a planning system that is ill equipped to respond. We may ask larger questions, therefore, about the position of citizens' rights within planning systems, particularly at a moment when a recently proposed revision of the English planning law included a removal of the right to public inquiry over local plans (DTLR, 2002; Owens, 2004)

In summary, the siting process outlined in this case study indicates that what was at stake here was not merely diverse perceptions of risk among different groups of managers, bearers and communicators. Such categorizations risk stereotyping 'the lay public' as a general body of non-scientifically informed people (or, perhaps, 'only' socially informed), rather than acknowledging heterogeneous associations with varied interests and beliefs. In this instance, we are dealing with a much more clearly drawn political question of the consequences of moving a nuisance to an environmentally conscious area. Clearly, members of the district council wished to bring the factory to the site and were not interested in providing environmental safeguards for the local population, however much the latter protested. Even so, they were able to adopt a discourse of sustainable development on the basis that they were providing local employment, where employees would not need to use private cars to reach work. This chimed in with their overall strategy for concentrating development at existing settlements. Had the factory been sited well away from a settlement, they would have been open to accusations of promoting unsustainable development.

What is, perhaps, surprising about this case is that the politicians were prepared to bow to capital under a rubric of sustainability within a population of highly educated and well-resourced professionals, and that they were also prepared to sideline planning procedures in order to disempower local dissenters. Although most examples of politicians ignoring constituents whose support they can do without occur in instances of disaffected, non-voting or small-opposition populations, in this case the politicians and planners were thought of by some villagers as deliberately antagonizing the local opposition with a sort of vindictive politics. Not surprisingly, furthermore, some villagers raised the specter of corruption to explain this otherwise erratic form of governance. Why, otherwise, would the local council favour the interests of a US-based transnational corporation over the well-being of its own residents when they could easily have found a more suitable site within the district, or could have ruled out the use of this particular site through its existing classifications, thereby putting the onus back onto the company to find a preferable site? The district had very low unemployment (one of the lowest rates in the UK), and would otherwise gain no direct benefits from the presence of the factory (especially since the company's headquarters were already within the district). Legitimate concerns that the planning system is supposed to consider for any resident, without prejudice, were simply cast aside under this rubric, despite there being no significant wider local or national interest at stake.

The only potential 'explanation' available for this particular incident concerns the different epistemologies of development adopted by the different parties,[6] and the inability or unwillingness of local political actors to withdraw from planning negotiations once a company has begun to invest in a particular site application. The fact that even two years later, after constant complaints from the villagers, opposition politicians from other parts of the district could address a public meeting in the village and state that the smells were 'not that bad' indicates that the district councillors severely misjudged both the concrete effects of their decision and the mood of the villagers in response to this. It also set the stage for a much more pre-emptive judicial conflict over housing sites that followed two years later. In this campaign, villagers who had no trust in district councillors or planners fought internally, first, to create a unified village argument against the district council's plans, drew support from national environmental and conservation groups, and employed their own solicitor to formalize their campaign (Murdoch and Abram, 2002). The cynicism created by the episodes described here also generated a more litigious, calculated and combative approach to future plans from within the village. At the same time, this made 'collaborative planning' or 'participative policy-making' almost impossible without any fundamental trust between planners, politicians and the public.

6 Living with Technological Risk: Industrial Encroachment on Sense of Place

Peter Simmons and Gordon Walker

Introduction

As the closed circle of policy-makers, regulators and risk managers is opened to admit the voices and concerns of those anonymous publics whose lives and localities are touched by the presence of environmental impacts and risks, new and challenging issues are forced onto the policy agenda. The debate about sustainability has broadened to include questions of quality of life and well-being. Alongside the calculability of technological risks and their socio-economic consequences there is, therefore, a need to understand and attend to the less tangible impacts for people living in the shadow of major industrial facilities. While considerable attention has been given to patterns of public risk perception, much of this work has approached risk in a way that is disassociated from the varied and complex contexts in which risks and hazards are experienced on an everyday basis. This is problematic, this chapter argues, because the context within which risk-producing technologies are situated may be as, if not more, important than the assessed risk in shaping local understandings of, and responses to, personal or community threat (Fitchen et al, 1987). Risky technologies are 'differentially constructed and consumed' (Irwin et al, 2001) within multidimensional contexts – cultural, economic, political, social, historical, geographical – creating a complex matrix of meanings in which technical representations of risk play only a small part.

For technological risks associated with particular places and communities, the spatial context may be particularly significant. This chapter focuses on one dimension of that context, people's 'sense of place', which we argue can play a crucial mediating role in the experience of living with hazardous sites. Specifically, this chapter explores how sense of place and place-related values (which, for brevity, we hereafter refer to as place values) can interact with and influence local constructions of risk. While a number of risk perception studies have recognized the significance of context for understanding risk perceptions and have given some importance to place in their analysis (for example, Baxter and Eyles, 1999; Bickerstaff and Walker, 2001; Bush et al, 2001; Wakefield et al, 2001), we would argue that there is scope for a more developed exploration of this relationship. A focus on sense of place enables us to develop a richer understanding of how technological activities and their associated risks can encroach upon people's feelings about where they live and compromise associated place values, which can affect both personal identities and social relations with others.

Our discussion takes as a case study a population living around a large chemical plant in Bradford in the north of England. We draw upon an analysis of group discussions with local residents to identify, first, the differentiated ways in which the presence of the chemical plant impinges upon the sense of place and place values of local people and, second, to examine the way in which the reactions of others outside the immediate community reinforce a sense of spoiled place identity. The case study has a number of characteristics that contrast with much of the existing research on public responses to site-based risks. First, the industrial installation presents a source of risk that is long established, rather than a potential hazard associated with a new siting proposal. Many studies concerned with community perceptions of site-based risk have focused on responses to the prospect of new developments, such as nuclear waste repositories, waste landfills or incinerators (for example, Couch and Kroll-Smith, 1994; Easterling, 2001). Second, despite the experience of a significant accident event in 1992, there has been relatively little community protest or opposition to the industrial site. Notwithstanding periods of intense local media attention, there has been an apparent, if sometimes uneasy, tolerance of the presence of the chemical plant, which provides substantial employment. Third, although the plant (and the associated risk) has been long established, it has evolved quite dramatically over its 50-year existence, growing from a small facility with 50 employees to a major chemical production complex employing more than 2000 people. It therefore provides an example of incremental encroachment, gradually rather than suddenly asserting its presence in the locality and in the lives of those who live around it.

Sense of place, values and 'community of experience'

The term 'sense of place' has been used by geographers as a way of emphasizing that places are significant not just as the physical setting for economic and social activities, but because they are the focus of both personal and shared feelings and values (Rose, 1995). Places have no inherent meaning, only the meaning that humans give to them – and this extends far beyond the drawing of boundaries, naming and locating, to incorporate place values, emotions, social relations and identities. These meanings are constructed, in part, by individuals, but are strongly shaped by the social context within which individuals are positioned (Eyles, 1985). As Rose (1995) emphasizes, both identity and sense of place are embedded within the social, economic and cultural relations that provide the setting for everyday experience on a more local level.

The term 'sense of place' is frequently used to refer to the positive and sometimes very intense feelings about a place that people can have, feelings that may be strong enough to be, in part, constitutive of personal or group identity. Sense of place is not, however, synonymous with positive place attachment but encompasses a wider range of relationships to place (Hay, 1998). Pred (1983) has referred to it as the 'felt sense of the quality of life at a particular place and time'. It is therefore important to recognize that, even where focused on a sense of 'belonging', identity and sense of place are also constructed by drawing contrasts with other places and identities to which a person or group do not 'belong' and which are seen as being, in some way, different. Positive feelings about one's own place can thus be constructed and reinforced by representing other places as less pleasant, more dangerous or in some other way alien and undesirable (Rutherford, 1990).[1]

Sense of place has been theorized in terms of a shared, place-specific 'structure of feeling' or community of experience (Pred, 1983). As Pred acknowledges, however, we cannot assume a homogenous sense of place to exist even among people living in a particular locale. That is not to say that sense of place is, as some treatments of the concept might seem to suggest, completely unique to each individual, but that differences in daily practices and experience, biography and place-specific social relationships will all affect an individual's sense of place. Rather than referring in the singular to a sense of place, implying a homogenous community of experience, it seems therefore more appropriate to speak of multiple senses of place. These different structures of feeling, which exist in the routine practices of everyday life, give structure to how we experience the world and to how we express that experience, and may, consequently, be associated with different identities or lifestyles (Hetherington, 1998). Empirical research has given support to this idea, demonstrating that diverse senses of place that reflect individuals' different relationships to place may coexist in a local population (Eyles, 1985). Even where there appears to be a dominant feature or characteristic of place that will be shared by all, we should also be sensitive to the presence of different configurations of experience and identity.

Hazardous industrial activities, particularly those with a physically or economically significant presence, may have both positive and negative relationships to local senses of place. For example, studies on local attitudes to the Sellafield nuclear reprocessing plant in the UK have revealed that, for some, Sellafield is an important component of local identity, while for others it is a key detraction from a sense of place which asserts the essential rural nature of the wider region (Macgill, 1987; Wynne et al, 1993). Furthermore, while it has been argued that responses to environmental risks are inextricably bound up with shared experience of, and commitment to, the neighbourhood (Klintman, 1995), a shared sense of place may not itself be a sufficient basis for citizens to take action in response to industrial pollution (Wakefield et al, 2001). For example, a study by Kaltenborn (1998) found that sense of place did not predict environmental perceptions, but that those with a strongly rooted sense of place tended to hold more positive images of their local environment and perceive their surroundings as less degraded than people with a weaker sense of place.

If the presence of hazardous industrial activity may be construed in a number of ways in relation to place, where those activities compromise place-related values they can assume a particularly transgressive quality. We can illustrate this in relation to the values associated with home. The cultural construct of 'home' can have a wide variety of meanings attached to it (Moore, 2000). One particular meaning that has been claimed for home – particularly homeownership – is its significance in the maintenance of ontological security (Saunders, 1990). Although the notion that this is the dominant meaning of home has been challenged by empirical analysis of the framings that people employ when talking about their home, which range from the moral to the economic (Gurney, 1999), there is evidence that in childhood home has, for many people, an association with safety (Harden, 2000), while in later life home ownership may be associated with a sense of security (Dupuis and Thorns, 1998). While this is not the only meaning that home may hold for people, when hazardous industrial activities make themselves felt within the context of home, we may therefore expect to find that, for some at least, they will be experienced both as a physical and a symbolic threat to a place that is valued for its associations with security and self-identity (Fitchen, 1989). Similarly, an activity that negatively affected residential property values would compromise the economic value that many people attach to their home.

The association between place and values is, we argue, central to understanding the structures of feeling that develop within a locality (Gustafson, 2001). Pred (1983) wrote of the 'felt sense of the *quality* of life'; we may analytically disaggregate 'quality' into a number of identifiable, if often interrelated, qualities which are positively valued and which may be more or less present in a particular place. Although we cannot assume place-related values to be universal, there are certain culturally constructed but commonly recognized qualities that most people appear to value about the places in which they live – such as amenity, community, safety and salubrity, or healthiness – the presence or absence of which will, in turn, have implications for people's own sense of identity inasmuch as that is tied up with the place in which they live.[2] The following section examines what happens when a place becomes identified as one in which certain of these positively valued qualities are compromised.

Stigma, risk and place

One strand of risk research that has perhaps most directly engaged with sense of place and place values concerns technological stigma (Gregory et al, 1995), where attention has focused on the process by which certain places become 'marked' by the presence of a technology or technology-related event and the consequences for those living there. Research has highlighted the stigmatizing effects of proposed hazardous technological facilities on the places and communities in which they are to be sited (for example, Slovic et al, 1991, 1994; Flynn et al, 2001). Although most often invoked in connection with economic 'blight', the stigmatizing effects of unwanted or feared hazards such as toxic pollutants have been found to have significant social and psychological effects – for example, in studies of 'contaminated communities' found to have chronic chemical pollution of their drinking water supplies (Fowlkes and Miller, 1987; Edelstein, 1988; Fitchen, 1989; Satterfield et al, 2001; Satterfield and Gregory, 2002).

A growing body of research has demonstrated that the presence of a stigmatized technology (for example, a nuclear, chemical or waste disposal facility) may, in some circumstances, lead to the place in which it is found being stigmatized and, in turn, to those who live in that place becoming stigmatized. Work on such technological stigma frequently acknowledges its debt to Erving Goffman's (1963) work on social stigma. Goffman's work, which may be seen as a development from classic sociological work on social labelling processes in relation to social deviance, defines stigma in terms of 'spoiled identity'. Edelstein (1988, 1991) has highlighted the consequences of such spoiled identities for people not merely in terms of how they are perceived by others, but also in terms of their experience of their own self-identity. Satterfield et al (2001) have also explored the ways in which these stigma effects may interact with existing forms of social stigmatization experienced by particular minorities and groups within society. Although Goffman's definition of stigma helps us to understand the relationship between technological hazard and the potential for stigmatizing effects on individual and place identity, we should be careful to avoid reifying the notion of stigma or of stigmatizing technologies. As work by Fitchen et al (1987) demonstrates, the identification of toxic contamination in a community is not in *itself* sufficient to generate acute public concern or to set in motion those processes of stigmatization. We cannot, therefore, assume the stigmatization of a place or its residents to be an inevitable consequence of the presence of a technological hazard. Furthermore, the object of stigmatization has to be socially negotiated and may be contested (Satterfield, 1996). This research in the risk field converges with anthropological and sociological research on the stigmatization of socially marginal communities, which has shown that affected groups may manage stigmatized identities by transforming them into something to be defended or even celebrated (Nadel, 1984; Hayden, 2000).

In the context of our discussion, it is important to note that most of this research has focused on the impact of developments that involve the introduction of major new technological hazards to a locality (as in the siting cases) or where toxic contamination that exceeds regulatory limits has been identified. Relatively little attention has been paid to the impact of the presence of existing technological hazards during normal operation (see, however, Bush et al, 2001). It is this situation of living with hazardous and stigmatizing industrial sites, one that is replicated in towns and cities around the industrialized world, that we are concerned with here. By combining insights from the literature on place with those from the risk literature and bringing them to bear on the case study outlined below, this chapter focuses attention on the impacts that the presence of 'everyday' risk can have on the 'life worlds', and therefore on the quality of life, of those who live with hazardous industries.

Chemicals in the community

The chemical plant that provides the focus of the case study was operated, at the time of the research, by Allied Colloids, a local UK company founded elsewhere in Bradford in 1935 which moved to the Low Moor neighbourhood in

1953.[3] At this time the operation in Low Moor employed only 50 people and occupied a few small buildings. Subsequently however, economic success led to the company transforming itself into a multinational operation with facilities in nine countries. As the scale of operations at Low Moor grew, expansion of the Allied Colloids works in Low Moor was achieved through incremental growth and extension of the original site, resulting in a densely packed 17-hectare site with more than 2000 employees.

Low Moor was once a village but is now an outlying district of Bradford, 5km south of the city centre. There had been industry at Low Moor since the 18th century, taking advantage of local iron and coal deposits. By the 1950s, most of this traditional industry had disappeared and Allied Colloids took over as the dominant industrial operation in the area. Today Low Moor is seen as a close-knit community that has tried to keep its own identity.[4] The area immediately around the site mainly consists of housing, most of which existed when the plant was first built, although there were substantial additions made during the 1960s and early 1970s (see Figure 6.1). Some housing is extremely close to the boundary fence of the plant with little or no separation from gardens, public footpaths or back lanes.

Figure 6.1 *Land uses around the Allied Colloids plant*

Housing in Low Moor is almost all owner occupied, with less than 6 per cent rented. Unemployment is uniformly low in the area, averaging less than 6 per cent. In a city known for its significant Asian population, the area is 98 per cent white. In 1995 Allied Colloids estimated that it contributed more than UK£50 million every year to the local economy through wages, taxes and rates, and at the time of the research it was the second largest employer in Bradford. The company had a long-established practice of recruiting trainees from the local community and had a close-knit internal culture, with many of its most senior executives having worked their way up through the organization. Many of its employees still live locally, although to a lesser extent than in the past.

At the time of the research the Allied Colloids site was designated as a source of major accident hazard and came within the remit of the Seveso Directive 'upper-tier' provisions due to the storage of flammable and toxic materials.[5] For this reason there is a full off-site emergency plan in place and the company regularly distributes information to local people about potential accident risks and how to behave in the event of a significant accident event. The company also uses a number of organic chemicals that have an extremely pungent odour. This has, over the years, been the cause of public complaint and of comment by the local press.

Allied Colloids was the focus of public concern and complaint for at least 20 years, although there was no significant mobilization of local people in opposition to the site. At different times over that period, various city councillors and members of parliament had taken up residents' concerns about smells, and environmental and accident risks. One longstanding local critic of the company gained considerable local media coverage in 1989 when he organized a petition and lobbied for a 50 per cent reduction in the annual property tax payable by residents living near the site because of a claimed fall in property values. About 60 households were successful in gaining reductions, but most of these were awarded for reasons other than the presence of Allied Colloids. In many cases the amount of the reduction was small. Claims about the effect of Allied Colloids' presence on residential property values re-emerged following a major accident in 1992.

Prior to 1992 there had been occasional small explosions, fires and releases at the site that had received local press coverage. In July 1992, the company attracted national media attention following a major warehouse fire. Forty-two people, including both Allied Colloids and emergency services personnel, were taken to hospital (Health and Safety Executive, 1994). The fire caused damage to the plant estimated at UK£6 million. A thick plume of smoke from the fire was carried several kilometres eastwards from the site. Local watercourses were polluted by the runoff of contaminated fire-fighting water, killing thousands of fish. As a precautionary measure, local people were warned not to eat fruit and vegetables from their own gardens and allotments. Subsequent monitoring of soil, grass, groundwater and crops by the city council's environmental health department did not reveal any harmful contamination, although the results of these tests took two or three months to come through. The incident resulted in a highly publicized prosecution by the Health and Safety Executive (HSE), which led to the company being fined UK£100,000 in January 1993.

The 1992 accident also led to substantial sustained local media coverage and a flurry of local community action, including public meetings and petitions. After the fire, in addition to a UK£2 million investment to improve safety, the company worked hard to improve relations with the local community. It appointed a community liaison officer to develop and coordinate its local activities and in 1995 launched a newsletter, with seven local residents from the liaison committee on its editorial board. The company also became increasingly proactive in supporting local community initiatives and activities, something for which it was given credit by many of the residents to whom we spoke.

The Low Moor case study was undertaken as part of a larger project that investigated public perceptions of the risks associated with hazardous industrial sites.[6] The Allied Colloids site was identified as an example of a site where there had been both a history of local environmental impact and a significant accident event. The initial stage of the research involved an extensive collection of information from local historical and media archives in order to obtain a good understanding of the development of both the site and the community, and the main issues publicized through media reporting. We also interviewed informants from the company, the regulatory authorities, the city council and other organizations in the local community. We then held group discussions with 6 groups of local residents, comprising 42 people in total. Each group met on two occasions, separated by a period of two weeks. The groups were recruited to include a cross-section of the local community, including both lifetime residents and some who had been there less than five years, reflecting to some degree the socio-economic make-up of the area as revealed by census and social classification data.[7] All the participants lived within the area identified by the HSE as being potentially at risk in the event of a major chemical accident at the site and received information on the precautions to take in case of an emergency.

Industrial encroachment and sense of place

Our group discussions with local residents began by asking people to identify good and bad things about living in Low Moor. We did not indicate that Allied Colloids was the specific object of our interest (although some undoubtedly deduced this to be the case), so we were able to derive some sense of the extent to which the plant figured spontaneously in their views about where they lived. In all but one of the groups Allied Colloids was identified as having a negative impact on the experience of life in Low Moor. Only one group was more circumspect, referring simply to the problems of living in an industrial city. This group included participants with various indirect links to the company or to other chemical companies, and one or two who were defensive about the way in which the area was represented by outsiders. One young man who spoke to us after the first meeting had ended, referring to the discussion of Allied Colloids' relationship with the residents of Low Moor, expressed his disapproval of what he described as 'airing the community's dirty laundry in public'. Nevertheless, despite an occasional sense of reluctance, most showed no inhibition when speaking about Allied Colloids or its relationship to Low Moor and would acknowledge quite even-handedly both good and bad aspects of its activities. As the discussions developed however, only a small number of people, almost all with strong work-related connections with the company, emphasized a positive view of Allied Colloids as a vital source of employment and local income. For example:

> *Jennifer:* I mean, in some respects, I mean obviously they're good, or they're good for the community 'cause they're providing employment. You see they're the second biggest one in Bradford (Group 1).
>
> *Robert:* They employ a hell of a lot of people. There'd be a lot of lads out of work if they weren't here (Group 2).

For most other participants the company was seen as a negative feature – sometimes the only negative feature – of Low Moor, detracting from the quality of their everyday lived experience and sense of place in a number of different ways. Most important were the direct experiences of odours from the site and the worry induced by the possibility of major accident:

> *Mary:* I don't like the fact that Colloids is down the road. Because, it's to me, it's quite dangerous and emits a lot of horrible smells (Group 4).
>
> *(Unidentified female):* Yeah. I mean it was here before I was. But growing up with it, I mean as I'm older now I've I noticed more what goes on there and I don't like it.
>
> *(Unidentified female):* You can walk down to the shop... [and] I mean you've got to hold your mouth and your nose because you're breathing it in and it smells and tastes so disgusting (Group 1).
>
> *David:* I like the area but the things I don't like [are] like everybody else has said... the chemicals, the threat of them; 'cause they'd a big fire. Every time you hear a bang you think... it's going to blow up (Group 6).

As part of the expression of such concerns there were repeated references to the immediate physical proximity of the plant, a continual threatening presence overlooking homes and schools:

> *Paul:* Well, I'm like everybody else. Really, my only dislike of living here is Allied Colloids now – as I look out of my front room window, right where them lights are (Group 1).
>
> *Mark:* The great worry I have is for the kids. Where the school field [is] you can actually... see the plant. You know it's there (Group 6).
>
> *(Unidentified female):* I mean, we're living at risk, really. I mean we're living day to day thinking: 'Well... is it going to be through the night? Is there another accident going to happen? Is it going to be worse than what it were last time?' We're living in fear because of them. They shouldn't be built round... a little community like we are.
>
> *(Unidentified female):* And then when you look at it and how big it's getting, I mean, it seems to be getting bigger all the time; then when they had a fire I started thinking more about, you know, what goes on there. And it's just... really close to people's, you know, close to houses (Group 1).

Comments on how the plant had grown and changed over time, as illustrated by the last quote, emphasized the dynamic nature of physical proximity. Indeed, central to people's negative evaluation of the impacts that Allied Colloids had on their experience of place was a strong sense of encroachment. It was not just that the company was physically dominant and produced unwelcome impacts, but that, especially for older residents, these intrusions had emerged over time to displace positively valued characteristics of Low Moor:

> *Dorothy:* And as far as the changing environment, where I live I look down over Raw Nook [the area of land occupied by Allied Colloids] 'cause I live on the main road and it has changed, because I used to have quite a nice view. I mean we live on the main road... but beyond that you could see trees and fields and what have you (Group 5).

The reference to 'science fiction' in the following exchange also conveys the sense of something alien and unnatural emerging in the place of what had seemed insignificant and innocuous:

> *Mary:* It's like science fiction.
> *Joseph:* It was a little research laboratory long ago.
> *Michael:* Yeah, yeah. When I came to live down here...
> *Joseph:* I could never have envisioned it.
> *Michael:* A tin shed plus a couple of office blocks when I come to live down here. Look at it now (Group 4).

The incremental growth of the company strongly enhanced this sense of a gradual and creeping imposition:

> *Patricia:* I mean it's, it's just taken over the whole place. I mean any bit of land they can buy and build on, they do, don't they? You know, it's just everywhere. Snapping it up (Group 2).
> *Maria:* It's just, it's just growed and growed, hasn't it?
> *James:* It has, it has, yeah.
> *Donald:* Well, like I say... I call it a mushroom field and there's fresh growth there every day (Group 4).

The analogy of the mushroom field conveys the 'organic' (and seemingly uncontrolled and uncontrollable) way in which the plant had developed. Each incremental addition had been relatively insignificant, but in combination had transformed the scale and nature of an industrial operation in the physical centre of the community. Local people had felt powerless to intervene and expressed deep distrust of the local authority's capacity and willingness to protect the interests of local residents:

> *Donald:* There's not many weekends go by without them cranes up putting new chimneys up... I will admit I don't blame Colloids at all for these problems. Colloids shouldn't really have been there; it's the Bradford planners that's at fault (Group 4).

Others followed a similar line, pointing to both the political power of the company and the consequences of economic dependency:

> *Linda:* Well, they [the company and the local authority] must have been hand in hand because they wouldn't have let them spread so much would they? Not in a residential area (Group 1).
>
> *Thomas:* They're too powerful because they can always sort of say: 'Well, OK, we'll take our business to another town', you know, 'and you'll lose thousands of jobs' (Group 2).

The sense of encroachment conveyed in discussion was not just physical. It was also aural – there were references to sirens going off and to bangs heard from the plant – and, most importantly, olfactory. The smell from the plant was not just unpleasant but had encroached upon and defiled people's homes:

> *Jennifer:* On a hot day it can make you physically feel sick.
>
> *(Unidentified female):* People who've come to my house have said: 'I don't know how you live with this smell' (Group 1).
>
> *(Unidentified male):* In summer you have to keep the windows closed 'cause the smell comes in the house and your house smells of this. Yes, I've had to close my doors many a time (Group 6).

This section has highlighted the experience of industrial encroachment on local senses of place. It is not that residents did not acknowledge the economic and social value to local people of Allied Colloids' burgeoning activities, but that these activities impinged upon Low Moor's valued qualities – not as the location of the biggest industrial employer in Bradford, but as a place to live, make a home or raise children. The next section examines one particularly acute aspect of this conflict: the stigmatization of place.

Sense of place and stigmatization

While there was a range of ways in which Allied Colloids directly affected people's feelings about where they lived, discussion in the groups also centred on how others viewed the area – and how Low Moor was viewed *in relation* to other places. To an extent, this theme emerged from complaints about property values, the local housing market and difficulties people had experienced in trying to sell houses. Several of the participants had moved to the area not knowing about Allied Colloids, or being unaware of the kind of impacts that it could have on the locale, and had been drawn by the affordable housing, the convenient road links and the proximity to open countryside.

Repeatedly in the discussions there were claims that Allied Colloids had marked Low Moor as 'not a nice place to live', a place where housing couldn't be sold at comparable prices to other areas and where selling some properties had become almost impossible:[8]

Richard: And [the estate agents] said: 'No, your house prices have not gone down. The ability to sell them, well, that's a different ball game after the large fire at Allied Colloids' (Group 2).

Christopher: See, housing property's low if you live near Colloids. That's if you can sell your house if you live near Colloids.

(Unidentified male): [One] poor guy must have paid, it's going back a bit you know, might be 12 months or so, he were trying to get compensation because [he] put his house up for sale for UK£32,000 or [something] and he couldn't even get £24,000 (Group 6).

However, there is more to stigma than depressed house prices. As noted earlier, the literature on risk and stigmatization has emphasized that risk can, in far more fundamental ways, 'spoil identities'. In their analysis of how the presence of polluting industry affected people's identity on Teesside, Bush et al (2001) identify powerful stigma symbols that 'discredited' the area as a place in which to live. This was manifested in the way that people attempted to distance themselves from this stigmatizing association by drawing attention to the far worse conditions experienced in other areas of Teesside, which were identified as the most polluted and unpleasant within the conurbation:

> Air pollution and poor health are used as discrediting characteristics to stigmatize an 'Other' place as dirty and unhealthy, whilst confirming the usualness – the relative cleanliness and healthiness – of the place where those doing the labelling ('normals') live (Bush et al, 2001, p54).

In our group discussions, there was evidence of similar processes of discrediting and distancing taking place. For many people, the whole identity of Low Moor and, thus, as residents of Low Moor, their own collective and individual identities had been tarnished and spoiled by the presence of the company. This revealed itself in how others were observed to talk about the area:

Maria: [If you say to somebody] 'I live in Low Moor', they go: 'Ugh.'

Michael: 'Yuck.' That's the attitude.

Susan: People who don't know us.

Michael: 'Allied Colloids' is the first answer back to you.

Charles: Yeah.

Michael: 'Allied Colloids, oh, Allied Colloids is there' (Group 4).

Elizabeth: As I say, we moved from the other side of Bradford and when we said: 'Oh, we', you know, 'we're moving to Low Moor', it's like: 'Don't you know? What do you want to move there for? What you going near Colloids for?' (Group 5).

Joseph: Allied Colloids is a centre-piece in the Low Moor. It... overshadows every single [thing]... If people [talk] about Low Moor, you can bet they're talking about Allied Colloids, you know (Group 4).

Some participants blamed the media, in part, for this spoiled place identity and the consequent negative image that others had of Low Moor. In particular, the 1992 accident was seen as having generated media images that produced and, through repetition, reinforced a greater awareness of Low Moor and of the presence of Allied Colloids as a source of risk to the community:

John: Well, most people didn't know where [Low Moor] is, did they – until Colloids blew up (Group 6).

Stigma was also reinforced by the jokes repeated by 'outsiders', which persisted in local culture far longer than the details of media coverage:

Lisa: But you just get fed up [with] the same old jokes about Colloids and having drums blasted into your garden and things like that. I mean, you know, the old jokes, they seem to be still going on, and that fire was quite a while ago now, wasn't it?
Margaret: I get quite a lot of flak about, you know, 'Haven't you noticed all the kids are green.' That's right. 'Keep away, you might be contaminated.' Yeah, I get a lot of jokes about it (Group 1).

It may be significant that the two women who complained most about being the butt of jokes about Low Moor were both relatively recent arrivals who had lived in the area less than five years and whose regular social circle included many friends from other parts of Bradford. The extent to which outsiders' jokes and views of Low Moor could affect residents' own sense of identity was only occasionally revealed in the groups' relatively public forum. The following exchange, however, demonstrates the strong connections between spoiled *place* identity and spoiled *personal* identity:

Barbara: It's like you're ashamed that you live in Low Moor; but you shouldn't be.
Elizabeth: No, you shouldn't.
Barbara: People who don't live in Low Moor have got such a negative attitude towards it. And it's not all bad. There's good and bad everywhere in every town.
Elizabeth: It's like, people that don't really know the area, they automatically say: 'Well, don't live down there by Colloids' (Group 5).

Residents adopted various, often creative, strategies for managing and negotiating spoiled identity. One was to construct Low Moor as 'normal' rather than different from other places, and to emphasize positive rather than negative qualities of place. For two participants, this normalization took the form of incorporating the rural characteristics of the surrounding countryside within their feelings about Low Moor:

William: I think the attraction is out of the door, into open countryside, and you can walk for a couple of hours into woodland across farmland and you'll never see a soul (Group 6).
Lisa: We'd seen that there was industry; but I don't think we realized quite what the nuisance of that was until we came, probably. But having said that, I think it's got other advantages. There's quite a lot of open land still round and about. There's, I mean, you can still usually get into fields in a couple of minutes, you know, even to just cut across up the back of the golf course and through the fields and down the beck [the stream] (Group 1).

For Lisa, normalization was aided by a retreat into the home:

Lisa: Once you're in the house a bit, you could be absolutely anywhere (Group 1).

The home here is constructed as a place of normality, enabling Lisa to shut out the presence of Allied Colloids and to reject the suggestion that her home is different from other places. When speaking to people from outside the neighbourhood, she engaged in a further form of stigma management, which Goffman (1963) refers to as 'passing' (that is, 'normal'):

> *Lisa:* I lie about where I live, I admit that. People say: 'Where do you live?' and I say 'Oakenshaw' [the adjacent suburb] (Group 1).

For others, however, stigma management involved defending the rationality of their own choice to live in the area and blaming others for stigmatizing the community, as in the following quotation in which Allied Colloids is not identified as the problem, despite its unpleasant impacts, but the stigmatizing outsiders:

> *Daniel:* There's [nothing] you can do about it and again I knew when we were going to move down there that [I] had to put up with the smells. I wasn't really bothered. It's other people again, you know. 'Oh, you don't want to live down there. What you living here for?' Yeah. That winds me up (Group 5).

It was evident from our discussions with local residents that many in Low Moor experienced a spoiled sense of place as a result of the presence of Allied Colloids. Even those with links to the company who emphasized its positive contributions to the locality acknowledged that some negative effects persisted. It was also clear that no one we spoke to was happy with the stigmatized identity that had been constructed for the place by others, whether they professed to be affected by it or not. All who spoke about it clearly resented the process of stigmatization, although by no means all resented Allied Colloids' presence in the neighbourhood. Some saw Low Moor's spoiled identity as an inevitable corollary of the presence of Allied Colloids, while others shifted the blame to those who perpetuated such views, whether the local press or those who repeated the lurid jokes and stories. In the often low-key but pervasive ways described, there was a widely felt impairment of people's sense of place and, in some cases, an impairment of people's own sense of self-identity. The following conclusion reviews the implications of the processes that have been discussed for future research and for policy practice.

Conclusion

The central argument that has been presented is that when considering the impact of technological development upon a place, we need to consider more than overt and measurable impacts, such as the effect on property prices. There has, of course, been growing recognition of the psychosocial impacts on those living in situations of toxic contamination. However, the more everyday impacts of hazardous industrial developments on sense of place, and therefore upon quality of life, have not hitherto received a great deal of attention. In this chapter we have attempted to convey the significance of these less tangible impacts through our description of the experience of living near to a substantial chemical plant for the inhabitants of one neighbourhood of a northern English city. In the case study, a strong sense of encroachment was central, particularly for older residents, to the way in which the chemical plant figured in local peoples' feelings about where they lived. The incremental growth and development of the plant had transformed how they and others viewed the area, creating a dominant presence that had 'spoiled' environments previously valued through both the day-to-day smells and pollution and the ever-present risk of a major accident. More generally, this encroachment was resented for its perceived inevitability, its transgression of the diverse values associated with 'home' and the stigmatization that identified the neighbourhood as a spoiled place to live – stigmatization that challenged both place and personal identities and therefore had to be managed in a variety of ways. Our case study thus demonstrates the multifaceted and often subtle nature of the impact of technological development on local structures of feeling. It also highlights the equally varied and often creative ways in which local people manage the stigma arising from those impacts.

So, what conclusions can we draw from our discussion? First, from the observations that we made in Low Moor, it appears that sense of place appears to be a significant mediating factor in the relationship between hazards, locale and people. That is not to say that it is a simple relationship; in fact, our analysis suggests that it may be quite complex. To understand the nature of the relationship we need to identify the salient place values and the way in which the presence of a hazardous site compromises those values. The discussion and case study analysis in this chapter has only begun to outline this issue and there is a need for more systematic research. This will involve building upon and synthesizing earlier work on risk and place, as we have indicated, but poses a distinct question about the place of local environmental values and identities in hazard management policies.

Second, we observed early in our discussion that the debate about sustainability has been extended to embrace a concern with well-being and quality of life, and that this poses new challenges to policy. The use of economic techniques and indicators in environmental policy, where they serve public decision-makers as a surrogate for heterogeneous social values, has often been criticized, not least for the attempt to incorporate non-market values into a monetary metric (see, for example, Sagoff, 1988). The values that people associate with the places in which they live may, to some extent, be reflected in property prices; but often, as we have tried to show, they include values that are not visible to the market (Norton and Hannon, 1997, 1998). Furthermore, the values of people who do not own property, which may be a substantial proportion in some areas, will also be invisible to the market. When we come to address the problem of how a technological development may impact upon local environments and communities, therefore, we need to consider these less tangible and more hidden values.

One of the possible ways in which this might be achieved is through the local land-use planning system. Land-use planning has a wide-ranging remit to control and shape patterns of development; therefore, in principle, it is able to consider risk not in isolation as a technical problem, but to view it 'in context', incorporating local views and opinions. However, in practice, there are significant obstacles to land-use planning performing such a role. While planning priorities are outwardly locally determined, they are, in reality, circumscribed by the legal definition of matters that come within the planning authority's remit by national and regional policy guidance and by the rationalistic culture of credible discourse within the planning system. As Davies (1999) has observed, even when attempts are made within the planning process to engage with the less quantifiable values of local people – for example, by the use of focus groups or citizen juries – there are major difficulties with utilizing such qualitative evidence in local decision-making. In our case study, the ability of the local planning system to balance the economic benefits of the Allied Colloids plant against its local impacts was also compromised by the incremental way in which the plant had grown, so that no single addition provided a measure of its longer term cumulative significance. The mechanisms through which local environmental and risk values may be integrated within decision-making processes therefore remain a challenging area for policy development.

Third, place consists of more than the physical locale and people's senses of place – it includes the relationship a place has to the wider socio-economic and institutional processes that shape the conditions for local action and experience, often referred to as location (Agnew, 1993). This is not an aspect that we have been able to address in this chapter; but it was, nonetheless, in evidence – for example, in repeated references made by participants to the relationships between the company, local government, regulatory institutions and the wider economy. Our case study therefore raises questions about the interaction between the senses of place (and associated place values) that exist in a particular locale and the power relations constituted by the wider processes of location. When considering sense of place and place values, we need to ask, how does location shape local experience and how does it make itself felt? In other words, we need to extend the analysis beyond that presented here and trace the operations of these structural and institutional processes in local experiences of place, and examine their relationship to the values that inform that experience.

Finally, with that wider context in mind, it is important to sound one final cautionary note: with all of this attention to local structures of feeling and place values, we must beware of reifying them or of overemphasizing their significance in relation to the experience of industrial hazards. Places, and the experience of places, change. There are, for example, wider cultural influences, not least that exercised by the mass media, which may subvert or blur a distinct sense of place and contribute to the (re)shaping of place values (see Meyrowitz, 1985). A fuller account of the significance of place values and local structures of feeling for our management of technologically hazardous industries should also, therefore, be sensitive to the mutability of place.

Acknowledgements

The authors gratefully acknowledge the UK Health and Safety Executive (HSE) for funding the empirical research upon which we draw and the

Leverhulme Trust for funding Peter Simmons's work on this chapter as part of the Programme on Understanding Risk. The views expressed here do not represent those of either body. We would also like to acknowledge our partners in the original research project, Alan Irwin and Brian Wynne, and an anonymous referee whose very constructive comments on an earlier version have helped to improve the chapter. Responsibility for any remaining shortcomings lies solely with the authors.

7 Visualizing Place and Belonging: Landscape Redefined in a Swedish Farming Community

Annelie Sjölander-Lindqvist

Building the Hallandsås train tunnel

The context of this chapter is the environmental crisis resulting from building a train tunnel through the Hallandsås ridge in the south-west of Sweden. When the local community, who lived on top of the ridge, learned that an 8.6km train tunnel would be built through it, few expected that the years following the start of the project in 1992 would bring sinking groundwater levels and a toxic spill. As private wells and surface water began to disappear and dry out four years after the initiation of the tunnel's construction, local residents began to be worried about changes occurring in their local environment. By early 1997 the situation was acute, with continually sinking groundwater levels. The building contractor and the Swedish National Rail Administration (Banverket) decided to start looking for an alternative method to seal the tunnel walls. Due to extremely high water pressure, it had proved difficult to seal the tunnel with traditional injections of concrete. In late September 1997, it was discovered that the toxic substance acrylamide, a chemical component of a sealant, had leaked into groundwater, soil and surface water. Cultivated fish died and cattle had to be slaughtered and disposed of. Empty or nearly empty wells, along with the prohibition to use water from contaminated streams, meant that Banverket had to provide households and farmsteads with water, delivered by tanker lorries to water tanks sited on affected properties. In some cases, Banverket financed connection of properties to the municipal water system or solved the problem by drilling provisional wells and pipes. Since construction work was halted in 1997, Banverket has worked continuously to seal the walls of the tunnel and halt the drainage of groundwater.

Since the first signs of these environmental effects, the local farming community has experienced tension and stress. Results from interviews[1] with community members whose situations had been particularly affected by the consequences of the tunnel project suggested a growing uncertainty and apprehension with respect to nature and the environment. The interviews indicated that members of the farming community suffered heavily from the restrictions placed upon the sale of agricultural goods,[2] even though compensation had been paid. To local residents, the destruction of farm produce meant much more than just complying with a restriction put on them by a national agency. In dumping milk away, they dumped hours and years of work. The disposal of milk into the manure drains represented a devaluation of their work and efforts, indicating that their dedication to their work had been in vain. In this region, farmers' everyday work is not only seen as an investment that yields good profits, but also as an investment in a way of life.

At the time of writing, the flow of water is minimal and the sanitation work to extract any remains of the toxic chemical sealant is nearly complete.[3, 4] In February 2003 the Swedish Environmental Court approved an application from Banverket to continue to release groundwater during the eventual completion of the tunnel. The drilling of the tunnel is likely to resume.

Photographing the local environment

The focus in this case study is on the perspectives of those affected by the environmental crisis that had its start during the early months of 1996 when the groundwater level began to fall. This second phase of fieldwork explored questions that were raised during the first part of fieldwork, which was carried out over a period of six months in 1999–2000. Collaborative photography and follow-up interviews were chosen as methods of providing a basis for exploring perceptions of landscape and community and to capture locally regarded vital assets of the local environment, both visual and intangible. The aim of this chapter is to display and discuss the motifs depicted by the photographers in their photos. In categorizing the photographs, I have considered both the motifs and the meaning of the motifs conveyed during the interviews. More formally, each photo has been sorted into one of four categories of representation (described in the next section). None of the categories, however, are clear cut and no sharp dividing lines exist. The analysis considered possible differences along gender lines, but no such variations emerged.

During the first part of fieldwork, it was found that the local environment was perceived as being vulnerable as a result of the project that was building a huge train tunnel through the ridge. Farmers whose farms had been in their family for generations did not know whether they would be able to continue to farm the land.[5] Plummeting groundwater levels were seen as a serious threat to the unique environment of the area. It was generally believed that the survival of agriculture intimately depended upon high groundwater levels as the copiousness of groundwater represented an insurance of good yields even if the summers were dry. People perceived a threat to their own future, the future of the community and that of the landscape itself. The tunnel project, above all, had introduced tremendous uncertainty into the lives of the people living on the Hallandsås ridge (Sjölander-Lindqvist, 2004).

In the second phase of the fieldwork, 15 members of the affected local community above the northern tunnel site received 'one-time' use cameras and were asked to photograph their 'local environment'. They were given only minimal instructions asking them to consider what they experienced as important in their local environment and what had meaning to them personally, either positively or negatively. What was to be understood by 'local environment' was left to them to decide. The gender distribution of the photographers was relatively even; 7 of the 15 were women, 3 were men, while 2 cameras were used by husband-and-wife teams. One couple returned an unused camera, having looked through their own photo albums where they had found all the motifs they valued in the local environment. All but one of the photographers lived together with a spouse. Although seven of the photographers were women, in most cases both husband and wife discussed what to photograph, either before or during the actual photography. People seemed to regard it as important that the project of photographing the local environment was communal. People were requested to return the cameras within approximately one month, and after two months all but one had done so.

The photography project yielded just over 300 photographs. The photographs were subsequently discussed in in-depth interviews with each photographer, following a semi-structured interview plan. Thirteen interviews were carried out in photographers' homes; the 14th photographer declined an interview due to a heavy workload since she was going to open her own business.[6] The follow-up interviews were taped. In the interviews, the photographers were asked to describe each picture and the meanings of the motif depicted. Each photographer was asked to categorize his or her photographs. The idea behind this method of collaborative photography was that the photos would serve as associative tools during the interviews that would follow. After these two initial tasks, some more general questions followed. Informants were asked to describe the landscape and the nature of the ridge for a hypothetical stranger. They were asked whether they thought that drawing a border around their local environment was problematic. They were also asked how they had planned and carried out the photography. Another question concerned what they thought, at that time, about the yet-to-be-decided continuation of the tunnel construction and whether they had any concerns about it.

Images of the local environment

To a neutral observer, a photo might be a picture of a tractor in a field or a cat in a garden; but to the photographer the motif in the same picture might be a Morello tree of specific significance (see Figure 7.1), symbolizing how five generations had lived and worked on the farm – and this kind of interpretation was consistently indicated in the interviews. From the interviews with the photographers it emerged repeatedly that their photos represented more than a single item or topic. For example, a photo of huge white balls of silage out in the fields represented small-scale farming; but the motif also symbolized life, good neighbours and a way of keeping the landscape alive and open (see Figure 7.2). Consequently, a motif could fit into several of the four categories, and linkages exist between the different groupings.

Source: Private collection

Figure 7.1 *Morello tree*

Source: Private collection

Figure 7.2 *White balls of silage in the fields*

The photos depicted a wide range of motifs. The analysis examines each set of photos through a categorization in which each informant participated. The motifs and images of the photos produced the following four categories of representation:

1. The category of *the estate and the household* comprises houses or farms. This category represents both the physical attributes of a household, such as buildings, and more abstract domestic attributes of family members. The 'house' is thus not only a physical structure; it is also a representation of the interrelations among the people who live in this physical structure, and their ideas and the daily life that is lived in the house (Carsten and Hugh-Jones, 1995).
2. The category of *beings* focuses on the people and the living creatures who are to be found on or outside the household and the estate. Although people did not photograph wild animals such as foxes, elk or roe deer, the wildlife constituted a noteworthy theme in the follow-up interviews. Though not visible in the photographs, these beings were associated with the photographs.
3. In this category, *the landscape* constitutes an overarching theme. Here, the frame of reference for the analysis is the house or the home as a point of perspective for looking at something – in this case, the landscape.
4. Finally, the category of *evidence* deals with what emerged as a documentary feature of some photos in relation to the tunnel project. Here, motifs of wells, appliances for water tests, cracks in house foundations and holes in the ground are examples of the images in this category.

The estate and the household

Representations of the estate category comprise several sub-groupings. Photographs in this category depict the home district, the livelihoods of people, their places of work and their homes. Gardens; the setting around the estate; cattle and buildings belonging to the farm; the estate and the house as an idyllic place (see Figure 7.3); and pets and family members – usually in gardens or in front of buildings (see Figure 7.4) – are the motifs of this category. Images related to the livelihoods of people and their places of work are also prominent. A salient feature of this category is the representation of estate members as *contributors* to the prospects of the site of the farmstead or the homestead. In the interviews, people stressed that activities of family members provided a foundation for both the domestic life of the household and for the future of the estate (see Figure 7.5). On the estate and in the household, people are engaged in activities that contribute to the well-being of the family and to the survival of the farmstead or the homestead. Through short-term and long-term planning, people take care of what are regarded as important assets of the estate and the household. By cultivating the area, farmers take an active part in the future of their farms and, at the same time, carry on the work of past farming generations. People feel that they have the responsibility both to replace what their parents planted some decades ago and to combine these traditions with their own ideas about the way in which the garden, perhaps, should look. By contributing to the maintenance of the estate's environment and the household, people contribute to reality: 'I am not a guest in reality, but a contributor to reality.'

Source: Private collection

Figure 7.3 *The idyll*

Source: Private collection

Figure 7.4 *Grandchildren swinging*

Another feature of the household and estate category is that it serves as a meeting point for neighbours and for family members. Here, people can meet and enjoy companionship at the same time as it is a place for social activity spanning the borders between generations: 'I'm not keeping this place up for nothing. I do it for my children and grandchildren, so we have a place to get together.'

The family, the next generation and the link across generations constitute the overriding dimension of continuity and temporality of the local community and of the landscape on the Hallandsås.

Beings within the local environment

Neighbours and animals are recurrent themes, both as photographic motifs but also in the verbal meanings of symbolic representations expressed during interviews. Neighbours hold a prominent position as they stand for companionship, the existence of social networks, memories and exchange of knowledge. Images of neighbours can also serve as links to other categories. One of the photographers took a picture of the son of one or her farming neighbours; when discussing the photo, she said that while the photo was a picture of the child, it was also an image of farming and of the importance of family (see Figure 7.5). In the outer circle of the household, wild animals such as roe deer and rabbits, and domestic animals such as cats and dogs, play an important role as they represent both untamed nature and tracts of land that have not been built upon. Sheep are also portrayed, linked to farming and farmsteads (see Figure 7.6).

Source: Private collection

Figure 7.5 *The son of a farming neighbour*

Source: Private collection

Figure 7.6 *Sheep*

The Hallandsås landscape

Images of the surroundings and the landscape focus on vegetation, wetlands, water and the cultural milieu. The Hallandsås landscape is portrayed through a number of themes, one of the most salient being the theme of farms and the farming community. Here, photos of cows and sheep, tractors and fields are recurrent. Another prominent motif is that of 'wild' and 'untouched' nature, such as the wetlands and moors (see Figure 7.7), as well as photos of landmarks, such as stone fences and watercourses, the views from the hills and the small roads. The photographers also generally agreed that these various landmarks gave character to the landscape and that they also serve as sites of memory for people in the area. The train station, a 19th-century red-brick building, was mentioned as an asset of cultural value. A new train station will be built a few kilometres outside of the town of Båstad, and some of the informants felt that this was a loss for both commuters and people who had memories connected to their train journeys as children.

The uniqueness of the natural environment is emphasized, sometimes in a melancholy way:

> It's unbelievable, but that part [the effect on nature] is very uncertain. What's going to happen? It's not fun pumping (up) water to fill these ponds. It's not natural. It's sad. If they drain the groundwater again, then maybe all of this will disappear anyway. Why the hell have we put all our time, sweat and tears into this, then? It's not fun anymore. When you start thinking about it... you shouldn't think about it. You have to be positive because otherwise it'll break you.

Source: Private collection

Figure 7.7 *Lya moor*

The tunnel project is disrupting the landscape on the Hallandsås. Informants employ the term 'artificiality' to refer to the unwanted consequences of the project – for example, the presence of small buildings for filtering water from newly drilled pipes on estates, or the presence of water tanks, another solution for the supply of water:

> ... the flow meter in the brook is also something constructed. I'd rather not see that either! And in that picture, the animals are out, but that little house [the filter shed], that's also constructed, something negative. I'd rather not see that at all.

Evidence

This last category can, in a sense, be said to reflect the ambition among many of the photographers to create a documentary. Many felt that they had the responsibility to record what was locally acknowledged as the consequences and 'future unknowns' of the tunnel project. During the follow-up interviews, they stressed that they wanted to make sure that the environmental consequences of the tunnel construction beneath their homes were made visible.[7] Images included motifs of one of the working access shafts of the tunnel (see Figure 7.8), dead trees, cracks in roofs and foundations (see Figure 7.9), dirty water, and wells known to have been contaminated, along with photos of wells and wetlands that, as people argued, had gone dry due to the sinking of the groundwater level in the ridge. These photos reproduce the 'facts' of the tunnel

Source: Private collection

Figure 7.8 *Working access shaft*

project; but they also portray the uncertainties connected with the project. Dead trees as well as trees that were losing their leaves were commonly mentioned during the interviews as proof of the consequence of the tunnel project and the lowered water table. Cracks in roofs and foundations were believed to be the result of blasting in the tunnel, an intrusion into people's homes and estates. In two cases, informants had photographed tap water stored in the bidet and the bath tub (see Figure 7.10). The water was brown-black as a result of manganese and iron precipitated from the water pipes that had been drilled into the ground to solve the water shortage. These factual images of the consequences of the Hallandsås tunnel project can be seen as a way in which the informants assessed their daily life and what for them was the 'reality' of the effort to build the tunnel deep down (see, for example, Morphy and Banks, 1997, on photographs as a record of reality). At the same time, these bits of evidence of the wrongdoings of the tunnel project have made people more aware of the importance of certain landmarks in their surroundings that now are under threat.

Heritage, present and future: An interface

The tunnel project on the Hallandsås ridge has set in motion a process of questioning and a discourse of doubt among local residents about the present and future of the local community. Aspects of the continuity of the local community have been incorporated within the process.

Source: Private collection

Figure 7.9 *Crack in a foundation*

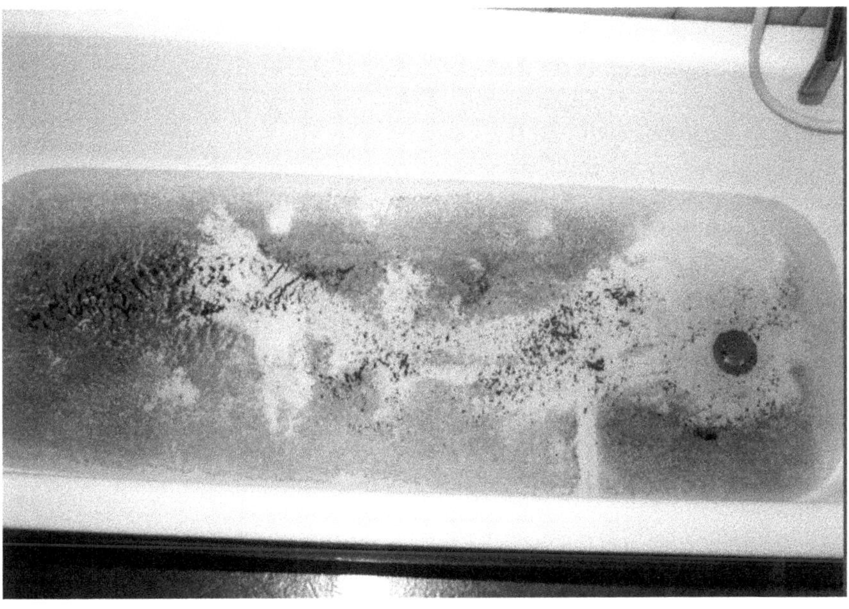

Source: Private collection

Figure 7.10 *Tap water contaminated with iron and manganese*

As argued previously, linkages exist between the different categories of photographs. In the analysis of these categories and in the content analysis of the interviews, the theme of continuity emerged as a salient issue again and again. Central in discussions of the photographs with each photographer was the question of the importance of keeping the history of the cultural landscape and the place alive. This theme of continuity was present in all four representational categories.

The theme of time, temporality and continuity can be divided into three interrelated categories: *the individual*, *the social group* and *the locality* – the last term referring to relational and contextual dimensions of a place (Appadurai, 1995). Images of homes, houses, family members, pets and gardens represent the individual perspective. From the group-oriented perspective, photographs of neighbours are prominent, while motifs representing the locality were more wide ranging. In this locality category, stone fences, farmsteads and cattle, an open landscape, small winding roads, the Lya moor, and the Branddamm (a centrally located pond) were recurrent motifs.

These three broad categories are all interlinked with regard to the continuity of the local community, the future prospects of the landscape and the local environment. None of the categories, from the individual perspective to the place-oriented one, are meaningful independently. The house (the estate), the home and the household are emphasized in terms of a connection between the individual and the surrounding landscape. Of importance is not what is inside the houses, but rather the connection between those who live in the house, their neighbours and the features of the landscape. There is a mutual relationship between people and the surrounding environment: neither can be understood without the other (see, for example, Croll and Parkin, 1992; Ingold, 1993).

There had been a small brook in the yard of one of the informants that dried out around the time of the tunnel excavation. The informant explained that the brook had been an important feature of the property and a source of joy for the family. As a natural feature of their environment, the brook, the shrubbery and the small birds all together contributed to the creation of a place where the sounds of birds and murmuring water could be enjoyed. The brook poses, in this case, a link between the home of the family and the local environment. This space can be seen as an extension of those who live in the house (Carsten and Hugh-Jones, 1995). At the same time, the dried-out brook is an ever-present reminder of the lowered water table and the tunnel deep underground.

The environment is collective in the sense that the immediate surroundings are shared not only with family members, but, above all, with neighbours. Stone fences, trees, shrubs and brooks are thus not merely visible features of the landscape; they also tell of a collective and inherited environment. Trees and avenues are memorials and landmarks of people's immediate environment:

> Every tree or avenue in this area holds memories or has unique traits... You see how people have worked this land for thousands of years. You see remains from that time and you want to preserve them (see Figure 7.11).

The sharing of the surroundings and the environment is also expressed in daily

Source: Private collection

Figure 7.11 *White beam alley*

and seasonal activities that are carried out in the surroundings. For example, in spring, people go picking lilies of the valley; in the autumn, mushrooming is another popular activity; while winter often presents the opportunity to go skiing or ice-skating. Every season has its enchantment and its type of activities. Many of the activities are performed together, and people share the landscape and the place where the activities are carried out. Some of the activities are carried out annually, and one might even say that they sometimes have ritual features that attach people and neighbours to each other, thus extending and deepening the relationships of neighbourhood. One example is the annual *Beskarunda* (the 'bitter round'), performed in the late autumn when people in the small villages gather to visit all of their neighbours to drink a home-made bitter. Such activities create bonds among those living in the area and the surrounding environment and landscape. Another such example is when people gather to have a picnic on a hillside covered with beech forests on an early morning every spring, commonly referred to as the *Gökotta* ('the cuckoo sings at daybreak').

Good neighbourliness is a significant value for the local community. Neighbours are acknowledged as an important part of life, providing an opportunity to share experiences and knowledge about their lives and work, about their well-being and shortcomings. The value is also important in the sense that neighbours take care of each other: 'We've gained incredible insight into farming and its necessary conditions by meeting and exchanging experience.'

Aspects of time and temporality are important in terms of this notion of neighbourliness since memories, to a large extent, are bound to neighbours and their houses. Neighbours depend upon each other as a memory resource, but also in other respects. Since some property and farm owners no longer actively work their farms, they lease out their fields to other farmers. In order to survive as full-time working farmers in a time when farming is becoming more and more rationalized, they need to extend their arable ground at the same time as the owners of the land have an interest in making sure that their properties are being well kept. A symbiotic relationship is developed where both parties benefit.

This leads us to another salient feature of the meanings and values associated with the category of motifs that depict the farming community. Small-scale farming in the local community is considered as vitally important in many respects. Farming is acknowledged as a crucial contributor to the shape of the landscape, giving character to the landscape and the local environment: 'It's this open landscape that's open precisely because farmers are cultivating it. It's not going to look like this if they are not here anymore.'

The existence of farms through generations of families and hundreds of years has contributed to the openness of the landscape, with its extraordinary views of the water in the coastal bay, the billowing hills and pastures:

> All that work and struggle. You can just accept and be grateful that it is as beautiful as it is... This small-scale farming is an extremely important part; it gives the whole area character and life, too.
>
> I've been around here since I was ten years' old... experiencing nature. That's really what I want to look at and I want to keep the landscape open by having cattle (see Figure 7.12).

Farming also contributes to the cultural history of the area and is acknowledged as an essential part of the lives of neighbours and their way of living. Cattle, tractors and combine harvesters give life and bustle to the community: 'We want to keep the countryside [as it is], with roads and all the activity. Among the farmers up here... Gösta has his red cows and we have our white cows' (see Figure 7.13).

Access to freshwater is considered the most important factor for the survival of the local farming community. Since farming depends upon reliable access to water for the irrigation of arable land, for watering animals and for the vegetation on the ridge, the residents are distinctly fearful of what will happen to the local environment and vegetation if the drainage and the lowering of the water table continues. In an area where lack of water has never been a problem before, there is a new uncertainty about access to water and the preservation of a steady, invariable water table that threatens to jeopardize the future of the farming community: 'We have about 15 acres of arable land and the tunnel runs underneath the whole stretch. If the crops were to fail... we'd lose the whole farm.'

A prevailing fear for the future of the flora and fauna remains:

> There's not so much groundwater here [anymore]... it changes the nature completely. Maybe the rosehips can survive... but the alders and such, they don't grow so well if there isn't any water in the ground. It's changing the vegetation.
>
> And if the groundwater level drops, then the crops get hit the hardest... It's the crops that are most important to us.

Source: Private collection

Figure 7.12 *Meadow with bay view*

Source: Private collection

Figure 7.13 *Country road with signs*

> …is it going to remain, the mixture of trees and other stuff, or is it just going to be black or green and overgrown?
>
> If the groundwater is lowered, how will [nature] react? It is both about my work and the work of past generations.

A growing awareness among residents of the vulnerability of the community and of the future of the local environment has been accompanied by feelings of responsibility. Among the informants, the area is seen more than anything else featuring small-scale farming. People say that the presence of family-owned farms is the most important reason why residents fight for their environment and their groundwater. Without the farms, the landscape risks losing its genuine character and traditional landmarks. The preservation of the landscape has come to the forefront, especially for people living in the area above the northern tunnel site. The widespread feeling of uncertainty about the local environment has furthermore contributed to an activation of memories of past generations' work and hardships:

> I sit up here sometimes and wonder what our ancestors thought when they sat here. What did they think about this? The same as I'm pondering now about how it will be in the future…We don't live forever, after all. I think it's nice for the next…generation to have this nature. Are we going to disturb these kinds of things that really are unique?
>
> We're not here forever; someone has to come after us. What am I actually going to leave here so they see what I've done?

Another salient feature in the photo interviews was the extent to which informants stressed the uniqueness of the local environment, the landscape and the local community. The ridge and the landscape are depicted in idyllic terms. Parts of the local surrounding nature are described as wild and more or less untouched. Juniper, beech trees, foxes, roe deer and badgers exist within a quiet landscape where cattle graze in fields alongside small local roads that connect the small villages with each other. The uniqueness of the area is vividly emphasized, not only for its natural beauty and the variety of nature, but also for the ways in which (and the extent to which) people value their neighbours and 'good neighbourliness'.

The landscape and the local community are, in a sense, described as a 'functioning totality'. It is an area, a landscape and a locality – a microcosm that is described as 'having it all':

> Well, this is, like, everything! It is very complete somehow.
>
> I often went out last summer…when the sun was going down. I'd go over to the little road to the intersection, and from there you can see the sunset. Completely calm, completely quite, you could see the sun setting. The blackbirds were singing in the woods and I'd say to myself that this has to be the next best thing to paradise.
>
> My mouth cannot describe what my eyes have seen. It's just not possible, no matter how nicely I'd describe it, because when you see it you just say 'wow!' It's this view and this…well, when you get a bit farther out, not where I live but out on the slope, it's like an aerial photograph…I just can't describe what the eye sees…you have to see it to understand.

These quotations indicate the importance of the landscape and the place on the ridge for the members of the local community. The local environment forms a unique whole and is perceived as giving perfection to the community and to the livelihoods of people. This perception indicates that specific and unique values can be associated with a certain place that is seemingly singular and irreplaceable (Kopytoff, 1986; Hornborg, 1994).

Discussion

Through visual representations we can gain an understanding of collectively shared meanings, values and traditional knowledge. In this case, the use of visual images has been an associative tool in understanding the views and perceptions of vital assets of the local environment. In the case of the Chernobyl accident, it has been demonstrated that visual images can be a way of verifying 'reality', while images at the same time can give individual interpretations of what is depicted (Boholm, 1998; Ferreira et al, 2001). By photographing reality, human experience is transformed into images (Sontag, 1973; Winston, 1998; Pink, 2001). Something of the photographers themselves is thus left in the images (Adelman, 1998; Winston, 1998). When collaborative photography is methodologically employed to gain insight and knowledge about cultural modes of life or, as in this case, about local views of landscape, place and locality, intuitive and emotive symbolic meanings and values can be elicited: 'We use images not only as representations of the objective world but also to communicate our deepest feelings' (Prosser, 1998, p1). Photographs report what we think, know and believe about our surrounding world, and they get meaning from their context (Becker, 1998).

The tunnel project has brought into question the future of the local environment. This process has led to increasing attention being paid in the local community to what people value in their community and in the landscape.[8] The environmental crisis that followed the sinking of the groundwater level, the toxic leak and other environmental consequences of building the tunnel has given rise to an awareness of shared responsibility for the local environment, the community and community values. At the same time as people form part of a society in the present, they also perceive themselves as members of a society that takes many of its bearings from the lives of past generations. An intensified recognition and re-evaluation of the local community and its collective social identity, as well as its past, present and future, has emerged.

The project of building a train tunnel through the Hallandsås ridge is a technological endeavour that threatens the way in which local residents construe the local environment in terms of memories attached to places and components of the cultural landscape, and how people relate to their environment. The tunnel has, in a sense, interrupted relationships with their environment and the landscape. Brooks where people used to go fishing are now dried out or contain less and less water. For the residents, elements in the surrounding environment, such as stone fences, beech forests, streams and creeks, are loaded with emotional sentiments and highly valued. These components are not only landmarks and monuments of nature, but are also significant for local identity.

A frequent motif in the photographs was a pond situated in one of the three small villages that form part of the local community on top of the ridge. This pond, the *Branddamm*, has played an important role in two senses, both as an anchor for shared memories and as a precautionary measure in case of fire. Several of the informants recalled how, as children, they used to ice-skate on this pond. When the pond emptied of water due to the sinking of the groundwater level, these childhood memories were activated and became a prominent topic when people started to question what was happening to the local environment because of the tunnel project. People simply began to recognize the importance of certain landmarks that hitherto had been taken for granted. The heritage of past generations was acknowledged and heritage landmarks reminded people that the local community owed its existence to previous generations. A telling example is the argument of both farmers and single homeowners that although the stone fences had an aesthetic value, they were also the product of the needs and efforts of earlier generations. The fences were created from the necessity of removing the stones from the fields that had to be cultivated at the same time as it was necessary to make fences so that cattle could be kept from arable land, a need that still exists today. The stone fences tell of the hard work of past generations. A landscape is a life story, narrating the lives and works of earlier generations as the totality of its people and their experiences in a specific historical context (Inglis, 1977; Brinckerhoff Jackson, 1984; Ingold, 1993; Hood, 1996; Stoffle et al, 1997).

Local interpretations of historically and culturally significant aspects of the landscape and environment above the tunnel site on the Hallandsås ridge demonstrate that the local community draws its basic references and values from a triangulate combining the individual, the social group and the place.[9] Earlier it was argued that none of the parts of the triangulate can have a bearing on its own; rather, they are interlinked and interdependent, relating to continuity and time. Local history and the work of past generations constitute the element of time and the temporality of a heritage, while the present local community represents contemporary time. Uncertainty is understood to be a constituent part of the future – associated with the potential consequences of tunnel excavation.

Views of the surrounding environment and the landscape are influenced by the negative outcomes of building a train tunnel through the ridge and by a collective reflection upon the surrounding environment. Otherwise, taken-for-granted conceptualizations of the landscape and the physical appearance of the community are suddenly challenged and questioned. The follow-up interviews confirmed the importance of the photographers' motifs; in many cases, they were associated with childhood memories, family history and more temporal aspects of the local community. This suggests that what people regard as personally important can also be associated with broader collective contexts relating to nature and social continuity. If your parents, for example, have given you something to look after, your feelings for the farm or house grow as time passes by.

Conclusion

The environmental consequences of the tunnel have not only contributed to a change in the conditions of the natural environment, but have also altered and threatened basic references within the local community. Anxiety about the future of the small-scale farming community as a basic symbol of the community's survival is prominent among local residents in the aftermath of both the toxic spill and the lowered water table. Normally, in good harvest years, cultivated hectares are highly productive. But with water tables low, drought can result in the farms above the tunnel losing good harvests. Due to a lowered water table, farming depends even more upon heavy rainfall. Disagreement among the experts about the future prospects for the groundwater, harvest yields and the flora and fauna (Florgård et al, 1999), adds to the anxiety, but also to the awareness of what people value and cherish in their surroundings.

A community who once could confidently rely upon the water supply has turned into a community where people depend upon external ways to manage their water needs. The tunnel is understood to affect not merely the private and domestic water supply, but the entire future well-being of the community. For the local community on the northern part of the Hallandsås ridge, the modernization of the railway on the west coast route implies a threat not only to private households but, more importantly, also to the survival and continuity of the farming community and the natural environment itself. The tunnel represents a threat to the natural and the cultural landscape:

> It's not supposed to change the whole landscape, that's just... that's just wrong.
> Before, it was more normal to think that it's always been this way and will continue to be like this for many years.

Community members see themselves as being attached to the cultural history of the area at the same time as they are contributing to the future of the area and the local community. In the shadow of the proposed tunnel, the awareness of the community's and the landscape's vital and cherished assets has intensified feelings of uncertainty regarding the future. Such feelings go beyond environmental concerns. The prevailing uncertainty about the future prospects of the landscape and of the local community disturb shared understandings of the past and the future. The past, present and future are recognized as interdependent. In the wake of the toxic leak and sinking groundwater levels, values attached to both physical and social characteristics of the cultural landscape have been evoked.

The findings of this study, which involved the active participation of the informants in producing visual imagery, suggests that when a local community is faced with the threat of a toxic spill or fairly negative outcomes of a lowered water table, assumptions of nature and the surrounding environment are challenged. The landscape is the result of human engagement with the local environment (Brinckerhoff Jackson, 1984; Hirsch, 1995). A landscape is a record of the lives and the works of earlier generations and a place where they have left something of themselves (Inglis, 1977; Ingold, 1993). Places, therefore, have the capacity to reinforce the past in the present. The physical environment, as well as events and occurrences, tie people to each other and to the landscape and local setting of everyday experiences – and therefore to themselves. The sinking of the groundwater level has turned out not only to pose a threat to natural streams, ponds and beech woods, but also to collectively shared cultural values and institutions.

ACKNOWLEDGEMENTS

The research on which this chapter is based has been supported by the Swedish National Rail Administration and the Bank of Sweden Tercentenary Foundation (Humanities and Social Sciences Donation). I would like to thank Åsa Boholm and Anna Bohlin at the Centre for Public Sector Research (CEFOS) of Göteborg University, as well as Alf Hornborg, Human Ecology Division, Lund University, and the anonymous reviewers for invaluable comments on earlier versions of this chapter.

8 Shifting Risks: Hoover Dam Bridge Impacts on American Indian Sacred Landscapes

Richard W Stoffle, M Nieves Zedeno, Amy Eisenberg, Rebecca Toupal and Alex Carroll

Introduction

This chapter is about a proposed bridge across the Colorado River that is designed to reduce the auto and truck traffic that currently passes directly over Hoover Dam. This bridge, or bypass, will not reduce the volume of traffic over the Colorado River, but is expected to reduce the risk of traffic to the people of the US by keeping most of it off the road across Hoover Dam. Planning the construction of this bridge has involved a number of major environmental and cultural debates, and the decision to place the bridge on a major American Indian ceremonial mountain has raised issues of shifting risks from those currently borne by the dominant society to a minority population. These risks are being shifted by using 'For the Greater Good' arguments, while ignoring the cumulative cultural impacts already borne by the minority society and the irreparable nature of these new risks.

This case of a siting controversy is placed within the social theory of the Risk Society that has been proposed by European social philosophers such as Ulrich Beck (1999), Anthony Giddens (1990), Barbara Adam (1998) and Scott Lash (1996) and that has been illustrated and expanded by Brian Wynne (1987), Elisabeth Beck-Gernsheim (Lash et al, 1996), Joost van Loon (Adam et al, 2000) and others. With few exceptions (cf Caplan, 2000), the theory of Risk Society lacks grounding in specific cases. Most risk cases that have been brought to the theory serve as passive illustrations rather than active tests. Thus, an important new effort by the European Science Foundation called Network for Research into the Construction of Environmental Risk (NRCER) is to provide grounded cases where certain aspects of the theory can be further illustrated, modelled, parameterized and tested. The NRCER has identified the following research goals that are important for grounding Risk Society theory:

- Employ conceptual clarity and precision.
- Provide sample of risk types for investigation.
- Describe the materialization of 'situated risk' and its influence on social movement and coverage by the mass media.
- Determine the institutional contexts of 'situated risk'.
- Consider the consequences derived from its action.
- Develop a methodology for the research of risk.
- Analyse the communication of risk.
- Consider issues pertaining to risk management in democracy.

The Hoover Dam case study is offered in an effort to forward the process of grounding Risk Society theory (Adam and van Loon, 2000, pp1–31) regarding the following topics, which at some point in the future may be sufficiently understood in order to be modelled as variables:

- greater good: shifting risks from the centre to the periphery;
- contesting risks: science versus lay knowledge debate;
- timescapes: short-term risks and solutions versus long-term risks and impacts, as well as spatially narrow versus wider project footprints;
- manageability: the insurability versus the non-insurable nature of risks.

The Hoover Dam analysis does not claim to contribute equally to all of these topics, but each is included to suggest that the model of the Risk Society should include operationalized and interacting variables. In addition, the case brings forth the issue of trust in science and bureaucracy, which – instead of being its own variable – is considered as an aspect of each of the previous topics. The concept of ontological security is also explored and a way in which it can be operationalized is suggested.

Risk Society as social theory

For Risk Society to exist it must be structurally and culturally changing (or have just changed) in response (or adaptation) to a series of factors that are qualitatively different (through either a rapid process or episodic change) than anything previously confronted by human society. Environmental examples include threats to human health and ontological security deriving from the nuclear explosion of Chernobyl; the widespread destruction of species throughout the planet; the hole in the ozone layer; global climate change; cloned sheep and the eighth day of Creation [The eighth day of Creation is a reference to the current status of biotechnology (genetically modified organisms and cloning) where new forms of life can be made by man, a task that had formerly been reserved for God.]; and the rise of transnational corporations and political affairs. These new threats to humankind can generally be categorized in five areas:

1. environmental change and pollution;
2. genetically engineered plants and animals;

3 globalization;
4 trust in science; and
5 trust in bureaucracy.

The latter two are analytically separate; but the fact of their frequent collusion often makes them a single variable.

According to this theory, Risk Society has come into being because of the newness of these threats. The number and magnitude of the threats to society has increased, and the threats are of a nature that all human populations on the planet share them. Arguments for this position have filled 30 books and numerous articles since the German sociologist Ulrich Beck proposed the theory in 1986 (Beck, 1992). The theory has sparked a raging debate; but few effective critiques have emerged. It has become the theory to be addressed by social scientists, especially those with access to data by which the theory can be explored, tested and further developed.

These new risks have undermined the confidence of people in their future. It is argued that many people on the planet now fear for their very existence. Giddens (2000) suggests this is a 'runaway world' and that people are riding a juggernaut of dangers that are, in most respects, beyond our reason and traditional ways of adapting to changes and threats to our selves and societies (Giddens, 1990, pp151–173). This array of risks has affected, and will continue to impact upon, our trust in expert systems and our feelings of ontological security (Giddens, 1990, pp131–134).

Adam (2000, p12) suggests that one problem that the Risk Society faces derives from those who have the power and the privilege to define risks. She notes that the language of risk, established as it is in terms of epistemologies of facility and truth, has been narrowly restricted so that it does not easily accommodate the language of injustice and local concerns. The essence of the 'badness' of risk has primarily been understood in medico-biological and economic terms and is known as calculated risks. Socio-cultural risks having to do with the structure of social relationships and the continuity of culture have no place in calculated risks. Social theory has been charged with the important task of challenging common sense – that is, the adequacy of reason and logic. Social theory must also challenge political and normality assumptions that are central to other cultural systems (for example, gender, class and race), and thus reposition risk through the explication of its meanings in alternative epistemologies. Perceived risk is the term used to describe these alternative views of risk, and the Hoover Dam case presents in sharp contrast these alternative views of risk.

The Hoover Dam case

Hoover Dam is located on the Colorado River at the mouth of Black Canyon, a place that is in the Creation lands of people who speak the Numic (especially the Southern Paiute people) and the Yuman (especially Hualapai and Mohave peoples) languages. This place is also connected to the Creation stories of the

Hopi, Zuni and Navajo ethnic groups. Wi'Kahme (Spirit Mountain) in the Newberry Mountains of Nevada is the centre of creation for all Yuman speakers (Hinton and Watahomigie, 1984). This mountain was formed when the Creator carved out the channel of the Colorado River and piled the Earth into a single place where Creation was to occur. The Southern Paiute people were created in the upper portion of Las Vegas Wash near the base of Nuvagantu ('where snow sits', or Mount Charleston) in the Spring Mountains (Kroeber, 1970; Laird, 1976). These Creation mountains 'stand on their toes and look at one another' according to Paiute beliefs, suggesting a mountain-to-mountain spiritual relationship. Lying in a north–south orientation to the east (Arizona side) of the Colorado River is a Creator Being mountain in the shape of a large lizard (the Black Mountains). Ha'tata ('the middle of the river') is the Hualapai word that describes where the Black Canyon and the Colorado River combine to form the ethnic boundary between two Indian ethnic groups.

According to an oral account recorded by John Wesley Powell during the early 1870s (Fowler and Fowler, 1971, pp76–77), for the Southern Paiutes the canyons of the Colorado River were produced:

> ...many years ago when wise and good men lived on the Earth. The great chief of all the Utes lost his beloved wife. Day and night he grieved, and all his people were sad. Then Ta-vwoats [one of the dignitaries in the mythology] appeared to the chief and tried to comfort him, but his sorrow could not be allayed. So at last Ta-vwoats promised to take him to a country away to the south-west where he said his dead wife had gone and let him see how happy she was if he would agree to grieve no more on his return. So he promised. Then Ta-vwoats took his magical ball and rolled it before him, and as it rolled it rent the Earth and mountains, and crushed the rocks and made a way for them to that beautiful land – a trail through the mountains which intervened between that home of the dead and the hunting grounds of the living. And following the ball, which was a rolling globe of fire, they came at last to the Spirit Land. Then the great chief saw his wife and the blessed abode of the Spirits where all was plenty and all was joy, and he was glad. Now, Ta-vwoats enjoined upon the chief that he should never travel this trail during life, and that all of his people should be warned not to walk therein. Yet still he feared that they would attempt it so he rolled a river into the trail – a mad raging river into the gorge made by the globe of fire, which should overwhelm any who might seek to enter there.

Today this same account is told as a vehicle for explaining the Black Canyon and its relationship to the Colorado River and the Southern Paiutes. The account is viewed as a true and exact representation; and the volcanic lined river is living testimony of the event. It is here that the epistemological problems begin when Indian people reason with Euro-Americans who would reshape this land.

Building Hoover Dam (originally called Boulder Dam) was either one of the greatest achievements of the people of the US in the 20th century (Bureau of Reclamation, 1946; Stevens, 1988), or one of the worst environmental and public policy disasters (Fradkin, 1968; Reisner, 1986). The story is well told from both perspectives and we only need to note that Indian people who lived here at the time spoke out against the dam and its damage, and were ignored – beginning a rift between science and Indian people that continues to grow.

When Hoover Dam was constructed during the early 1930s, there was evidence of Indian people's ceremonial use of the immediate area. At the junction of the Las Vegas River and the Colorado River was an ancient agricultural village that used both the floodplain moisture and new soil of the Colorado River and the quiet flow of the Las Vegas River for agriculture (Kelley, 1936, field notes). This village probably was the service community where individuals seeking ceremonial contact with the Black Canyon stayed while in the area. Just to the east of the Black Canyon was a large and old turquoise mine, which also provided red paint (Ompi in Numic language) for use in ceremonies. Just to the northeast of Black Canyon was Song Cave – in English called Gypsum Cave after the large crystals of gypsum found there. This is no mention of Sugarloaf Mountain in the written records of the time except to suggest that it, too, had a turquoise deposit.

The mouth of Black Canyon was chosen as the site of Hoover Dam because it was the first major constriction of the Colorado River since the Grand Canyon hundreds of kilometres upstream. The site also was more proximal to major communities in southern California and the small town of Las Vegas, both potential consumers of electricity. Given the lack of a way to cross the Colorado River, there was no major road to Black Canyon and no town along its 64km length. The area was isolated and distant from the meaningful centres of US society.

Most US citizens viewed this part of the country as a wasteland, raw and needing civilization. A few citizens, however, had developed a desert ethic and strove to represent the greater American southwest in positive ways through art and literature (Van Dyke, 1901; Teague, 1997; Pyne, 1998). Except for the Grand Canyon, some rugged mesas in Monument Valley and a hand full of Indian icons, the region remain far from the minds and centrality of American life.

The wild Colorado River was viewed as dangerous and needing to be tamed. A report to the US congress outlining plans to dam most western US rivers, especially the Colorado River, has the title *The Colorado River: A Natural Menace Becomes a National Resource* (Bureau of Reclamation 1946). In this report under the heading 'Primitive peoples' the ancient peoples 8000 to 10,000 years ago were said to have been forced to leave due to volcanic activity. Contemporary Indians either practised irrigation or roamed hunting animals and collected herbs. The latter, the Utes, Paiutes and Chemehuevi ('Digger Indians'), are among the least progressive, according to this report. To the south the tribes along the Gila River – the Pimas, Maricopas and Papagos – are among the most advanced Indian tribes found in the US. Clearly, the irrigated agricultural systems of the Paiutes that were located all along the Colorado River and up each of the feeder side rivers were either not known, not respected or viewed as a water-right issue that would not be addressed by the Bureau of Reclamation as it requested from congress the permission and funds to flood these Numic farms.

When construction of the dam began, a very small portion of the funds was devoted to any type of science other than engineering, geology and hydrology. Some funds, however, went to the science of archaeology. Mark Harrington, who had worked in the area for more than a decade, was funded by Hoover Dam project funds to study the ancient Indian cultures of the area. He had little interest in the contemporary culture of Southern Paiutes or Hualapai people. In fact, when a contingent of Paiute shaman came to him to complain of his excavation of their spiritual song cave, he simply ignored their requests and continued with what they defined as a defilement of a sacred place (Harrington, 1933). He also studied the turquoise mine across the canyon from Sugarloaf Mountain, noting that it was deep and had been used for thousands of years, as indicated by the pottery types scattered about its rim (Harrington, 1929). Between 1936 and 1937, the mine was studied and put on display by out-of-work men in the Civilian Conservation Corps (CCC). According to McBride (1995, p39):

> The boys excavated some of the ancient turquoise mines the Pueblos had worked in Hemenway Valley. In cleaning out these pits, the CCC boys uncovered potsherds and stone hammers, many of which were put on display later in the Park Service museum in Bounder City.

Harrington also studied the ancient salt cave at St Thomas (located upstream at the edge of the river and soon to be flooded by Lake Mead), which he also identified as having been mined by Indian people for thousands of years, as indicated by the artefacts remaining there (Harrington, 1970). More concerned with saving the ancient past than contemporary Indian cultures, he apparently never conveyed any sense of the cultural inappropriateness of either his excavations or the dam construction to his sponsors or his scientific colleagues. Science and Indian culture were separated by these events, while the relations between science and federal agency were strengthened.

Greater good

Hoover Dam was constructed in 1933 and a two-lane road was built on the top of the dam linking east to west, Arizona to Nevada. As the west grew and tourism increased, the dam became a destination site for tourists, who came with the purpose of viewing the wonders of modern engineering. Soon honeymooners would stop and photograph each other on top of the dam on their way to or from Las Vegas. They were to create a shared 'national viewscape' that has come to be considered worthy of cultural preservation by federal management agencies.

Sixty years after construction, the road is filled daily with trucks and automobiles trying to save a few kilometres by crossing the dam instead of travelling across highway bridges to the south. In direct proximity and conflict with these vehicles are thousands of tourists who stand centimetres away from the traffic taking photographs of Lake Mead or Black Canyon, while being awed by the hydroelectric power lines emanating from the belly of the dam. The mix is hazardous and standing lines of vehicles have become the norm.

The Hoover Dam bypass project was designed to reduce the traffic delays and volume over the dam by either diverting traffic to one of the existing bridges to the south or constructing a new bridge. Fourteen possible proposals were considered during the project's ten-year long life span. All but three bridge locations at the dam site were rejected by 1997 when the final environmental impact statement (EIS) was begun. After seven years of environmental impact studies, and all but 3 of 14 alternatives had been rejected, American Indian tribes were initially consulted and ethnographic studies began.

Consultation between American Indian tribes and US federal agencies is a formal process largely defined by law and regulation (Stoffle, 2000). Key in the process is Executive Order 13175, which specifies that consultation will be on a government-to-government basis, thus reflecting the dependent nations status of tribes within the US (Deloria and Lytle, 1984). Critical to consultation is the willingness to share power on the part of the federal agency. Consultation without shared power has been characterized as co-option, while co-management occurs when real partnerships are established between tribes and agencies (Parenteau, 1988).

Multiple jurisdictions always provide social and political complexity, and the Hoover Dam bridge EIS had a great number of institutions and levels (see Table 8.1).

The Federal Highway Administration (FHWA) undertook the assessment of how to reduce traffic and increase safety at Hoover Dam under the direction of the US congress. The final three bridge alternatives at Hoover Dam would be constructed on lands managed by the Bureau of Reclamation (BOR) or the National Park Service (NPS). All of these agencies have administrative divisions at the regional and national levels. The local NPS and BOR agencies have their own cultural resource and archaeology specialists. Cultural assessment is reviewed and evaluated by the State Historic Preservation Offices (SHPOs) for Arizona and Nevada; at the regional and national level, cultural assessment is made by the Advisory Council for Historic Preservation (ACHP) and the National Register of Historic Places (National Register), respectively. Departments of Transportation (DOTs) for the states of Arizona and Nevada are partners with the FHWA in the study. A private management consulting firm with local, regional and national offices was contracted to produce the final EIS with funds provided by the FHWA. The University of Arizona ethnographic contract was funded by the management consulting firm with funds from the FHWA. The final three alternatives all continue the existing flow of traffic in front of the only casino hotel near Hoover Dam, and the owner of this casino is a Nevada State legislator.

The web of interrelationships among involved institutions at various levels in the Hoover Dam bypass project is so complex that it would take a separate analysis to simply describe the formal patterns. The informal patterns are beyond any external analysis and could probably not be reconstructed because informal or 'off-the-record' discussions are where so much of the power brokerage occurs. For this analysis it is appropriate to simply define the institutional matrix and to address those situations where the process is known and was influenced by one or more relationships.

Table 8.1 *The web of institutional relationships in the Hoover Dam EIS*

Institutions	***Management Levels***		
	Local	Regional	National
Bureaucracy			
Highway Administration	Departments of Transportation (DOTs) (Nevada, Arizona)	Federal Highway Administration (FHWA)	FHWA
National Park Service (NPS)	Lake Mead NRA	Rocky Mountain region of NPS	Washington office of NPS
Bureau of Reclamation	Hoover Dam		
National Heritage offices	State Historic Preservation Offices (SHPOs)	Regional	National register
Elected governments	Boulder City Council	Nevada State Legislature	US congress
Universities	University of Arizona		
Capital			
Local business	X		
Casinos industry	X		
Consulting firms	X	X	
Media			
Newspapers	X		
Radio	X		
Television	X		
Internet	X		
Science			
Archaeology	Bureau of Reclamation (BOR), NPS	Consulting firm	
Ethnohistory	W&S Consultants		
Ethnography	University of Arizona	NPS	
NGOs			
Sierra Club	X	X	

Contesting risks

An ethnographic team from the University of Arizona was awarded a contract on 1 April 1998 from the FHWA through the EIS management consulting firm to conduct the American Indian impact assessment study. The task was to:

1 contact culturally affiliated tribes;
2 design the field studies, including interview instrument development and team training;
3 conduct four days of field interviews to ascertain Indian concerns; and
4 produce a final impact assessment report for the EIS.

The list of participating tribes was given as 11 Southern Paiute tribes and the Hualapai Nation.

The University of Arizona team was chosen because it had conducted EIS ethnographic studies since 1976 in the immediate area with various Indian tribes, including both the Southern Paiutes and Hualapai. These studies included almost a decade of ethnographic studies and consulting between Southern Paiutes and the BOR upstream at the next dam – Glen Canyon Dam – and the recent assessment of a highway-widening project in Las Vegas.

The study design was disputed from the outset. Representatives of different institutions brought divergent perspectives regarding how the study should be designed. The tribes and the ethnographers at the University of Arizona argued for a much more extensive study that would involve at least two elders to be present from each tribe and more time to visit places in and around the study area. Such studies had become standard in agency–tribal consultations that lasted for decades (Stoffle et al, 2001). The scientists from the BOR and NPS were of the opinion that no Indian study was needed because their archaeology studies had not revealed significant evidence of Indian use of any portion of the study area. The FHWA project manager wanted to keep on track and within budget and insisted on two major cuts in the original study estimates. The consulting firm's archaeologist from Oregon supported the Indian studies because an Indian member of his survey team had indicated the place was important to Indian people.

The actual study proceeded in the summer of 1998 more as a scoping endeavour than as a scientifically sound ethnographic analysis. It proceeded, nonetheless, with 21 tribal representatives participating in private ethnographic interviews for two to three days. The report addresses both site-specific and cultural landscape issues.

The completed study reported in December 1998 that Indian people believed all three alternative bridge locations were in the same religious location. At the centre of this ceremonial area was a medicine area called Sugarloaf Mountain. At the top of this mountain are cleared areas identified as vision-questing or dancing circles. The views from the mountain are only partly affected by the current dam. Directly connected with the power of this mountain were mountain sheep that serve as spirit helpers for some shaman, medicine plants, crystal deposits and healing stones. A single figure is pecked on a large stone on top of the mountain. [These peckings are made by using a rock to hit another larger rock, creating a large image of a man. Such images are often termed petroglyphs (Whitley, 2001).]

Just across the Colorado River from Sugarloaf Mountain, but still within the ceremonial hub, are a series of hot springs in Goldstrike Canyon, where in those sections near the river hot water showers down to the hot creek from high cliffs.

The place was used for purification before and after ceremony. Across the canyon was a traditional turquoise-and-red paint mine; both substances were needed for ceremony. The Black Canyon is a place of volcanic power and is especially forceful where it constricts the Colorado River. These elements constitute the hub of ceremonial activities; but essential and powerful places exist nearby, forming the spokes of a ceremonial wheel which is about 26km in diameter.

Gypsum Cave is a significant place located nearby (about 13 direct kilometres away from Sugarloaf Mountain) in the Frenchmen Mountains. The opening to this deep cave can be viewed from the top of Sugarloaf Mountain. The cave is known as a place for receiving songs needed in curing and in transporting the deceased to the afterlife along the Salt Song trail. Shamen regularly return to such places to get new powers and new songs. To the south-west of Sugarloaf (about 13km) are two major rock pecking and paint sites. At each one is a figure (one in red paint and one pecked on a boulder) that closely resemble the pecked figure at the peak of Sugarloaf Mountain. One rock pecking site has a special shape, referred to in its name as a keyhole. The site is known as a place of powerful activities between both the Paiutes and the Mohaves. Knotted string motifs (*tapitcapi* – literally, something that is tied) occur, suggesting that it is a place on a medicine trail that is used by medicine people. Such rock pecking sites are viewed as places where ceremonial performers would stop on the way to the hot springs, Gypsum Cave and Sugarloaf Mountain. After the ceremonies, this site would be revisited to give thanks for a successful trip into and out of such a powerful place. On the Hualapai side of the Colorado River (about 13km from Sugarloaf Mountain) is a similar rock pecking site at a constricted point along what would have been a major trail into the Black Canyon area. Knotted string motifs also occur at this point, suggesting a similar function to the eastern keyhole site.

Taken together, the sites at the ceremonial hub appear to be connected with those nearby to form a ceremonial landscape (explained by the Indian people as a ceremonial wheel). The components of the landscape are each culturally important and essential to ceremonies in this area. Their centrality in Indian culture, however, derives from their interrelationships with each other and their location at the junction of Black Canyon where it constrains the Colorado River.

The Indian ethnographic report was not well received by any of the involved agencies. It constituted a potential fatal flaw in the proposal and was to be interpreted by some as reflecting basic errors of both science and the EIS process. Scientists who had determined that nothing would be found were now confronted with cultural resources of great importance. For those who had guided the EIS process, the findings suggested that the tribes should have been involved at least seven years earlier in the process when more alternatives were available for consideration. Basically, the Indian study suggested that the three bridge alternatives being studied were proposed for the same place. Two of the routes physically touched Sugarloaf Mountain. The Goldstrike route touched the hot springs canyon used in association with ceremonies at Sugarloaf and cut away a portion of the south side of Sugarloaf. The Sugarloaf route clipped the northern side of the mountain and would damage the healing stones deposit. The third route, Promontory Point, was located over the pool of the dam and would negatively impact upon medicine animals and plants and the viewscape to the north. None of the alternatives were acceptable because all would adversely affect this ceremonial cultural landscape shared by both Hualapai and Paiute people. Sugarloaf was the least acceptable and Promontory was the most acceptable if the project were to go through in spite of Indian protests.

Representatives of key agencies went into denial and began to contest the Indian view of these places and this ceremonial landscape. The consulting firm's Oregon archaeologist's study was challenged and he was even required to return to the study area and rediscover artefacts that had been identified and drawn as a part of his report. The ethnographic team's methods and objectivity were challenged, suggesting that even the way in which questions were asked could have artificially created the report's conclusions. These debates were conducted away from the public's eye, often solely between the agency staff.

The findings of the first study were basically held in check for a year, during which time the EIS proceeded and the findings were debated. It is important to understand the procedural implications of delaying during an EIS. At an Indian consultation meeting, the FHWA project manager described what happens as an EIS proceeds: it is like building a brick wall – that is, even though it is not completed until the end, it becomes increasingly more difficult to change as it contains more bricks. The scientists in BOR and NPS were unanimous in their belief that nothing culturally or archaeologically significant was really present at any of these locations. The hot springs lacked either artefacts or rock markings that might indicate being used for ceremonies. Sugarloaf Mountain was surrounded by rock chips that were interpreted as mostly natural breaks; the Indian identification of medicine stones and crystal deposits were viewed as spurious; and the pecked figure on top of the mountain had yet to be discovered by Indian people.

Eventually, another American Indian consultation was initiated on 11 January 2000. Officially, it resulted because of new federal regulations regarding what government-to-government consultation should involve and an expressed desire by agencies to clarify and make more scientific the findings of the first study. A neutral third party ethnographer from the regional office of the NPS was hired by the FHWA to design and guide the next round of consultation. He was assisted by an Indian person who works as a Native American specialist out of the Santa Fe Regional Office of the NPS. Together, they would conduct all future American Indian consultation meetings. As a part of the new consultation, it was decided to greatly expand the set of consulting tribes. A letter was sent to all tribes in the state of Arizona inviting them to participate in the consultation. A number of new tribal representatives (Apache, Navajo, Zuni and Hopi) attended the first meeting. After hearing about the project and coming to understand what was at issue, the tribes met in executive session and determined that the meeting itself could not be counted as 'government to government' because of procedural issues.

A second meeting, and the first official government-to-government consultation meeting, was held on 30 March 2000. The tribes decided that they would like to have the ethnographic study expanded by adding Mohave elders to the study and increasing the number of Hualapai and Paiute elders interviewed.

One elder walked on the mountain and then reported back during the meeting that he had heard his ancestors singing. The agencies, responding to a request by the SHPOs, decided to fund an ethnohistory study through a third-party study team to gain some perspective on the findings. Both studies were independently conducted in May 2000, and the reports were finalized by October 2000 (Stoffle et al, 2000; Whitley and Nabokov, 2000).

The expanded ethnography study and the new ethnohistory study completely supported the findings of the initial Indian study. At the third meeting (August 2000), the tribes reviewed the two studies, supported their findings and recommended that Sugarloaf Mountain and Goldstrike Hot Springs be nominated to the National Register of Historic places as one or two traditional cultural properties (TCPs). The regional ethnographers of the NPS and a representative of the Washington office of the ACHP supported the recommendation. All of the federal agencies argued against this decision in the meeting, and at one time it appeared that consultation would be halted. Eventually, the agencies agreed to fund an Indian committee to help prepare the TCP nomination, and to forward the combined TCP nomination to the two SHPOs and get an informal ruling as to whether or not the sites were potentially eligible. After months of writing the TCP nomination, and having it reviewed by the agencies and the tribes, it was sent to the two SHPOs. Their review was quick and positive; these two sites were assessed as being potentially eligible as a single TCP. At the next consultation meeting the tribes requested that the agencies send the TCP nomination formally to the National Register for a final evaluation and placement on the register. Today, the EIS process has been completed (January 2001) and the record of decision (March 2001) was issued to build the bridge at Sugarloaf Mountain; but the TCP nomination was held for years by various involved agencies and not forwarded. In 2003, the new project engineer who was charged with constructing the bridge asked in a FHWA meeting that the TCP nomination be further delayed so that it would not interfere with his construction schedule. The TCP nomination was eventually forwarded to the Federal government in July 2004, well after bridge construction was underway and could not in any way be influenced by the nomination. Tribal distrust of these federal agencies seems well founded.

The final EIS (see www.hooverdambypass.org/) did reflect the Indian interpretation that all three of the bridge alternatives are located within a TCP. The EIS team decided, however, that because significant cultural features were present everywhere, they could not be used in a triage decision. As a result, Indian culture ceased to be a variable in the decision to build and in the assessment of where to place the bridge. In addition, it was determined that because the tribes were in formal consultation and the FHWA had agreed in a memorandum of understanding to continue government-to-government consultation, there would be no irreversible and irretrievable commitment of resources (3-147), and impacts to Sugarloaf can be mitigated simply by continuing to talk with the tribes. [(4-2) consultation under US federal law means talking and explaining the impacts of projects, it does not mean the projects cannot destroy the cultural places under discussion; thus, the destruction is mitigated (or made better) simply because it has been explained.]

TIMESCAPES

Adam (1998) encourages those who would assess the impacts of projects or actions to broaden the temporal and spatial limits of their assessment to fit what is being considered, rather than to artificially limit both to standard cost-benefit analyses. In the Hoover Dam case, proponents clearly have short-term goals and a narrow project footprint perspective. The federal goals of the project pale in comparison with what is at stake from a tribal perspective. The dam was constructed during the 1930s and was expected to last only a few hundred years. The traffic problem is less than a generation old and there is no assurance that the bridge will continue to resolve the problem for as long as a generation or more. There is no proposal to close the road over the dam, thus traffic can be expected to continue to be an issue. From an Indian perspective, Sugarloaf Mountain has been used since the beginning of time. Its ceremonial function is specific and largely not replicated by other power areas. If irreparably damaged by any construction activity, it simply cannot be replaced. Thus, tribal cultural damage is permanent, while the bridge fix is, at best, temporary.

When debating what the bridge will affect, the agencies continually tried to reduce the footprint of the project. They restricted the archaeologists to a very narrow few metres on either side of the centreline of the project. Archaeologists were not permitted to visit the top of Sugarloaf and nearby areas because, a priori, these were not being harmed directly by the project construction. Only during the Indian studies were accompanying archaeologists to visit the top of Sugarloaf, and they were never permitted to fold these new observations into their report of findings and impacts. Issues of Indian visual and auditory impact were simply not considered in any formal way. From an Indian perspective, Sugarloaf is a part of the ceremonial hub, and tribes repeatedly requested that the agencies formally study and discuss potential impacts to nearby areas. Such studies were denied as being beyond the footprint of the study and beyond direct impacts. Furthermore, the Indian people wanted the entire ceremonial landscape (or wheel) to be the unit of impact analysis. While the EIS did talk about the landscape in general, the agencies kept the impact debate focused on Sugarloaf and Goldstrike Hot Springs, and failed to either study or seriously discuss the potential cultural impacts that could derive from damage to the landscape as a whole. Instead, the agencies recommended that the tribes' repeated concerns for landscape impacts become a part of project mitigation to be studied and considered during construction.

MANAGING RISKS

Risk theory seems right on target in the Hoover Dam case by raising the contrast between insurable risks and uninsurable risks (Beck, 1996, pp30–31). At this time the major problems being solved by the bridge are insurable risks. Trucks hit cars and people are hurt: sad events, but well within what normal insurance is designed to cover. These are also events that both truck drivers and pedestrians are carefully trained to avoid, so there is an element of personal responsibility that comes with awareness. Contrast these known and insurable risks with those that accompany physical, visual and acoustical damage to places that help individuals, communities and the world itself achieve balance. When in history since Creation have Indian people had to address such issues? These actions must seem like madness and teeter at the edge of the unimaginable. Elders in this project continue to express concern that this bridge could have extreme and irreversible adverse impacts upon Indian culture and people. The tribal elders said:

> What are we to do if the songs are destroyed in Gypsum Cave, if the hot springs are insulted by human behaviour and do not clean us, and if we cannot hear the messages we need in order to heal ourselves and the world on top of Sugarloaf Mountain? It is just too much for us. Where will we go? Will this destruction never stop? Why won't white people listen?

There are two variables (trust and ontological security) that are commonly raised in Risk Society discussions that are variously portrayed as both causes and outputs in relationship with other variables. Neither variable has been directly measured by the Hoover Dam study, but both have served to modify the process and contribute to its outcomes.

TRUST

Trust is a difficult variable to understand and measure, perhaps because it really is much more complex than it at first appears. Studies of trust suggest that it has two major dimensions when talking about people's responses to projects that might hurt them (Stoffle et al, 1990). The first dimension is trust that the people in charge (of some aspect of the project) have the ability to understand the technical nature of the threat and to do something to isolate or eliminate the threat. The second dimension is trust that the people in charge have the interest or willingness to protect people from harm. When studied together, these two issues often do not co-vary because threats are recognized as being technically complex and the people in charge of the project are from somewhere else. In turn, people who can be trusted to look after the concerns of people are well known and live locally; but they rarely have the technical knowledge to know what to do to isolate or eliminate the threat.

People indicate that trust issues are evaluated in terms of past experiences with either the agency in charge of the project or the technology itself. These comparisons and frames of reference are called *project analogues*, and they must be formally studied in order to understand how they contribute to trust (Stoffle et al, 1987). In general, people will go to increasingly distant and apparently unrelated analogues the less experience they have had with either the technology or the project agency.

The Indian impact assessment portion of the Hoover Dam bypass project began after seven years of activity, so tribes felt that they had been eclipsed and left out of the process. Most of the tribes had some experience with the BOR and the NPS at the local and regional levels. A few tribes had direct experience with the FHWA, which recently had studied the widening of a nearby highway and chose the alternative that favoured the American Indian position. All tribes had experience with their respective state DOT. In general, early consultation dialogue was neutral to positive regarding past experiences with the agencies. There were strong concerns expressed about the adverse impacts of dams along the Colorado River; but it was generally believed that the BOR knew how to operate a dam and the DOTs knew about how to manage highways.

Trust to listen, respond to and be concerned with Indian issues in the project began to decline rapidly as soon as the first ethnographic study was presented to the agencies in December 1999. The most fundamental issue in the ensuing debate was that respected tribal elders had come to the site and identified it as a sacred place in the middle of a number of other sacred places. Agency resistance to this issue, while couched in terms of how scientific the findings were, simply translated into their not listening to respected elders. The requests for more elders to come to the site stemmed not from the tribes doubting those who had come before, but from an agency effort to build up the body of elder opinion to the point that it was considered a scientific finding. When even the second report was doubted by the agencies, a number of Indian women cried because they were angry and the men threatened civil disobedience. There was little trust at this point in the process. Finally, EIS was issued selecting the Sugarloaf Mountain alternative.

There is a risk associated with trust. Perhaps when tribal government are more willing to trust agencies and to participate in the normal EIS process they have largely unrecognized opportunity costs. If the EIS process co-opts the tribal governments they would have wasted their time and lost access to alternative routes for reacting to the EIS. One such route would have been talking to the media and having the tribal position become public knowledge. Almost no interviews were given by tribal leaders during the three years of consultation at the request of the involved federal agencies to insist the tribal voice be heard and respected. Once the final EIS emerged, the media was given access to tribes, and the first detailed newspaper article to fully convey the tribes' concerns was published (Walters, 2001). By this time in the EIS process tribes had no power over the final decision.

Ontological security

What of ontological security? What does this concept mean to a people who are potentially loosing a place that is culturally central, essential for maintaining the balance of the world and unique? What are the ontological securing impacts? (ie what does it mean for Indian people to lose faith in and hope for their future because balancing places are destroyed? What happens when whole cultures lose a sense of agency?) How does one frame such studies, translating profound and yet basic questions into not one but three ethnic cognitive systems? Does it require a study to be conducted beyond the project in order to obtain objectivity, or should such a study become a standard part of the EIS research toolkit?

Statements made during elder interviews convey a sense of loss and of hopelessness that reflect ontological 'insecurity'. The statement of hopelessness could be translated into one of the more standard measures of how people evaluate their lives and assess the hope for their future. This measure is called quality of life (Campbell et al, 1976) and is suggested as a possible way of carrying out ontological security.

If ontological insecurity does occur, will it translate itself into direct action and, if so (for example, as a public display of protest), does the action itself become a remedy for the insecurity? If the action is successful, does the victory in some way make people more secure? Can political protest somehow replace ceremonial activities to balance the lives of individuals, communities and the world? Is it possible to bring back to communities a sense of power and instrument, while loosing powerful places and their access to solutions? These are questions beyond the scope of this chapter, but rightly suggested according to the theory of Risk Society.

Conclusion

Will the damage caused by the Hoover Dam bridge result in American Indian social disorganization or reorganization? Certainly, the new bridge will weaken the power of this place by further intruding upon the quiet viewscapes and presence of the mountain. Only time will tell whether or not the site will become unusable for contemporary and future generations. As one Indian woman said when the Glen Canyon Dam studies were begun in 1994: 'In the long term, both the dam and the white people will go away and we will be left alone with our river and canyon.' Within this cognition of the environment and time, the river will reclaim its natural ways and the canyon walls will release the sides of the dam. Perhaps Sugarloaf Mountain will be usable again if it is not physically cleared of its gifts, such as the healing stones and the minerals, or irreparably dug away by construction. After all, this powerful mountain made these things for Indian people, and potentially it can do so again.

But what of Indian people and the continuity of Indian culture? Without this place in a condition (physical, auditory and spiritual) that will facilitate the learning of lessons for the practice of healing ceremonies at personal and world scales, the Indian people are at risk that generations will not learn and practise ceremonies and the world will become 'further out of balance'. Can the condition of the world become so skewed that it cannot recover? Of course it can, and millenarian events have happened a number of times before, according to Indian beliefs. Many Indian cultures record the ending and recreation of the Earth due to human mismanagement of the planet. The ghost dance movement of 1870 and 1890 was a millenarian event that almost occurred (Stoffle et al, 2000). Each time the world has been destroyed, the Creator selected some humans with a good heart to escape the destruction and have another chance to live in ecological balance in the next world. Evidence of current ecological imbalances are apparent everywhere in the study area. Already the Las Vegas basin has been tipped over 15 centimetres, the major salt caves have been drowned, Indian villages have been covered by the lake, and agricultural fields have been flooded. Some scientists have scientifically documented that the weight of the water in the pools of giant dams around the planet have changed the way the Earth rotates. Where will these impacts lead?

Perhaps it is more within our ability to predict the short-term responses of Indian people who are culturally attached to this place. These actions have already been discussed and expressed as possible in consultation meetings. Indian people have threatened civil disobedience. Such action by elders and youth has been successful in expressing the cultural points expressed in this chapter. One example are the Ward Valley protests against the siting of a low-level radioactive waste (LLRW) isolation facility in a valley that is both spiritually and hydrologically connected with tribes along the Colorado River. There, after years of study and consultation, project planners shifted the site of the facility to one of the most spiritually sensitive areas within the Indian landscape. Resistance by occupying the site occurred after months of fruitless debate and consultation. After months of occupation and heightened public debate, the LLRW proposal for Ward Valley was withdrawn. Will the Hoover Dam decision to build a bridge at Sugarloaf Mountain result in a similar action? In a sense, the project and the consultation have already brought the tribes together and laid the foundation for a collective response. The arrogant response of the Hoover Dam EIS team towards Indian concerns could stimulate yet another step in American Indian identity politics.

9 The Invention of a Minority: A Case from the Aragónese Pyrenees

Gaspar Mairal

Introduction

This chapter explores how a situated social conflict surrounding the construction of several large dams in the Pyrenees became globalized as a result of the efforts of those who considered themselves adversely affected. In this globalized conflict, a new kind of discourse developed in which notions such as 'equity', 'general interest' and 'minority and human rights' played a fundamental role. The point of departure here is the emergence of a social movement whose *raison d'être* is preventing the construction of large dams in one specific territory, namely the Spanish Pyrenees. This chapter focuses on the discourses that this movement has constructed and sheds light on some of the concepts that sustain it, equity being a case in point. The movement directs criticism at the public administration in charge of water policy in Spain for the way in which it has been equating democracy with the concept of general interest. The effects of controversial water dam projects in Spain surpass the locally bounded implications of such projects. This conflict involves diverse and antagonistic political and civil society parties, who all use arguments of democracy, each in their own way and according to varying interpretations, with the aim of managing the conflict according to their interests and eventual triumph. The argumentative strategies employed by the opposing parties merit analysis in that they raise significant challenges for the way in which we understand and practise democracy.

Water policy in Spain and Aragón

The geographical space is the Ebro valley and the Pyrenees in the north of Spain. The political cultural space is Aragon, one of Spain's 17 *Comunidades Autónomas* (self-governing regions). At the beginning of the 20th century, a new model of development was defined in this territory, ignited by major changes in the Spanish political landscape at the end of the 19th century. Decadence has been pervasive in the contemporary Spanish consciousness. The awareness of decline was heightened following Spain's defeat in the war with the US in 1898, which resulted in the loss of Cuba, Puerto Rico and the Philippines, the last substantial colonies of the old Spanish empire. This was the 'Crisis of 1898', and this year also figures in the name of a political and intellectual movement calling for the regeneration of Spain, the 'Generation of '98'.

Thus, an ideological movement known as 'regenerationism' subsequently grew among members of the Spanish elite and eventually filtered through to the whole of Spanish society. The main purpose of this movement was to modernize and revitalize the nation. Joaquín Costa, an Aragonese lawyer, emerged at this juncture to proclaim a future of prosperity resulting from a new policy that promised to transform the extremely poor agriculture of the age through the development of large-scale irrigation systems (Cheyne, 1972). This ambitious programme for the construction of major dams and canal systems became known as the water policy. Costa died in 1911, convinced that he had failed in establishing such a policy. However his main ideas on the development of a water policy, brilliantly expressed in speeches and writings charged with images and metaphors of water, had by then become widespread, even reaching the farmers of the arid plains of Aragon. This idea of a unified national water policy, together with the figure of Costa himself, had a decisive influence on the formation of an Aragonese identity based on the promise that the regional identity, people's own definition of 'us', would be redeemed by water. Twentieth-century Aragonese regionalism owes the formation and nurturing of its identity to Costa and his ideas.

The *Ley del Plan de Riegos del Altoaragón* (Upper Aragon Irrigation Act) was approved in 1915. The purpose of the proposed plan was to exploit the rivers that flow down from the central Pyrenees in order to irrigate the extensive arid plains of the Ebro valley. At that time, the goal was to transform approximately 300,000 hectares (ha) into irrigated land. Work began on 29 March 1915. To date, roughly 110,000ha hectares[1] have been transformed. In Aragon, this attempt at modernization adopted the form of a development model; the water policy became a generalized idea for the promotion of collective prosperity. Indeed, in the case of some regionalist movements, the model was endowed with an identity-related dimension that was later to become the main plank of a programme not only for development but also for the political redefinition of Aragon, which by then also aspired to political autonomy. As a result of the public works carried out under the water policy model, Aragon today has three major irrigation systems (*Bárdenas, Riegos del Altoaragón* and *Riegos de Aragón y Cataluña*), providing water to over 250,000ha of new irrigated land in the 20th century. This endeavour has provided new strength to Aragonese agriculture, even though the mainstays of the Aragonese economy today are industry and services, with agriculture accounting for no more than 5 per cent.

Water policy and the development of further irrigation systems, nonetheless, continue to be a crucial issue in Aragon, not only because of historical inertia but also because of the cultural assumptions that have made water a leitmotiv of Aragonese identity. In 1976 the plans for the construction of a dam on the River Esera,[2] close to the village of Campo, was publicly announced. This project was supposed to create a 600hm^3 (cubic hectometre) reservoir and entailed flooding several villages inhabited by some 800 people. For the first time, however, the affected population reacted against the flooding of their communities and their own displacement. From then on, water projects became controversial issues, giving rise to social and political conflict. The conflicting collective interests of the populations affected and of those who stood to gain from irrigation were defined. In geographical and cultural terms, those affected by dam schemes are the inhabitants of the Pyrenean valleys, while the beneficiaries are the farmers of the plains, who need the water to irrigate their arid land.

The social conflict over dams in Spain involves numerous actors and groups: the people directly affected by the construction of new dams; the beneficiaries of major irrigation projects; government agencies; political parties and trade union organizations; the environmentalist movement; and experts who hold diverging views. Two main camps have formed, the battle lines being fairly clearly drawn.[3]

A basic feature of the research undertaken has been its local focus. The objective has been to understand the local discourses, implications and aftermath of a specific area of land-use policy. During recent years, however, this conflict over irrigation and water dams has widened as local movements have expanded their efforts and activities, mainly as a result of increased communication and interaction between the various local groups involved. In Spain, this movement has now become increasingly salient in the media and relevant at the national level. This development can only be understood in the context of the historical development and the current realities of water policy in Spain. A few basic figures are sufficient to cast light on the situation. In the first place, Spain has more dams per million inhabitants than any other country in the world.[4] Around 40 per cent of all surface water flows have been dammed, the result of intensive dam construction throughout the 20th century. Second, water has become a major political issue, and the National Hydrological Plan (Arrojo Agudo, 2001), which the Spanish parliament recently voted into law, has been the subject of heated debate. This plan envisages the construction of approximately 117 new large dams, a matter that has sparked fierce opposition.

At the same time, the conflicts generated by the construction of new dams have become increasingly global, a development that has made it necessary for researchers to adopt a new stance in the question. Purely local research is therefore no longer sufficient. The situations must be related to a wider context and this methodological requirement can no longer be ignored. The actors in these conflicts have themselves come to rethink the conflict and what it is about and they have sought new ways of representing the issues at stake. This has caused the affected population to go beyond the established limits of the context, while others, those who have benefited, have tried to keep the situation within its traditional bounds by employing the concept of the 'minority'.

Recent events

Any discussion of recent events in this long-running conflict requires consideration of the results of almost a century of water policy in Spain and, therefore, of existing major dams. At the same time, their social and territorial impact must also be taken into account. In the Aragonese Pyrenees, a part of Spain that is sensitive to the effects of social disruption caused by dam-building projects and the area where opposition to the new schemes is most intense, the capacity of the ten largest dams is 2809hm^3. These dams, which were built between 1920 and 1975, flooded or made it necessary to abandon dozens of villages, displaced several thousand inhabitants and, in particular, destroyed some of the best land on the valley floors, which is essential to any development or land-use plans in such a mountainous area. Overall, this has had a severe impact on the Pyrenean region, as some of the best, flattest and most accessible land has been flooded while the local population has suffered the loss of a significant part of its territory.

Table 9.1 *Large dams built between 1920 and 1975*

Dam	*hm^3*
Barasona	160
Bubal-Lanuza	89
Santa Ana	240
Yesa	466
Grado-Mediano	835
Sotonera	189
Canelles-Escales	830
Total	*2809*

The turning point in Spanish water policy came with the end of the Franco dictatorship and the arrival of political liberties, which allowed the groups affected by the dams to organize their opposition publicly. Since 1976, opposition has taken the form of demonstrations, public statements, manifestos, strikes, the boycott of elections and sporadic acts of passive resistance, as well as occasional sabotage in order to halt or delay work on certain schemes. Initially, the promoters of these projects, mainly the state, hydroelectric-generating companies and irrigation communities, were not a little disconcerted by the increasingly local opposition; but this did not stop them from imposing the schemes, at times with the help of the police.[5]

In 1992 all of the political parties represented in the Aragonese Assembly,[6] including conservatives, Aragonese nationalists, socialists and communists, voted in favour of an agreement to build various new dams, in principle designed to extend the area irrigated by adding a total of 200,000ha of new land to the three main systems. This agreement was known as the water pact, and at the time it faced criticism only from organizations representing the population affected by the new schemes in the valleys of the Pyrenees and a few university researchers who were already proposing far-reaching changes in water policy. Criticism and controversy has grown increasingly intense since then, and cracks have appeared in the unanimity of the political parties since left-wing nationalists first won seats in the Aragonese assembly in 1996 and, having rejected the water pact, began opposing most of the new schemes proposed.

Finally, local opposition movements have increasingly influenced public opinion and succeeded in making themselves heard. Expert criticism has also become more consistent, influencing thinking on the left of the political spectrum.

Table 9.2 *New large dams planned in 1992*

Dam	*hm*^{3}
Biscarrués	225
Jánovas	180
Santaliestra	80
Yesa (reconstruction)	1059
Total	***1544***

The water pact made by the Aragonese assembly in 1992 has been incorporated within the National Hydrological Plan, including all of the schemes for new dams (Table 9.2). In fact, these projects have already successfully passed the preliminary planning stages, including environmental impact assessment,[7] and work could commence in 2001. Nevertheless, the populations affected have appealed against the outcome of the preliminary procedures, and especially the positive environmental impact declarations. However, the courts have yet to issue any rulings.

In this time frame, the associations formed by the various groups affected by these highly controversial projects called a two-hour general strike throughout the Aragonese Pyrenees on 25 October 2000. This was an enormous challenge for these groups, as the strike was proposed for a sparsely populated and eminently rural area with little industry and few businesses employing a numerous work force. Nevertheless, it was well supported and succeeded in bringing virtually all industrial and commercial activity to a halt for the two hours of its duration, while several thousand people attended the demonstrations arranged by the organizers. This action showed the extent of opposition to the construction of new dams not only from a minority of those affected, but throughout the area. This is the issue that forms the basis of this chapter.

This brief summary of events in recent years, and even in recent months, shows how a controversy that was initially confined to a few valleys in the Aragonese Pyrenees has gradually spread to become a matter of national debate, involving many more, and more powerful, protagonists. The events that are analysed here must be considered both from the point of view of their historical origins and in light of the critical point reached at the end of 2000.

EQUITY AS AN ARGUMENT

Equity has been the principle argument put forward by the movement of the affected populations during recent years, particularly in moments of confrontation between the self-perceived losers and those they consider to be the beneficiaries of dam-building schemes. This confrontation involved a sally from the purely local context, since it was not considered that any of its inhabitants could benefit from these projects. The condition of beneficiary was thus attributed to the population of the arid low country, who would be able to transform their parched land into prosperous irrigated fields. Furthermore, the construction of new dams was seen as the continuation of the same unequal exchange that had taken place in the past, when the inhabitants of the mountains lost their land to permit the irrigation of the plains, significantly improving the productivity of lowland farms. By couching the argument in these terms, the conflict spread out from the purely local and community bounds within which it had hitherto been confined, and a new, much more political, debate was proposed in terms of the principle of the equitable distribution of wealth in a democracy.

The term beneficiary alludes principally to the condition of those farmers whose formerly arid and unproductive land was transformed due to irrigation. Geographically, these lands are situated in the plains of the Ebro valley, which are much more densely populated than the Pyrenean highlands and have now become vastly more productive and richer. During the 20th century, three major irrigation systems were developed, which today cover a total of 257,082ha of irrigated land. The water supply for these irrigation systems is stored in autumn, winter and spring in the reservoirs of the Aragonese Pyrenees. The expansion of these already large irrigation systems is the main justification today for the construction of the planned new dams. Consequently, the conflict has centred mainly on this situation, causing frequent clashes between the populations affected by the construction of new dams and the lowland farmers who stand to gain from the further extension of the irrigation systems.

These farmers may be seen as embodying the ideal of redeeming arid land through water, and they have been the bearers of a symbol of identity that contributed (as explained above) to the formulation of an uncompromising Aragonese identity around the promise that water would save the country from poverty. During the last years, a constant debate has been developing that is considering if Aragon is a nation or a region. The *Estatuto de Autonomía de Aragón*, the fundamental law of the Aragonese political autonomy, was reformed during the 1990s to include a new definition of Aragon as a '*nacionalidad histórica*' or 'historic nationality'. In order to avoid the debate, the word 'country' is used in this chapter in the sense that England, Spain, Corsica, Scotland, Catalonia or Aragon are countries, which is not necessarily the same thing as a sovereign state. During his time, Costa did not consider this difference as something very significant and he really used the terms 'nation', 'region' and even 'homeland' (patria) indistinctly to refer to Aragon. This is the 'promise of water',[8] a rhetorical pledge made by Joaquín Costa at the end of the 19th century, which was inspired by the biblical story of the Exodus and has fed the collective imagination of the people of Aragon for decades.[9]

This complex of identity concepts, inspired in Joaquín Costa's ideas, is, of course, also a form of 'culturalism',[10] and fieldwork[11] has shown that the lowland farmers have activated their own culturalism around the symbol of the 'arid land waiting for redemption through water' as a representation of 'us', a community suffering an imbalance and threatened with poverty. However, this identity matrix has been greatly weakened to the extent that the great dam-building programmes, particularly during the second half of the 20th century, have largely satisfied needs and expectations. Many of the farmers in dry areas have long since become agricultural entrepreneurs, concentrating increasingly on intensive agriculture, livestock and industrial food processing. Other farmers in communities that benefited less from the new irrigation systems have opted to raise pigs or sheep, or have sought employment in the industries that have sprung up in nearby towns. Moreover, the subsidies provided today by the European Union (EU) via the Common Agricultural Policy (CAP) have had a decisive effect on maintaining the incomes of the most vulnerable part of the farming population who own little or no irrigated land. It has become increasingly difficult to maintain a culturalism based on the redemption of the land through water in the face of this changed reality.

In fact, there is a significant move away from the conceptualization of water as a vehicle for representation, and thus from its symbolic value, towards a concept of water as an essential economic resource that is the object of detailed and exhaustive pricing. This community has thus deactivated its own cultural identity in its day-to-day practices. It is therefore something of a paradox that the irrigators themselves, and especially those who now employ the latest irrigation technologies, should advance the arguments of both cultural and economy depending upon the context in which they find themselves at any given moment. They continue to demand that the state complete old projects which have not yet been carried out in order to achieve the irrigation of wide areas of land, and in this context they recall the 'promise of water'.[12] The same thing happens with the demands made of the political parties and in public declarations intended to influence public opinion. In their relations with the communities affected by dams and associations opposing new schemes, however, the irrigators deactivate their own cultural identity and adopt a fiercely economic outlook, continually pointing to the low value, from their point of view, of the land to be flooded compared to the productivity of irrigated farming. They also tend to demand that the state pay generous compensation to those affected.

All of this highlights a fundamental fact: the cultural nature of equity as argued and, above all, as perceived in a social conflict of this kind. Equity has to do with a complex of signs and meanings activated to channel the conflict and operating around a concept of 'us' against 'them'. Undoubtedly, many social and political conflicts take on a similar structure. The basis for equity in relation to local conditions and to the global frameworks that inspire them need to be better understood, since an affected person in the Aragonese Pyrenees may refer alternatively to his or her own tradition, to the Spanish constitution and to European directives in seeking to rationalize a conflict of this kind.

The social sciences, and particularly social anthropology, have an important role in the study of situations of this kind. In the case analysed here, research has indicated that a conflict[13] of this kind requires the comparison of the key cultural features of those involved (at times as antagonists) since the economic arguments used by one or the other party are generally strategic considerations aimed at achieving a final end, which is none other than to win the debate. To reveal the true nature of the problem, it is necessary to strip away layers of argument, which in themselves may, of course, be significant in order to get to the heart of the matter. I believe that the heart of the conflict over the construction of new dams lies in the affected communities' identity construct, which incorporates arguments of equity and is negotiated against the 'outsider'– that is to say the communities of irrigators. The supposed beneficiaries have adopted the strategy of blocking any debate regarding equity that may be raised by the communities affected by the schemes, either by ignoring such positions or responding exclusively in terms of the exchange value of all of the elements involved, such as the land, the house or the community upon which the affected population have constructed their own notion of risk. The affirmation of a cultural dimension in many similar controversies to the situation I have described here may seem rather obvious; but in spite of this my experience tells me that government agencies frequently ignore this aspect, which is so evident to us, when considering problems of this nature.

In our research on the conflicts generated by the Esera River project, we have suggested that common ground needs to be found between the cultural identity of the populations affected, both as losers and as beneficiaries, in order to bring about a cultural dialogue between the parties in which each would first and foremost be able to tell the other 'who we are' and 'who we wish to become'. It would only be after such a dialogue that economic, technical or legal arguments could be advanced. Thus far, however, the decision process bears no resemblance to this proposal and it is, instead, the state itself which has burst upon the scene with its economic, technical and legal viewpoints, ignoring any hint of 'culturalism'. The beneficiaries are aware that the protective umbrella of the state favours their own interests and have gladly taken shelter while waiting for the state to press ahead with and complete the works that they demand.

Development has a cultural aspect which is decisive for its success and it is in this context that the communities involved situate their own concepts of equality. This is the path taken by the populations of the high valleys of the Aragonese Pyrenees, who have argued for equality in terms of what it means to be a loser or a beneficiary of such schemes. The root of the question is whether, in a democracy, these conditions should be shared equally among the population on a random basis in such a way that today's loser may be tomorrow's beneficiary. And, of course, the highland communities have argued that they have already been the losers and will continue to be so if the new schemes are carried out. Thus, there is something perverse, as affected people claim, in the practice of a development model that is based on the construction of major dams in order to extend irrigation schemes, thereby making a whole region into a continuous loser. The communities affected have grounded their assessment of the situation in terms that they define as 'subservience', describing their valleys and land as 'an area of subservience'. Accordingly, the inequity of water policy in its current form is based, above all, on the fact that it makes the rights of one territory depend upon those of another.

The impact of big dams on highland areas is not just quantitative in terms of the number of hectares of farming land or pasture flooded, the number of people displaced or the villages abandoned as a result of expropriations. It is also qualitative, because the dams render the valley floor unserviceable, and in mountain areas this is an essential strategic space for any development option. The valley floors are the spaces that provide opportunities for agriculture, service infrastructure and the development of a good-quality communications network. During recent years, the population of the highland areas has become increasingly concentrated in the towns and villages on the riverbanks, though on a small scale. The Pyrenean districts have already lost a significant part of their valley floors and rivers as a consequence of the construction of major dams and the few that are left are key assets for any development options. For the mountains, therefore, it is not just a few thousand hectares that are at stake, but the essential territorial support for the future.

The future of the water policy proposed by the affected communities should be discussed within a framework of dialogue, equality, equity and shared development. To cede water without losing land, population, territory and natural spaces are the ideal terms of this exchange as proposed by the Pyrenean population. Technology, economics, the law and politics should, accordingly, make this possible.

A controversial 'general interest'

The existing dams and water infrastructure and the schemes currently at the planning stage have been carried out or proposed within the framework of the law. Thus, behind all of these schemes there is a body of laws, and when administrative measures are carried out in accordance with the law, it should guarantee their legitimacy. Logically, it is the state which promotes, guarantees and, almost always, undertakes and finances these works.[14]

This points to another key feature of the conflict itself – another element of the debate that goes beyond its local boundaries. Over the years, the affected populations have clashed with the state and successive governments regardless of the prevailing political ideology, whether centrist, socialist or conservative. The devolved regional structure of the Spanish state since 1978 has also brought the autonomous government of Aragon into the conflict. Finally, the affected communities have carried on an intense struggle with the water authority, in this case the *Confederación Hidrográfica del Ebro*,[15] the institution responsible for exercising the powers of the state in water management and planning in the whole of the Ebro basin.

As pointed out earlier, the dams that have already been built and those now planned are appropriately supported by the relevant legislation. This legality is based on the legal and political principle of the 'general interest', in accordance with which a minority may be obliged to suffer some disadvantage in order to benefit a majority, provided that the minority is appropriately compensated. This is, of course, a basic principle of any state where the rule of law prevails and forms a part of democracy in its present-day form. There is, moreover, nothing to object to in the formulation of the principle, which tries, above all, to guarantee the common good, while at the same time recognizing the rights of minorities. In Spain, it is the government, through the Council of Ministers, which is responsible for declaring any project to be in the public interest; thereafter, expropriations may be carried out. Nevertheless, the rights of the affected party are further safeguarded since the law provides for such administrative decisions to be appealed through the courts.[16] This is, in outline, the legal process by which big dams are approved and built. Beyond the legal process as such, however, this section analyses the interpretations of legality made by the parties to the conflict in order to highlight the importance of the terms in which that legality is made tangible.

In order to understand better the interpretation of this legality by the affected communities, let us consider their own words in a text, almost a programme, published in 1998 under the title *Manifesto for the Dignity of the Mountain*:

> Furthermore, the old discourse of the majority and the minority frequently hides a double meaning: the people of the highlands are in the minority against those of the plains, who are, in turn, in the minority against the cities of Aragon, while Aragon itself is a minority compared to the rest of Spain and, of course, the world. The truth is, the minority which we all form at some time should not be against anything, but should serve as a constant reminder to the majority that everyone has a right to development, but that this does not imply the right to beggar your neighbour. This doublespeak is also used to claim that certain actions are in the 'general interest' or of 'public utility'. Without doubt, actions have fairly been taken in the public interest; but it is no less true that other interests have sometimes been ignored. These are the private interests which are sacrificed to the public interest. For a century now, in matters to do with water, the mountains have been placed at the service of a general interest, which has frequently been shown to be less than general.[17]

The use made by the affected communities of concepts such as 'minority' and 'general interest' is worth noting, as well as the manner in which they enter a field of discourse that no longer refers to the particular circumstances of an affected population within the confines of its own small world but to general considerations related to democracy. On this occasion, the criticism strikes at the play of majorities and minorities, one of the foundations of democracy, which is defined as 'old' not so much because it is considered inappropriate, but because it is perpetual. In reality, we are told, everyone is in the minority at some time. The voice of the affected communities is expressed around arguments related to a basic question, since what is really important is development. However, the discussion no longer centres on projects, objectives or policies, but on something much deeper and more substantial. It now concerns rights. This is the ethical and political dimension of the voices and discourses of the affected communities when they raise the matter of the 'right to development'. On this basis, the whole critique is aimed at the concept of the 'general interest' and 'public utility' and, above all, at the manner in which such principles are used. What the affected communities are really criticizing, therefore, is not democracy but a particular manner of putting democracy into practice, since the objective is for them to truly participate in democratic debate.

A first question is, therefore, 'How is the general interest established?' or

'Why is the construction of a big dam in the general interest?' For many years, the affected communities did not object to this principle as applied to specific dam-building schemes. It was possible to show that the negative effects were much less than the benefits if they were calculated in terms of the hectares of irrigated farming land, as the area flooded was always smaller. Similarly, consideration of the overall productivity gave rise to a comparison that was overwhelmingly in favour of building the dams because the land flooded was poor, fields were small and the mountain climate was unfavourable to agriculture. The wide plains of the Ebro valley that would be irrigated by each scheme enjoyed a considerably gentler climate and would be far more productive. It was therefore clear where the general interest lay. Things started to change, however, from the moment when the evaluation of the impact of each individual dam began to give way, at first among a minority of the people affected and later much more generally, to a more holistic stance that considered the results of building a number of dams in a territory with the social, cultural and economic characteristics of the Aragonese Pyrenees. As a result, a new viewpoint developed and with it new arguments that had not been raised earlier. All of this began during the 1980s and was finally consolidated during the 1990s at the same time as the movement opposed to the construction of new dams developed.[18]

The main action taken by the affected communities in order to arrive at a concept of themselves and to represent themselves as the 'losers' was to bring the problem out of its local bounds and situate it within a wider context. This also meant bringing into play a collective memory that narrated the events arising in other nearby valleys which had already suffered the consequences of dam-building. This 'us' multiplied to become the voice of a whole territory. The leaders of the various movements of affected communities were, without doubt, the prime movers of this transformation, which resulted in collective action with wide-reaching effects, such as the two-hour general strike held on 25 October 2000. This new voice, capable of speaking in the name of a whole territory, was already to be heard in the *Manifesto for the Dignity of the Mountains* published in 1998:

> The big Pyrenean dam schemes imply the end of our rivers and the definitive dismemberment of the human territory in the north of Aragon. Before we continue with this policy, we must discuss holistic needs and find alternatives to solve individual problems.

The manifesto is referring again to something that attracts a great deal of interest: the relationship between the local and the global. In this way the affected communities are claiming the global nature of their problems, and in order to face these problems, they say, it is necessary to establish a global dialogue and find solutions to local problems. From the position of the affected people, the global understanding of a local situation has been the most important contribution to redefining an old conflict.

Globalizing a local controversy

In 1999, Spain was visited by a commission from Chile representing the Pehuenche community. Their objective was to report on the situation of the Pehuenche people, whose land was threatened by the construction of various dams on the Bío-Bío River and who were facing eviction. Two years earlier, the American anthropologist Ted Downing, who had been contracted by the construction company IFC to prepare a study of the social impact of the Pangue and Ralco dam projects, complained to the American Anthropological Association (AAA) that the very company which had requested the study had withheld the results of the study from the community affected on the Bío-Bío River: the indigenous Pehuenche people. The AAA, which represents over 11,000 professional anthropologists in the US, opened an investigation through its Human Rights Committee and raised the matter with the World Bank, which was involved in financing the dams, in order to inform it of events and make the following demand, among others:

> ...adoption of a single and obligatory commitment to guarantee the human rights of the communities impacted by [the World Bank's] development projects.[19]

The World Bank has contributed significantly during recent years to financing major dam and hydraulic projects in developing countries. Recently, the World Bank itself and the World Conservation Union have created an international commission, the World Commission on Dams, which has spent three years evaluating dam-building policy worldwide. The documents produced by this commission reflect a set of criteria for the review of dam-building policy. Together with multiple economic, technical, political and ecological variables, this set of criteria reflects a new concern for the relationship between these projects and human rights. With each day that passes, new testimony is provided of numerous situations of conflict arising throughout the world as a consequence of building major water infrastructure projects. Recently, the campaign led by Arundhati Roy, India's best-known writer, has been widely publicized. This campaign condemns the fact that over 50 million people have been displaced in India as a result of the construction of big dams.

For those like this author who have been involved in researching the conflicts arising in connection with big dam-building projects for some time, it is evident that behind the immediate reactions of those who consider themselves affected lies a whole complex of ideas, values, feelings and emotions. As the issues evolve, this complex becomes charged with symbolic expressions alluding basically to the defence of a territory which the community affected considers its own. The Chilean Peheunches came to Spain to discuss this matter with those communities in Spain who have been under threat from the possible construction of big dams and who express themselves in similar terms. This view of territory and water clashes with the accounts of the Spanish government. The few lines given over to this issue in the *White Book on Water*[20] reveal a range of technocratic prejudices regarding a cultural valuation of water. For the authors of the *White Book*, to assign any social or symbolic value to water is proper to 'indigenous peoples' and is 'atavistic', while the notion of ownership of territorial values in relation to water use is 'tribal'. All of these expressions have found their way into the *White Book* in a diagnosis that is implicitly exclusive with regard to any more or less organized expression of a symbolic world with its own values. Any cultural representation of water expressed by a community who has historically been linked to a territory where this resource is freely available is banished to the realm of the 'quaint'.

It is worth pausing a moment to consider these matters because the people affected in the Aragonese Pyrenees have linked their situation to that of communities affected in other parts of the world, and particularly to the case of the Pehuenche Indians in Chile.[21] On occasion, the Aragonese opposition movements have represented themselves as 'indigenous people', pointing to the similarities between their situation and that of communities such as the Pehuenche. For the same reason, they have also begun to donate a part of their limited financial resources to help such communities. On this point, the manifesto cited above has the following to say:

> Wrapped up, as we are, in our own problems, we rarely notice that the debate concerning the protests against certain projects has by now become an international movement on several continents. Although it may seem that each community defends its own interests, we form a part, whether we like it or not, of a new water culture, defending the rights of minorities in mountain areas throughout the world to the flow of rivers through their territory as a source of development.[22]

The manifesto also notes the existence of international legislation and charters protecting ethnic minorities, the survival of which is favoured precisely in view of their minority status. Arguments based on a quasi-ethnic representation, postulating the Aragonese highland communities almost as a reservation, are, of course, an exercise in irony. The arguments intend to show how a member state of the EU ignores the specific value accorded by the community to its territory and the continuity of life there, while most international institutions increasingly recognize the value of local territories inhabited by ethnic minorities.

These arguments are not trivial. They touch the heart of the matter, laying bare the crucial problem for the future of local life in Europe, especially in mountain areas. On 23 October 2000, the European parliament approved the new Framework Directive on Water, the objective of which is to harmonize water policy in all of the member states of the EU.

The prime objective of this new directive is to ensure the environmental quality of water use in the future. Nevertheless, priority is given to the defence of the water user conceived basically as a consumer. This typology relates, above all, to the European citizen who wants a quality water supply and to enjoy the environment with reasonable guarantees regarding its conservation. Naturally, the objectives of this directive are basic and valuable; but it lacks any vision of the social and cultural value of water. Thus, the notion of the environment which is repeatedly reproduced in the directive is overwhelmingly biological; indeed, this is a very one-sided approach since it hardly recognizes the social and cultural aspects of the environment.

The use and exploitation of water can activate culture because the inhabitants of a given region are linked to such uses through tradition and history. Water is a basic element of the territory, and as such it forms a fundamental part of the interaction of the population with the land. From this standpoint, the concept of 'environmental water quality', which is fundamental to the directive, cannot be defined exclusively in terms of ecological and bio-chemical parameters, but must also include cultural factors. Recognizing that water and its use contribute to the identity of communities should therefore also have formed a part of the directive. It seems, however, that no importance was attached to this question. As a result, an exclusively urban concept of the European citizen prevails in connection with water, which is reduced to an object of consumption with the highest levels of quality.

The representation of a territory's water as a symbol of identity is not considered by the new European water policy, although it would probably be supported by the European institutions in the event that such a concept were to become visible in developing countries and among indigenous communities. It is because of this that the inhabitants of the Aragonese Pyrenees have defined themselves, somewhat ironically, as the 'indigenous people' of the Pyrenees. They felt that the only way to resist dam-building was as a community who stresses the importance of its roots in a territory at risk. It might, therefore, be wondered whether the construction of the citizen within the heart of the EU is capable of assimilating identities rooted in the land without having recourse to ethnicity, a definition as a specific minority or the need to retreat into a reservation. In many places the local populations of Europe have transformed their territory, the life-supporting space in which they have lived for generations, into an object of representation that identifies them, and it is in this global context that the struggle of the inhabitants of the Aragonese Pyrenees against the construction of further dams is situated. This is not a specific action, but an example of the culture shared by millions of Europeans.

Conclusion

The case of the opposition to the construction of new dams in the Aragonese Pyrenees has been used in order to throw light upon the fundamental tensions involved in a controversy such as this, which is situated within a specific local environment. One of the parties involved in this conflict considers itself to have been adversely affected and injured, and has therefore tried to widen the conflict outside of its purely local confines, while the other has tried to block the debate and keep it within local bounds in order to neutralize it. Both parties have constructed concepts of themselves by creating cultural representations which, strategically, may help them to win. This chapter has also tried to clarify the arguments underlying these efforts, along with institutional and legal aspects, and to describe the actions taken to make those arguments visible.

The concept and definition of the 'minority' is at the centre of the debate. The affected communities have shifted between two types of argument, demanding respect for the minority, on the one hand, which means considering themselves as forming that minority, while at the same time claiming not to be a minority at all. The main argument in this chapter is that 'minority' is not an 'objective' definition of a group, community or collectivity. Minority is the political construction of a community and it is not necessarily a 'bad' (oppressive, authoritarian, anti-democratic) construction. In this case, the affected people who have been defined as being a minority by the state by means of the law, are beginning to refuse this construction, and sometimes they are ambiguous and even contradictory since they are moving from the status of a minority to an increasing awareness that their problem does not depend upon the play of majorities and minorities, but on equity. This chapter suggests that in the context of a state based on law, we still have to discuss what a minority is. Democracy, furthermore, should surpass a narrow definition of this basic conception. This claim has been made possible on the basis of growing territorial awareness, enabling the Pyrenean communities to globalize their situation in view of the fact that the social and environmental impact of the dams already built, as well as other plans, were highly detrimental to their own 'general interest', which is to maintain the territory as a life-supporting area. The notion of survival has thus begun to appear in the voice of the affected communities:

> Considering that future generations of inhabitants of the Pyrenees will have grave difficulties subsisting in changed times without useful land for human life, and that the current generations, as well as being directly or indirectly affected, are those able to defend our territory, and considering that the fact of being a majority confers no right to oppress the minority where better alternatives can be found for everyone concerned, we hereby sign this *Manifesto for the Dignity of the Mountains*.

As can be seen from the *Manifesto for the Dignity of the Mountains*, the argument in favour of the survival of a territory leads to the definition of what the affected communities clearly consider to be a 'general interest', and it is at this point that they object to the 'general interest' imposed by the state, which is defined in terms of the prosperity of outside territories which have been, and will be, revived. On this basis, a simple comparison is made to raise the question of whether the highland territory is to be considered of less value for development. The controversy surrounding the nature of a minority arises from this evaluation

I believe that at the root of the problem is an underlying discourse related to the foundations of democracy and the play of majorities and minorities. The general interest has been defined until now on the basis of numerical calculations of the proportions constituting the majority and the minority in relation to an 'interest' defined in accordance with just that calculation. Against this, what is at the root of the proposal made by the communities affected by the construction of dams in the Aragonese Pyrenees is nothing less than the consideration of qualitative criteria in defining the general interest with regard to work intended to favour development. These qualitative criteria are even presented as human rights, which is not unconnected to an increasing awareness of international events. This fundamental link cannot be violated in order to further a supposed general interest. From this point of view, there can be no majority or minority, but only equity. This is the deeper meaning of the *Manifesto for the Dignity of the Mountains*:

> The truth is, the minority we all form at some time should not be against anything, but should serve as a constant reminder to the majority that the right to development does not imply the right to beggar your neighbour.

These words emphasize that it is not a natural condition of any people or community to be a minority, but an accident that depends upon multiple factors. The facts presented here are intended to help show that the villages of the Aragonese Pyrenees have been made into an 'invented minority' by a policy to which they object.

10 Schismogenesis in a Swedish Case of Railway Planning

Per Binde and Åsa Boholm

Introduction

Large-scale industrial and infrastructure projects, such as this case of a modernized double-track railway for high-speed trains on the west coast of Sweden, are long-term endeavours that take decades to accomplish with regard to planning, legal and administrative implementation, finding technical solutions and construction work. There may be many competing definitions of the project and its various parts, and substantial ambiguity as to its nature (Latour, 1996). This makes such projects highly sensitive to contexts and contingencies and to rhetorical ways of articulating advantages, risks or uncertainties.

A systemic approach to studying such projects is, therefore, needed – an approach that focuses on public debate as a context that has its own principles of organizational logic. Using Chaïm Perelman's analytical framework of the 'New Rhetoric', a theory of 'practical reasoning that accounts for both the social and semantic aspects of sense-making', Hervé Corvellec (2000) analyses the controversy in Stockholm over a planned third rail track, parallel to two existing ones, crossing the historic old town of the capital of Sweden. The debate about the modernization of the west coast railway line has much in common with this case. This chapter takes a close look at the debate concerning the west coast railway, as it occurred in towns along the route, to discern some of the features not only of the rhetorical logic of argumentation, but also of its social nature as a process of discordant communication. In this, Gregory Bateson's (1973) concept of schismogenesis will be used as an analytical tool.

The case of the west coast railway

The modernization of the west coast trunk line, approved by the Swedish government during the late 1980s, is the most substantial railway project in Sweden since the railway boom at the end of the 19th century. This investment, originally projected to cost 40 billion Swedish kronor (approx. 4.4 billion euros), is part of an ambitious plan to modernize Swedish infrastructure to meet the needs of the 21st century in terms of efficiency and environmental sustainability. The overall idea is to create an efficient railway link between the west coast of Sweden and the European continent, as well as to increase the capacity, in terms of train speeds and transportation volume, on this part of the Swedish railway network. Connected to this transnational infrastructure project is the Öresund Bridge (inaugurated in 2000) between Malmö and Copenhagen, which has railway tracks and a motorway for road traffic.

Current Swedish transportation policies aim to secure a socially and economically effective and long-term sustainable system of transportation for citizens and industry (*Trafikutskottets betänkande*, 2001/2002, TU2). The ambition is that transportation should:

- be accessible, answering to the needs of citizens and industry;
- be of high quality, in terms of being functional for industry;
- be safe so that no one is killed or seriously injured in traffic accidents;
- contribute to creating a good and healthy environment for all, where nature and built environments are protected from damage, and natural resources, such as land, water, and energy, are conserved; and
- contribute to regional development and allow different parts of the country to develop on equal terms.

The west coast railway is 370 kilometres (km) long and connects two major cities on the Swedish west coast, Göteborg and Malmö. For decades it has been one of the most intensely trafficked railways in Sweden, but was among the trunk lines with the poorest track standards. In 1990 this railway was almost entirely single tracked. The topography of the coastal landscape, with its bays, hills and seaside communities, meant that the century-old line was winding, with occasional steep gradients. Thorough modernization was therefore given top political priority.

The new west coast railway will have double tracks suited for both ordinary trains and the X2000 high-speed tilting trains. Level crossings are being replaced by underpasses or overpasses. Sharp curves and detours are largely being eliminated, and steep gradients are avoided through tunnels and embankments. Many changes affect cities and towns along the route. In some cases the tracks and the railway station will be moved out of the centre of the community; in others, a tunnel will be built underneath or near the city centre; and in still others, the route will be modified to allow for higher top speeds and traffic efficiency.

Among the more prominent sub-projects in this effort is building a double-tube, 8.6km railway tunnel through the Hallandsås, a rock–sand–clay horst that forms a natural and regional boundary between the provinces of Halland and Skåne. The building of this tunnel – which has been fraught with technical complications, environmental damage, legal examinations and resulting work interruptions – has been the subject of intense political and public debate. The tunnel building at Hallandsås has, in Sweden, become the epitome of large-scale projects that are economically and environmentally questionable, and it is regularly cited as a cautionary example when similar technical endeavours are debated. One third of the tunnel has been built to date, and work is to be completed by 2010-2011 at the earliest. Another major investment related to the modernization of the west coast railway is the 8km-long City Tunnel in Malmö. It will connect the trunk line north of Malmö with the Öresund Bridge and will also be used by regional trains in the south of Sweden. The City Tunnel project, planned to be completed in 2009, includes a new underground railway station.

Almost 300km of the west coast railway line has so far been rebuilt, meaning that about four-fifths of the entire route has been modernized. Travel time between Göteborg and Malmö has been reduced from over 4 hours during the 1990s to 2 hours and 40 minutes (with X2000 trains). Faster trains make rail traffic more competitive, and train passenger and cargo traffic along the west coast are expected to increase at the expense of road traffic, which is both less safe and more polluting (in terms of toxic emissions and greenhouse gases). However, in spite of the faster connections, the volume of passengers on the west coast railway decreased by 42 per cent over the ten years ending in 2001. The E6 motorway follows the same route, and only recently have trains become as fast as or faster than travelling by car. This, however, applies only when trains run on schedule – often not the case because of delays caused by construction along the line.

The governmental authority responsible for this large-scale reconstruction is the National Rail Administration, which is in charge of the railway system in Sweden, including tracks and the signalling and electrical systems. The trains themselves are run by the state-owned Swedish State Railways (SJ) or by private companies, hiring rail capacity from the National Rail Administration and managing the actual transporting of passengers and goods. The west coast railway has been rebuilt piecemeal by the west and south regional branches of the National Rail Administration. The completed stretches of double track are interrupted by sections of single track totalling about 70km. These interruptions occur at sections of the line where there have been disputes, impending court decisions, delays in obtaining necessary permits from supervising authorities, technical problems, or where rebuilding was scheduled for later stages of the project due to economic or technical constraints.

Modernization of the west coast railway through the northern part of the city of Lund was, for instance, delayed by at least four years because of appeals against the local implementation of the plans by a group of residents living close to the railway; this 5km section of the railway will be completed by 2005. In Varberg, the whole planning process had to start anew in 1999 following enactment of the new environmental code and its stricter demands for environmental impact assessment; construction work here has been postponed until 2010–2015. At Hallandsås, tunnel building, after having been halted in 1997 after a toxic leak of acrylamide, was finally given the go-ahead in October 2003 by the Swedish Supreme Environmental Court. One month earlier, the same court approved another long-delayed sub-project: the tunnel through Skrea Backe near the city of Falkenberg.

During the early 1990s, the modernization of the west coast railway was planned to be completed in 2000, at the same time as the inauguration of the

Öresund Bridge. Today, the most optimistic estimate of when double tracks will connect Göteborg with Malmö is about 2013. The multibillion investment in the reconstruction has paid off badly, since full efficiency of the line will not be reached until all sections have been modernized – the old sections of rail currently constitute bottle-necks for the train traffic. Communities and counties along the railway have criticized the National Rail Administration since the mid 1990s for its inability to keep the reconstruction on schedule, and the implementation of the project plan is generally considered to be a failure. Money has been wasted, and road traffic along the top-class E6 motorway, rebuilt a few years ago, has increased its advantage over the train traffic.

Local reservations: The three phases of controversies

Modernizing the west coast railway could potentially benefit Swedish industry and citizens, and is generally regarded as environmentally sound. Except for a few critics who question the overall economic soundness of favouring train over road and air transportation, as well as its environmental advantages (see, for example, Swedenborg, 2002), the project has received resounding endorsement. Politicians at the local, regional and national levels belonging to all political parties, as well as both industrialists and environmentalists, have all supported the project.

As to the more specific plans for rebuilding and relocating particular sections of the railway, there have been serious reservations, even fierce opposition, in communities along the proposed route (Boholm, 2000). A number of local action groups have been formed to mobilize citizens against National Rail Administration plans, and citizens have engaged in various protest actions to put pressure on local politicians and the authorities involved. Citizens have worked out alternative plans for relocating the route according to what they think will be better for the community. Individuals and interest groups have written complaints to the various authorities involved, such as municipal authorities, the county administrative boards, the environmental court (formerly the water court), various other supervising legal authorities, the Swedish government and even the European Commission.

The modernization project's national aim is to reduce travel time, increase transport capacity and, since train traffic is conceived to be environmentally friendly, to contribute to 'sustainable development'. Locally, however, the project requires the expropriation of property, significantly alters local rural and urban landscapes, and has awakened fears of catastrophic accidents and risks to health and safety. Residents of several towns along the route have criticized the National Rail Administration for not considering or consulting those most immediately affected (Boholm, 2000). Contamination of groundwater, resulting from the construction of the Hallandsås tunnel, has further aggravated local sentiment as it casts doubt on the competence of public authorities, particularly the National Rail Administration (Boholm and Löfstedt, 1999; Löfstedt and Boholm, 1999; Sjölander-Lindqvist, 2004).

The local controversies about the new railway characteristically have three distinct phases. The initial phase commences the moment the National Rail Administration decides upon a *particular* alternative for rebuilding. Though various alternatives were discussed and opinions voiced beforehand, considering the intensity of debate that follows selection of a particular alternative, the initial discussion appears as merely an embryonic conflict. As soon as a decision has been made, strong protests are voiced by those directly affected. The criticisms primarily concern the overall spatial or physical consequences of the rebuilding. Arguments such as 'the community will be lacerated', or 'a whole agricultural district will be devastated', are voiced.

The focus of this debate are the immediate consequences of the project: properties will be expropriated, houses have to be demolished, farmland will have to be put to other uses, fields and meadows will disappear, the landscape will change, and neighbourhoods will be intruded upon by the new rail line and other new infrastructure, such as relocated roads. Those who will be immediately affected demand that the rebuilt railway should be located elsewhere. Hence, the arguments raise concerns about what is certain to occur if the plans are implemented – although expressed subjectively, emphasizing local disadvantages – rather than about 'risks', which by definition include a measure of uncertainty (Rosa, 1998).

The National Rail Administration and the municipal governments, in turn, justify their decisions by referring to transport efficiency, and technical and economic calculations. Their arguments concern rail capacity, time saved for train traffic and the benefits of freeing up attractive space in urban environments by relocating existing tracks. They argue that all alternatives have been thoroughly considered and that the one chosen is the best. Eventual drawbacks for particular individuals and groups have been weighed against the 'common good' and found to be of lesser weight.

After a period of spontaneous protest, opposition takes on a more organized form, involving not just those directly affected; others who have views on the railway issue enter the debate. Issues that are discussed are the project's economic soundness and technical feasibility, and a wide variety of issues relating to its impact on the community, regarding, for instance, the natural or urban environment, and the future of agriculture, tourism and commuting. Other aspects of the project might also be considered, such as the legal issues it raises regarding expropriation of property, and its influence on the interests of various stakeholders such as farmers, ornithologists and sport fishers (mainly from a local perspective but also, in some cases, from a European Community perspective).

In this second phase of the controversy, when opposition has become more organized, questions of risk are forcefully activated in the debate. Thus, the risks of railway transportation are greatly amplified compared to the level of interest and engagement that they normally attract in the public consciousness. Research in Sweden and other Western countries has shown that the general public perceives railway traffic as safer than other forms of transportation, such as road traffic (Drottz-Sjöberg and Sjöberg, 1991; Alm and Lindberg, 2000). As will be demonstrated, the critique of the new plans is organized by mobilizing arguments – the more, the better – for or against specific alternatives.

Opposition groups, in a weak position in relation to the local authorities and the National Rail Administration, will employ every argument they can in favour of the alternative proposed by the group. It is this situation that amplifies the discourse on risk.

The third and final phase of the railway controversy commences when organized resistance is given up because it appears useless. The final court of appeal may have rejected the complaints by local interest groups, or reconstruction work may already have begun. It is evident to all that the plans will soon become reality. The controversy does, however, linger in concerns over details of the plans or the execution of specific construction works. It might concern the location of overpasses, changes made to local roads or the design of noise-reduction fences. In this waning phase of controversy, risk issues are not commonly emphasized.

Planning and counter-planning: The cases of Varberg and Falkenberg

The second and most intense phase of the controversy is exemplified by the experience of two communities along the west coast railway, where there has been organized resistance against the railway plans for over a decade. These cities, Varberg and Falkenberg, are particularly interesting because the arguments for and against the railway plans are inverted. In Varberg, where the railway will continue to run through the city centre, protesters demand that it should be relocated to the outskirts of the town. In Falkenberg, the railway will, indeed, be relocated; but here protesters instead demand that it should be kept in the city centre.

In the city of Varberg (population 50,000), the National Rail Administration started the planning process by investigating three major alternatives. One was to build the new double tracks on the same route as the existing railway through the city centre. Another was to move the station a few hundred metres to the north and build a 3km railway tunnel under the city centre. A third alternative was to abolish the old railway altogether and relocate the west coast railway east of the city, which meant that a new station would have to be built at the fringe of the built-up area. The town council opted for the tunnel alternative and the National Rail Administration accepted the decision on the condition that the city of Varberg contributed to the higher cost of this alternative. The local politicians in office argued that the removal of the railway track from the city centre was a great advantage: the railway would then no longer constitute a barrier between the centre and the harbour area, with its picturesque marina and historic fortress facing the sea (a major tourist attraction on this part of the west coast). The tunnel alternative also allowed the city to keep a centrally located railway station. To move the tracks and the station east of the city was considered less attractive since travelling to and from Varberg by train would be made less easy. The regional Train Commuters' Association strongly agreed with this argument and supported the tunnel alternative.

As soon as this decision was made, protests were voiced and counter-arguments began to flourish. Opponents maintain that the tunnel will be too expensive and that there is a risk that the municipality, in order to pay its share of the high costs, will eventually be forced to cut back on essential services, such as education, healthcare and care for the elderly. Other arguments claim that the building of the tunnel threatens to damage parks and buildings in the city centre, and that car traffic would become highly congested as a result of people using cars to reach the station. The safety of traffic through the tunnel, to be used by both high-speed passenger trains and cargo trains that regularly carry toxic or flammable chemicals, is questioned. The alternative of moving the railway from the city centre, and locating it east of the town parallel to the E6 motorway, was early on brought to the fore by opponents. The interest group, the Eastern Track, has, for over ten years, strenuously protested against the tunnel plans. This letter to the editor, published in a local newspaper in July 1999, is a typical example of its argumentation:

> We have been informed that the horrible tunnel will cost the municipality at least 100 million [Swedish kronor]. We have not been informed that it will cost the state around 1 billion, and the state is us. We have not received one word of guarantee against those endless risks that this fatal decision creates. What will be the cost of the concrete lining, what will be the cost of redirecting traffic during the five years of building, causing stress and chaos? Who is going to pay for all those fancy, empty brochures and all the fringe costs?
>
> That road traffic is one of the biggest threats to our environment and our health is correctly stated in the latest brochure, *Fresh Air in Varberg*. This giant problem will now be solved by our politicians in their own special way by forcing people in the entire municipality to try to find, through narrow passages in a heavily exploited city ghetto, the way to 'their own railway'.
>
> We still do not find a word about the alternative of an eastern railway route that a clear majority of Varberg citizens want; a route for the line that in the future would open up the city for all citizens, provide plenty of space and room, and be a dream for architects, community planners and for the entire city of Varberg.
>
> The planning and building of the new double-track railway in Varberg has been delayed due to financial problems, environmental investigations, the tunnel catastrophe at Hallandsås, other toxic scandals throughout the world and dreadful traffic accidents in tunnels. All this adds up to hardly any rational person any longer believing that this crazy tunnel decision can ever be implemented (*Hallands Nyheter*, 1999).

In the city of Falkenberg (population 37,000), located about 30km south of Varberg, there were two main alternatives for the railway modernization. One was to replace the existing single-track railway through the city centre with double tracks. The other was to relocate the railway to the east of the city – a solution similar to the one advocated by the Eastern Track interest group in Varberg. There were several eastern alternatives; one of these, in a slightly modified form (alternative 'E4'), was preferred by a majority in the town council and accepted by the National Rail Administration. According to this solution, a new railway station would be built about 2km from the town centre. The northern part of the old track through the city would be kept for cargo transport to and from Falkenberg, and the railway would run through two tunnels, one at Skrea Backe and another through Tröingeberg.

When this decision was made public, there was outcry from the small rural community of Stafsinge, northeast of the city. The relocated railway was planned to run right through the village, intruding on farmland and buildings. People felt that the community would be 'lacerated' by the tracks, and some were shocked to learn that they would have to abandon estates that had belonged to their families for generations. 'Build the railway further to the east' was the initial reaction to the railway plans.

Soon, however, the critique against the railway plans of the politicians in office and the National Rail Administration assumed a different character. The core of the criticism was now, and it still is, that it is wrong to relocate the railway. If the station in the city centre is closed and a new one built 2km away at the outskirts of the community, the city centre will lose a vital element, and those commuting by train to nearby cities, such as Halmstad or Varberg, will be at a disadvantage. In addition, these critics argue that the eastern alternative is highly objectionable in itself, since people living along the new route would have their local environment harmed by the rail intrusion. After a time, questions began to be raised concerning the two tunnels. Would they have adverse effects on the environment, and were there risks during the construction period? The Committee for a Living City Centre was founded to organize public resistance to the plans of the National Rail Administration and the city council. The following excerpt from a letter to the editor in the local newspaper illustrates the character of the arguments put forth in the debate:

> Those among the politicians in the municipality of Falkenberg, who obstinately cling to the proposal of the E4 alternative [the fourth version of the original eastern, 'E', alternative] for the double track, are taking on a big responsibility for the mutilation of the community. Terrible environmental destruction threatens our beautiful rural countryside at Stafsinge and Tröingeberg… The living environment of around 100 homeowners, above and along the tunnel route through the Tröingeberg neighbourhood, will be destroyed for all time. Those who can stay will have to tolerate disturbances from noise and vibrations, which will penetrate buildings, as well as electromagnetic disturbance and radiation that will particularly harm children, with risks of cancer and leukaemia. Due to the shallow depth of the tunnel under the buildings, the disturbances will be greater than from a deeper tunnel. All such risks for people have been entirely ignored by politicians and by the National Rail Administration.
>
> All of these intrusions, disturbances and risks are entirely unnecessary. There is alternative A – the current location of the railway line – as well as alternative D, 'the Falkenberg model' – both causing much less environmental damage and intrusion than the E4 alternative. In both these alternatives, our current centrally located and well-functioning railway station and travellers' centre, with buses, etc, will be saved. Protests from citizens against the E4 alternative have been many and well founded; but politicians have, being jealous of their prestige, not listened to their voters.
>
> The public has also, in letters to the editor and other contributions to the debate, criticized the decision by the politicians; but hardly ever have the responsible decision-makers answered. The over 10,000 signatures on lists of protest have also been ignored (*Hallands Nyheter*, 1996).

Organized resistance against the National Rail Administration and municipal politicians in office often has a high level of ambition. When an organization has been established, it assumes the role of an alternative authority aiming to investigate the matter thoroughly, compiling alternative facts, expert opinions and calculations that favour solutions other than the one chosen by the authorities. The Eastern Track in Varberg is a good example. This group has compiled a substantial file of documentation on the railway issue in Varberg. According to a formal division of labour, leading members have been assigned various responsibilities for recording and responding to the railway issue as it develops. The organization has regular meetings, where its membership votes for representatives, listens to opinions and invites outside speakers. Several active members are of high technical and administrative competence, formerly being high-ranking civil servants or highly qualified engineers. The investigations and reports issued by the National Rail Administration are scrutinized in detail; officials at the administration, as well as politicians, are regularly contacted and exposed to questioning; and the members frequently write letters to the editor in the local press. The group has arranged several well-attended public hearings and their own opinion polls in Varberg. Some of the more active members have been engaged in the issue since the early 1990s and presumably know a lot more about the local context of this issue than do officials of the National Rail Administration.

An important circumstance for the dynamics of the controversy, not only in Varberg but also in several of the other affected communities, is that several of the most active members of the opposition groups are, as mentioned, retired engineers or public officials. During their professional careers they occupied leading positions that required great technical or administrative competence. They now see it as their duty to educate and supervise the younger project staff and technical personnel sent out by the National Rail Administration to undertake massive and substantial changes in their community. They have been leading local figures of technical expertise in their community, and feel that they have a responsibility to closely scrutinize National Rail Administration plans. They see themselves as responsible for the well-being and future of their home town.

The escalating controversy

Opponents of the planned new railway mobilize all kinds of arguments against the plans of the project proponents: essentially, the National Rail Administration and local politicians in office. The arguments, as mentioned, concern all thinkable aspects of the plans for the new railway: economic costs, the nature of the 'common good' invoked to justify expropriations and environmental harm, consequences for local planning, conditions of commuting, effects on the natural and built environment, and disturbances in terms of noise and vibration for those living nearby.

Local opponents have also voiced numerous arguments about risk: environmental and health risks, risk management and security standards. These arguments are brought forward in letters to the editor in the local press, in brochures and leaflets, on websites, and vocally at public meetings. The following list includes the major risk issues that have been raised by opponents in communities along the west coast railway:

- Building tunnels can harm the environment. The uncontrollably sinking water table and toxic leakage at the Hallandsås tunnel has, since 1997, invariably been cited as a cautionary example. It is argued that such things could easily recur when building other tunnels.
- A train accident in a tunnel can be catastrophic. Two recent cases are cited as cautionary examples: the fires in the Mont Blanc and Tauern road tunnels in 1999 killed many, as did the fire in a mountain railway tunnel in Kaprun, Austria, in 2000, when 170 ski tourists lost their lives.
- Tunnel construction can damage buildings in the vicinity.
- Accidents when transporting dangerous cargo can have catastrophic consequences if they occur in a densely populated area. An often-cited incident is when, in 1996, railway cars carrying ammoniac derailed on the west coast railway outside the small town of Kävlinge, and 9000 people had to be evacuated. A similar accident, involving railway cars loaded with liquid petroleum gas, which also necessitated massive evacuation, occurred in Borlänge in 2000.
- Increased track capacity with more and faster trains seems logically to imply that the associated risks will increase proportionally.
- Accidents involving high-speed trains have more disastrous consequences than those involving ordinary trains. The accident in Germany when a high-speed train derailed north of Hanover in 1998, leaving about 100 dead and 300 injured, illustrates this argument. Not only passengers may be killed; a catastrophic accident could occur if a derailed high-speed train hits houses, a school or a day-care centre. Traffic with high-speed trains through residential areas should, therefore, it is argued, be avoided.
- Electromagnetic fields created by the railways' aerial power lines may constitute a health risk of unknown and potentially great magnitude. These arguments are connected with debates in Sweden about 'radiation' from computer monitors, 'electric allergy' and, most recently, the possible hazard of electromagnetic waves from cellular phones and mobile phone masts.
- A new railway with better communications means that new categories of people can be expected to visit the community. Social risks are therefore another type of argument that has been brought forth in the debate. In the small town of Glumslöv there were concerns that people from Christiania (a community in Copenhagen where drugs are, in practice, tolerated and liberally used) would take the opportunity of convenient travel to bring drugs for sale into the community. In Varberg, there are fears that the new underground railway station, planned by the National Rail Administration, will attract drug addicts. It could become a meeting place for derelicts and dangerous people, as in some subway stations in Stockholm, threatening the youth of Varberg.

Confronted with this rich plethora of arguments from opponents, the National Rail Administration and municipal authorities must defend their decision. Each argument needs a counter-argument, and every new argument bolsters the position of the side that puts it forth. The debate has a tendency to be carried out in rounds – for example, by means of letters to the editor in the local press. The arguments in favour of the decided-upon planning option, and that relate to risk, include the following:

- Rail traffic is much safer than road traffic. This can be statistically demonstrated by pointing to the fewer dead or injured per kilometre of rail travel.
- Rail traffic is better for the environment than road traffic since the electricity powering the trains largely comes from hydropower. Road traffic produces considerable toxic emissions and greenhouse gases, while rail traffic is environmentally 'clean'.
- Along the modernized double-track railway, overpasses and underpasses will replace virtually all level crossings. This means traffic will be safer since the risk of a road vehicle colliding with a train is minimized. Except for people committing suicide by jumping in front of a train, collisions between road vehicles and trains are the most common cause of death and injury involving train traffic in Sweden.
- New and stable tracks with modern state-of-the art signalling systems make train traffic safer. Increased traffic volume thus does not make the railway more risky, since the increase in volume is offset by more efficient security measures.
- Double tracks are safer than a single track since the risk of a frontal collision between trains is considerably reduced.
- Train accidents can be catastrophic, but the risk is very small. During the mid 1990s, the National Rail Administration made a risk assessment of a train accident involving dangerous cargo in the small town of Frillesås, situated along the route 45km south of Göteborg. It was calculated that such an accident causing ten deaths would occur once every 500,000 years. In comparison, it was stated that the risk of someone living in Frillesås dying in a traffic accident was once in five years; of dying in a domestic fire, once in 100 years; and of being struck by lightening, once in 5000 years. These calculations were presented in a brochure that the National Rail Administration distributed to the residents of Frillesås in 1994 as part of its information campaign about the plans for reconstructing the railway.

Arguments pertaining to risk bear great weight in the debate, since such arguments have a solid moral foundation. An intuitive ethical principle is that it is morally wrong to put other people's life, health or well-being at risk without a truly good cause (Hansson and Peterson, 2001; Peterson and Hansson, 2004). In the case of each specific decision, a balance must be struck between risks to people and benefits: how much risk can acceptably be taken to achieve a certain benefit? As there is no ready-made and agreed-upon model of how risks and benefits can be balanced in all contexts, every issue is, in principle, open to negotiation and dispute.

During this second and more intense phase, local media focuses keenly on the controversy – not least because members of the opposition actively seek media attention. Pamphlets are distributed in the streets, protest petitions are circulated, public meetings are arranged, and numerous letters to the editor are published. In the local newspapers of several communities along the west coast railway route where the issue has been controversial, coverage of the issue has been dominated by articles reporting criticism of the National Rail Administration or of decisions relating to the rebuilding made by other authorities. The daily regional newspaper Arbetet (closed in 1999), which drew most of its readership from Malmö, Lund and other areas in the south of Sweden, serves as an illustration. From 1997 to 1999, a total of 55 articles, editorials, letters to the editor and shorter news items dealt with the plans to rebuild the west coast railway in Lund. Of these 55 items, 52 focused on the controversy surrounding the rebuilding plans. Many of these texts specifically discussed risk issues, while others referred to actions expressing discontent over risks, problems and disadvantages thought to accompany the rebuilding.

Schismogenesis in environmental conflict

We suggest that people, confronted with an unwanted industrial or infrastructure facility close to their homes, become engaged in a schismogenic communicative process with the authorities responsible. The theory of schismogenesis had already been proposed during the 1930s by Gregory Bateson, a social anthropologist, psychiatrist and cyberneticist. The term 'schismogenesis' is a compound of the Latin and Greek words *schisma* and *genesis*, signifying 'split' and 'origin'. Bateson's theory has been applied in social anthropology, psychology and other social sciences (see, for instance, Muskens and Kinnear, 1993; Brox, 2000), but not, it seems, in risk research. The theory can, however, cast new light on the communicative dimensions of the social amplification of risk in siting controversies.

It is generally assumed that notions of risk are largely socially construed and contextualized, and that risks are socially amplified as well as attenuated (Kasperson et al, 1988; Kasperson and Kasperson, 1996; Pidgeon et al, 2003). There are real risks in the world, and there is individual psychological variation in how risks are perceived; but people's ideas of these risks are shaped within specific social and cultural contexts (Boholm, 2003). Some risks, which in a statistical sense are minute, can be of great concern to people, while other risks, which pose a serious threat to health and safety, are largely ignored. It is within the collective experiences and discourses of local communities, corporations and interest groups that the extent and contours of many risk objects take shape. Grabill and Simmons (1998) sum up this analytical position as follows:

> The meaning and value of risk in a given situation is a function of multiple and sometimes competing discourses. In this way, controversy about risk is reframed not as a problem or a negotiation between two parties (the risk-maker and the audience), but as a complex web of stakeholders and positions that contribute to the meaning of risk in any given situation.

The conceptual framework of the 'social amplification of risk' originally referred to the metaphor of a stereo receiver, which may filter and intensify incoming signals; individuals or groups act as 'amplification stations' for risk signals (Kasperson et al, 1988; Renn et al, 1992; Kasperson and Kasperson, 1996). The schismogenic model, however, focuses on a series of signal exchanges between two parties. Thus this model fits well the ongoing and dynamic siting controversy, where two parties are engaged in a battle over a particular issue. It adds a new dimension to the basically linear 'amplification of risk' model. A 'social amplification station' (an interest group) is, through the application of Bateson's theory, found to interact in a predictable way with institutions in society (political and technical authorities).

Gregory Bateson's (1973) theory concerns patterns of interaction between pairs of individuals or two distinct groups of individuals that lead to schismogenesis or differentiation; differentiation means, here, an increasing polarization of positions. Each party interprets and responds to signals, consisting of verbal or non-verbal communication from the other party. Their responses, in turn, constitute new signals.

The theory distinguishes between processes of 'symmetrical' and 'complementary' schismogenesis. In the symmetrical type, each of the two parties interprets a given signal in the same way and also responds to it similarly; the response constitutes a new signal of identical significance. An example on a global scale is an armaments race between two nations. When one of the nations declares that it now has more powerful weapons and has achieved military superiority, this constitutes a signal to the other nation that it has to intensify its armaments development to gain an advantage. When this nation has succeeded in doing so, and its military superiority becomes known to the other state, this constitutes a signal to that state that it has to make an even greater effort in arming itself – and so on. Many relationships that are characterized by competition and rivalry include symmetrical schismogenic elements.

In the complementary form of schismogenesis, the promoting actions are dissimilar, but mutually appropriate. The behaviours of a dominant and a submissive person, for instance, reinforce each other. The dominant person becomes even more dominant when interacting with a submissive person and the submissive person, in turn, becomes even more submissive. This pattern of interaction leads, by necessity, to a polarization of positions or behaviours that need not take place in the case of symmetrical schismogenesis. According to Bateson (1973), the two types of schismogenesis are logically incompatible: they cannot occur simultaneously in a single sequence of communication since the signals and their interpretation then would not reinforce each other.

The railway controversies include features of both types of schismogenesis. A symmetrical schismogenic process commences when the local opponents, in their effort to win the battle over where the railway line should be located, mobilize as many arguments for their case as possible. Such mobilization is, as has been described earlier, apparent when the local conflicts are viewed over time. The arguments used belong to all kinds of discourses: whether the economic costs of the contested route make good sense; whether it is fair that a number of citizens will have their immediate surroundings changed for the worse; or whether the overall advantages of the new railway line outweigh the local environmental disadvantages.

Among the most powerful of the opponents' arguments are, however, those relating to risk – arguments claiming that the authorities, on dubious grounds, are putting the life and health of the citizens at stake. When the opponents emphasize a particular risk, the National Rail Administration or local politicians in charge typically counter with a statement that the danger is minute and that every reasonable precaution to minimize the risk further will certainly be taken. They may also present arguments stressing the improved safety of the modernized railway in order to counterbalance the risk arguments with safety arguments. The opponents then emphasize another risk, and again the authorities answer that there are no real reasons to worry. As will be described below, the emotive content of the critics' discourse also increases. It is in this situation, when every new argument is a new 'weapon' in the battle over the railway plans, that issues, which to an outside observer might appear as marginal or far fetched, are brought forth in the debate.

Of particular weight are references to actual hazardous events, well known through the mass media, that have occurred when rebuilding the west coast railway or recently in railway traffic in Sweden or abroad. As mentioned, the 'scandals' and misfortunes surrounding the building of the Hallandsås tunnel are brought to the fore again and again by opponents in other communities where railway tunnels are to be built. References are also made to the incidents in Kävlinge and Borlänge, when thousands of people were evacuated from their homes following the derailment of cars carrying toxic or highly flammable cargo. These events prove that there are, indeed, risks connected with rebuilding the west coast railway and with its future traffic.

Thus, the controversy over the location of the railway line can be likened to putting weights in the pans of a balance. The authorities put their initial arguments into one pan; then the opponents start to put theirs in the other. This competition is public as every new major move is announced in the mass media. The party who puts the heaviest weight in its pan will win in terms of reason and morals, and therefore in principle – though certainly not always in practice – will also win the struggle over where to locate the railway line. Every new argument put into one pan compels the opponent to put an argument in the other, so there is an active search for, and production of, new arguments that could be used to tip the scale in one's favour. In this escalating competition, arguments carry unequal weight, and risk arguments are among the heaviest. Certainly, train passengers might save a few minutes if a specific route for a section of the west coast railway line is chosen rather than another. This, however, appears to be a trivial benefit compared to the risk of innocent people being poisoned by chemical contamination of their drinking water or children contracting cancer because of exposure to electromagnetic fields extending from the railway's aerial power line into their bedrooms.

If a particular argument turns out to be weak, it is simply disregarded and another and stronger one is put to use in the rhetorical battle. The building of the Hallandsås tunnel, for instance, was initially motivated by time savings for cargo and passenger trains. By means of complicated calculations, it was computed that the tunnel would be socio-economically justified. This argument turned out to be weak: tunnel opponents scored points in the debate when they questioned whether it was worth spending 6 billion Swedish kronor (approximately 660 million Euros) and destroying the environment of the Hallandsås to save merely ten minutes of travel time. The tunnel has consequently been redefined by the National Rail Administration as, essentially, an environmentally friendly project. The tunnel favours rail traffic over motorway traffic, and is thus assumed to counteract global warming. In order to stop global warming, the argument goes, no price is too high. This environmental argument has proved to be effective against the tunnel opponents, taking the sting out of their own environmental arguments concerning the damage caused by the tunnel excavation (Boholm, 2005). The protesting local farmer, whose livestock has been poisoned and whose well has gone dry, is made to appear as a polluter himself, and a much more dangerous one. If his demand that tunnel excavation should be stopped were to be approved, road traffic on the E6 motorway would continue to increase, contributing to the global warming that threatens the future of all mankind.

To win a debate by presenting sound and rhetorically powerful arguments is, however, not the same as having an influence on political decisions. The political authorities invariably state – and this also constitutes an argument in the debate – that decisions have been taken in due order, considering all aspects of the problem, and should therefore not be reconsidered. It is, however, evident that if a decision turns out to be very unreasonable – the arguments in its favour are actually few and weak and those against are many and strong – then the opponents feel that there is a good chance of having decisions reconsidered. From the viewpoint of the interest groups, their position becomes stronger with time since their array of arguments against the railway plans becomes more and more extensive. In their view, the 'failure' of the politicians in office and the National Rail Administration to accept their argumentation becomes increasingly outrageous, to be explained (as the two letters to the editor cited above show) as proof of idiocy, self-interest, jealous guarding of prestige, or blatant disregard for the well-being of the citizens. As mentioned, it is only when there is no hope at all of having the decision altered that the organized resistance to the railway plans is given up.

Not only a symmetrical, but also a complementary process can be discerned in the controversies. The arguments proposed by the National Rail Administration and the politicians are usually impersonal and claim to be objective. 'Facts' about the various alternatives for locating the modernized railway are compiled, and the planning option chosen is supposed to give the most advantageous balance between benefits and drawbacks. Among the opponents, there are always some who feel that such a 'rational' way of treating the railway question lacks something important: a consideration of the personal consequences for those who are negatively affected. In the debate, therefore, they put forth personal and emotional arguments. They speak of the suffering that the reconstruction will cause those who have to leave their homes, about the distress felt when the neighbourhood or landscape is changed beyond recognition, about the worries over environmental harms and other risks, and about the helplessness of the individual in confronting the power of the authorities.

In attempting to influence the authorities, there is, therefore, escalation on the part of the opponents of the emotive content of their risk discourse. Vivid images of suffering, catastrophe and death come to the fore, and anxiety in the face of the unknown – such as the subterranean realm where tunnels will be dug and the invisible electromagnetic field of the railway's aerial power line – forms a dark undercurrent beneath the surface of such arguments.

The authorities have no adequate response, as they think that emotional issues do not belong in the debate. They cannot possibly react emotionally themselves (for instance, by exclaiming that they have had enough of all these 'exaggerated complaints') since that would severely damage their image as 'rational' and objective servants of public administration. They have to stick even harder to the 'rational' and objective position, presenting more statistical figures that show how low the risks 'really' are, and reminding the public that sometimes the interests of the individual must yield to the common good. This response constitutes a signal to the opponents in the debate that their emotionally framed opinion was not understood, and they therefore must intensify their efforts in that respect. Thus, the more personal and emotional the arguments of the opponents become, the more impersonal and technical are those of the National Rail Administration. This occurs foremost at public meetings, when the two parties face each other in person. Under the force of its own logic, the complementary schismogenic process leads to an increasing polarization of standpoints and meanings.

Just as Bateson (1973) postulated, the symmetrical and complementary forms of schismogenesis are incompatible. The 'planning and counter-planning' is a purely symmetrical process: the competing accumulation of 'good' arguments, pro and contra. There is a shared definition of what constitutes a 'good' argument: it should be objective, reasonable and preferably scientific. The 'counter-planner' who becomes upset and emotional would, like a representative of the National Rail Administration reacting in the same manner, ruin his image and credibility. What he or she can do – and this is common – is to refer to the pain and emotional suffering of others affected by the railway plans, and state that this is a fact that must be taken seriously, thus transforming the emotional outbursts of others into the building blocks of rational arguments. It is equally improbable that a person, arguing in an emotional vein, in the same breath would raise scientific arguments; it is precisely such arguments that this person feels overly dominate the debate.

Conclusion

This discussion should not be understood as leading to the conclusion that opponents to rebuilding the railway speak of risks simply in order to persuade the National Rail Administration to change its decisions. Without doubt, a substantial number of people in the affected communities are worried about risks relating the rebuilding of west coast railway (Binde, 2000a). The risks they worry about are not *individually* but *socially* constructed, as are, to a large extent, risks in general. The particular evaluation of risk takes shape within a complex process of competing interests, information exchange and creation of meaning. To the risk object, in this case a railway, are attached notions of fairness and justice, and about hierarchies of values, about the intentions and agenda of the opposing parties. Risk is, therefore, so deeply embedded in values and particular circumstances that it cannot be assessed on its own.

Kasperson and Kasperson (1996, p99) noted that when 'risk becomes a central issue in a political campaign or a source of contention between social groups... polarization of views and escalation of rhetoric by partisans typically occur'. Gregory Bateson's theory of schismogenesis provides an answer, compatible with the social amplification of risk approach, as to why this takes place. The theory predicts important aspects of the behaviour of, and interaction between, interest groups and the responsible authorities in contested large-scale industrial and infrastructure projects. This cybernetic model for information exchange captures the dynamics of the controversy and shows that its rhetorical dimension follows logical rules of symmetry and complementarity.

Acknowledgements

This chapter is based on research conducted within the framework of the project *Understanding Siting Controversy: The Case of the West Coast Railroad, Sweden*, financed by the former Swedish Transport and Communications Research Board (KFB) and the Swedish National Rail Administration (Banverket). Some of the arguments presented here have appeared in a conference paper (Binde, 2000b), as well as in a chapter of a Swedish book on risk issues (Binde, 2002).

11 When Complexity Becomes a Problem: 'Law' and 'Fairness' on Separate Tracks in Sweden

Ralph Heiefort

Introduction

Modern society is complex. Conceptually, it is a manifestation of 'modernity', implying a dynamic process of change that began in Europe during the 16th century, giving rise to institutions such as science, industrial production, market economy and democracy, and to processes of urbanization and globalization. Two essential features of modernity are the differentiation of institutions and the division of labour. In this respect, modern industrialized society significantly differs from pre-modern agrarian modes of society.[1] The institutions and agents that comprise modern societies are, in other words, highly specialized and are assigned very specific tasks in all areas of the social system. Institutions and agents can thus interact and interrelate in infinite ways.[2] To characterize such specialization as 'complex' can simply mean that the system is composed of many interacting components, the behaviour or structure of which is difficult to grasp (Casti, 1997). Analytically, however, the interaction is not only difficult to grasp – in the sense of being highly complicated. That a system is complex refers to the fact that it is counter-intuitive and that the outcome of the process is unpredictable (Casti, 1997). The difference between a *complicated* and a *complex* system is that whereas the former can be completely described in terms of its individual components, the latter cannot be fully understood from simply analysing each of its elements (Cilliers, 1998, pviii).

The 'rhetoric of impossibility' – that is, Post-modern theorists' preoccupation with what is no longer possible by way of text-centred deconstruction – is opposed by Niklas Luhmann, amongst others, who argues 'that there is something to be said' (see 'Foreword' by Knodt in Luhmann, 1995). Still waiting for what is to come after deconstruction, 'the need for more pertinent analyses of today's complex social reality' (Knodt in Luhmann, 1995) might be initiated from shifting the focus from what is 'possible' or 'impossible' to what is intentional, or rather what is *unintentional.* Are values – as manifested in a de facto outcome – of a given relation or constellation intended *by* and *in* the social system and the administrative network, or is a de facto outcome unintentional?

The constituent parts of social systems might be systematically mapped out and designed with the best intentions by a government itself, or by its democratic institutions and organizations; but certain components in certain constellations may, nevertheless, generate unintentional outcomes. Sometimes an unintentional outcome can be eliminated by fine-tuning the system or the administrative network. Sometimes a complete overhaul is required. The (questionable) idea of social engineering is precisely this belief in the intentional design and management of society (Scott, 1998).

The 'network society' (see, for example, Castells, 1996) is a widely employed concept and metaphor used by social scientists to describe an emerging new structure or phenomenon of society which breaks with modernity.[3] Social scientists are not the only ones who have been dealing with the network society. From a philosophical perspective, Deleuze and Guattari have suggested the concept of 'rhizome'[4] to describe complex – social, as well as cognitive – horizontal networks (Deleuze and Guattari, 1987). 'Neural networks' are yet another model and metaphor that prevail in the natural sciences. The basic idea, then, despite academic origin, is that the metaphor of modern society is the vertical structure of the tree with its 'foundation' and 'origin', whereas the general metaphor used for describing the structure of post-modern or late modern society is the 'floating' horizontal network with no beginning and no ending – without any centre of excellence.

Conceptually, the emerging (post-)modern network society seems to indicate that the evolution of society is moving from small and simple *Gemeinschaften* to large and complex *Gesellschaften*.[5] Recent research (Scott, 1998) suggests, however, the opposite tendency. Paraphrasing a review article (Yoffee, 2001) of Scott's book *Seeing Like a State* (Scott, 1998), we are actually dealing with the evolution of simplicity when it comes to modern society. According to Scott (1998, p2), the ultimate driving force of modern states is the attempt to make society legible:

> I began to see legibility as a central problem in statecraft. The pre-modern state was, in many crucial respects, partially blind; it knew precious little about its subjects, their wealth, their landholdings and yields, their location, their very identity. It lacked anything like a detailed 'map' of its terrain and its people. It lacked, for the most part, a measure, a metric, that would allow it to 'translate' what it knew into a common standard necessary for a synoptic view (Scott, 1998, p2).

Scott's argument, in brief, is that the modern state, in trying to get an overview of the pieces of reality it wishes to control, necessarily had to transform this complex reality into a simpler and, thus, relatively more manageable one. Against this background, one wonders whether modern society is a complex society or if it is essentially becoming more and more simple and uniform – or is it, to rephrase Latour (1993), rather the case that we have actually never been modern? The answer is equivocal inasmuch as modern society is simultaneously becoming both more complex and simpler. This dual tendency towards increasing complexity as well as increasing simplicity is, however, not as paradoxical as it initially might seem. To distinguish reality itself from the administration of reality eradicates the paradox, if not the problem.

The differentiation of institutions and the division of labour has, when seen from a systems level, made reality more complex; therefore, institutions and professionals act to simplify[6] reality in order to make it possible to administer, bringing it under control through management regimes: 'The reduction of complexity is the condition of evolutionary differentiation – that is, the internal elaboration of complexity which embraces both natural and social evolution' (Roberts, 1995, p7). Accordingly, there is no disagreement between Scott (1998) and, for instance, Luhmann (1995) regarding the desire or aspiration of the state or the system to reduce the complexity of the environment; disagreement on the normative implications of that enterprise is quite another issue.

Complexity itself is, like the social system, not problematic by default. But when the complexity of the social system brings into being unintentional outcomes, then it does become problematic. This chapter focuses on the unintentional outcomes in a Swedish social system arising from the complexity of the social system itself in interaction with a complex social sub-system (the legal system). The centre of attention is primarily an institutional or structural level, and only secondarily an individual or agency level – that is, the focus is primarily on the differentiation of institutions and secondarily on the division of labour.

One indicator of a problematic complexity within the social system and the social sub-system emerges when citizens experience a discrepancy between the law (as it is exercised by the juridical system) and fairness (as an intuitive moral understanding). Since the overall context in the case to be presented in this chapter is that of a democratic state, it is somewhat astonishing that in laymen's view there exists a discrepancy between law and fairness. Is it not at the very foundation of the democratic state to provide legal rights – rights that should be fair towards its citizens? If this alleged discrepancy between law and fairness is grounded in laymen's inadequate knowledge of the law as such, then the solution to the problem is plainly to provide them with better knowledge. Education for the masses is, however, not the sole possibility and remedy; the discrepancy might be grounded in a far more fundamental opposition than that between knowledge and ignorance.

The fact that people in a specific local context, such as the context described in this case – rightfully or wrongfully – experience a discrepancy between law and fairness is the point of departure for this chapter. Here, an empirical case of a 'contested local environment' is presented: first, in a general account of the case, and then through an overview of its legal history. In short, the primary focus is not the publicly expressed discontent in its various forms, or private 'nagging' between or among involved parties, but rather the formalized arguments that have been presented in court.[7] This chapter's main concern is to elucidate the perceived inconsistency between 'law' and 'fairness', and it gives an account of such inconsistencies, asking whether they should be understood as an unintentional outcome of a well-intended arrangement, and thus not synchronous with society's prevailing values.

General context: Tunnel vision

Building a railway tunnel through the Hallandsås ridge in the southern part of Sweden in the municipality of Båstad is part of a major upgrading of the west coast railway line (*Västkustbanan*)[8] from a single-track railway into a modern two-track railway. The railway traffic between Göteborg in the northwest and Lund/Malmö in the southwest (a distance of 370 kilometres (km) between Sweden's second and third largest cities), and further on to Denmark and the rest of Europe, was, amongst other issues, considered in need of improvement with regard to travel time and carrying capacity (see Boholm and Löfstedt, 1999; Löfstedt and Boholm, 1999; Boholm, 2000). The building of the 8.6km Hallandsås tunnel, within a nature reserve area, started in 1992[9] by order of the Swedish government and was scheduled to be completed in 1997. The project is still unfinished and the tunnel is forecast to be open to train traffic in 2011, according to the Swedish National Rail Administration (the state authority responsible for building and maintaining the Swedish railway system). To date, two-thirds of the tunnel has yet to be drilled.

The major reasons for the delay are threefold. Most important is the complex geological nature of the ridge. In some parts of the ridge, the rock mass has completely decomposed, while in other parts it is extremely permeable. Owing to these geological circumstances, the Hallandsås ridge contains huge amounts of groundwater; and the drilled part of the tunnel – one third of it – has turned out to be extraordinarily difficult to seal off. Deriving from the geological complexity, another main reason for the present incomplete condition of the tunnel project has been the use of the water-soluble chemical sealant Rhoca Gil, which contains the toxic substance acrylamide.[10] Rhoca Gil was used during spring and summer 1997 as a sealant to stop the groundwater from leaking into the tunnel. The effort failed and, what is worse, acrylamide leaked out into the groundwater and into wells and streams. The construction of the tunnel was discontinued in October 1997 as a direct consequence of this. Besides these two more tangible reasons for the incomplete state of the tunnel, there are also significant bureaucratic problems – namely, a six-year legal intermezzo.

The decreased groundwater level is a direct consequence of drilling the tunnel.[11] Besides the long-term implications of the toxic contamination of the environment, the decreased groundwater level had several negative consequences for the local residents: wetlands dried up, wells ran short and, in many cases, the quality of the water in private wells[12] deteriorated and became unfit for consumption.

The tunnel project, it could be argued, is a 'techno-logical' failure. Looking at a map of the present railway, which winds through the scenic hilly landscape, it is evident that there is a possibility of rationalization: the shortest distance between two points is a straight line. The idea of the Hallandsås tunnel as an instance of high-modernist state planning (Scott, 1998) can thus be condensed to the tenet of the straight line. In other words, it is not the internal *raison d'être* of this logic that is questionable. Nevertheless, it is exactly this quest for legibility of the terrain, to evoke Scott's term (Scott, 1998), which is the source of the massive aftermath in the courts of law – amongst other forums.

AN OVERVIEW OF THE LEGAL HISTORY OF THE TUNNEL PROJECT

The failure of the tunnel project since the discharging of Rhoca Gil into the environment in September 1997 has led to a whole array of legal consequences. Legal proceedings took place at Ängelholm District Court (*Ängelholms tingsrätt*) in May 2002, in what was expected to be the largest environmental legal process to date in Sweden. The trial was initially scheduled to begin in September 2001 and to be finished by late December 2001 (with a break in proceedings during October). Instead of having one major trial, the trial was, however, divided into several sub-trials. One sub-trial dealt with the 'environmental issue' of the case while another sub-trial related to the 'water issue'. In addition, there was a separate trial regarding violation of the law concerning chemical products. Last, but not least, individual claims for damages were singled out as a separate part of the legal course of action.[13]

The legal forum for these four sub-trials was, as mentioned, the Ängelholm District Court; but these were not the only trials to be held in connection with the tunnel and its legal aspects. In order to resume the construction work of the remaining projected tunnel, the Swedish National Rail Administration had to obtain a new permit (*vattendom*) from the environmental court (*Miljödomstolen*).[14] The first main hearing in the environmental court was held in Grevie, a small village on the Hallandsås peninsula, in April 2002. The result of the proceedings was that the environmental court decided that the material presented by the National Rail Administration was inconclusive, and the agency was required to present complementary and supplementary material at a resumed main hearing, which was held in October 2002. Finally, in September 2003, the case was addressed at the environmental court of appeal. The following section provides, first, an overview of the legal history of the tunnel project with respect to the trials held at Ängelholm District Court, then an overview of the two main hearings at the environmental court and, finally, an overview of the main hearing at the environmental court of appeal.

The part of the criminal trials relating to violation of the law concerning chemical products (*Brott mot lagen om kemiska produkter*) – that is, the matter of the acrylamide leak – was the first sub-part of the trials addressed in Ängelholm District Court. In June 2001, the court found the defendant chief executive officer from the Swedish sales office of the French chemicals corporation Rhone-Poulenc, who had sold the sealant, guilty as charged for not complying with the regulations on information concerning chemical substances affirmed by the (Swedish) National Chemicals Inspectorate (*Kemikalieinspektionen*). The judgement was not appealed.

On the 'environmental issue' of the criminal trial, a division manager from the contractor Skanska, one of the largest building contractors in Sweden, was, in January 2002, found guilty as charged for causing damages to the environment (*vållande till miljöstörning*). Another division manager, also from Skanska, was charged with criminal violation of the working environment law (*Brott mot arbetsmiljölagen*).[15] The latter manager, however, died before the case went to court. Both division managers were, in various ways, in charge of the use of the Rhoca Gil sealant manufactured by Rhone-Poulenc. The contractor Skanska, also in January 2002, was found guilty as charged and directed to pay the maximum fine (företagsbot) – 3 million Swedish kroner (approximately 330,000 Euros) – stipulated by the law for the use of Rhoca Gil. This judgement was not appealed either.

Only two weeks before the 'water issue' of the trials was scheduled to begin, the chief prosecutor (*överåklagare*) – as a complete surprise to most of those involved – decided to withdraw the indictment against the three chief executives of the Swedish National Rail Administration (Banverket) for violation of the water law (*Brott mot vattenlagen*). This pronouncement by the chief prosecutor was widely debated in the public forum. The violation of the water law was, in many respects, regarded as the most important sub-trial, and it was questionable whether the trials, seen as a whole, really could be counted as 'the largest environmental trial in Sweden'. The prosecutor general (*Riksåklagaren*), however, overruled the chief prosecutor's decision only a few weeks later, and the trial thus took place in May 2002 – with a new public prosecutor. Eventually, the three chief executives were found not guilty in June 2002 by the district court. The chief public prosecutor, however, filed an appeal against the court's decision. The formal setting for this appeal was the court of (civil and criminal) appeal (*Hovrätten*). The court of appeal confirmed in May 2003 the verdict of the district court.

The legal proceedings that took place at Ängelholm District Court were, from the point of view of Swedish jurisprudence, not unique by any means – the court sessions were conducted according to customary standards. Sociologically, on the other hand, it is remarkable that besides the media (reporters from radio, television and newspapers) and a few researchers, only an occasional handful of local residents attended the trials. The reason for the low attendance in court was perhaps that it was geographically situated in the nearby township of Ängelholm and not in the municipality of Båstad, where the tunnel site is located; or possibly it was that the proceedings were held during working hours. If such practical circumstances were of any importance, however, the attendance would have been expected to be similarly low at the hearings at the environmental court.

At the environmental court, the scenario was, nevertheless, strikingly different. Lawyers, a multiplicity of technical and environmental experts, and media representatives in plenty were vastly outnumbered by local residents. The hearings were held at two different locations, which, admittedly, in terms of distance, were closer to the tunnel site than Ängelholm District Court; but it would be missing the point to account for this fact in terms of geographical distance. The reason why so many locals attended the hearings was due to sociological or social–psychological factors. People were anxious about future implications of continued tunnel drilling; they considered themselves to have been 'steamrollered' by various – and numerous – instances of the bureaucratic apparatus; last, but not least, many locals had devoted a considerable amount of time and mental energy to follow the matter. The sociological or social–psychological interpretation also makes sense when the setting and, more importantly, the 'role' of the attendants are taken into account.

The setting at Ängelholm District Court is a traditional court setting: the court is situated at the front centre of the courtroom (in this case, in a slightly higher position – looking down at everybody else in the room), while the prosecutor and the defendants are facing each other to the right and left of the judges. The audience faces the court at the opposite end of the room. The main difference between this 'permanent' court setting and the hearings at the environmental court is that the setting of the latter is 'non-permanent' in light of the ambulant nature of this court. There are five environmental courts in Sweden – each with a specific geographic location and jurisdiction of its own. However, the environmental court, as well as the environmental court of appeal, have conducted *on-site* hearings and *inspections of the physical environment* relevant to the case.[16] This non-permanent character of both the environmental court and the environmental court of appeal means that the formal or physical setting of the court, when ambulating, is arbitrary – the first hearing was held at a community centre, whereas the second hearing was held in a spacious room at a conference centre.[17] At the environmental court, the applicant (the Swedish National Rail Administration) faced the court at the far end of the room, with the audience on the right and left, leaving one end of the room empty. In short, the physical setting of the two courts differed in that one was perceived as more hierarchical and institutionalized, whereas the other was perceived as more egalitarian and intimate.

The major difference between the two courts, however, is not simply the distinction between being hierarchical and egalitarian – rather, it is the 'role' of the audience. At the district court, participation is restricted to the conventional definition of 'audience': mute observation, which, at most, only allows for an occasional murmur of pleasure or displeasure. Only those summoned by the court exercise the right to speak. Specialists discuss matters within the same frame of reference – that of law – but do so according to their different agendas: prosecution, defence and judgement. In contrast, the role of the audience at the environmental court is not restricted to mute observation. Everyone is invited and everyone has the option to speak – to have their voice heard. The role of the audience is thus of a group of potential participators. With this in mind, it is therefore not at all surprising that so few local residents attended the trials at Ängelholm District Court – at the proceedings, they had no right to seek to influence the verdict of the court. At the environmental court, on the other hand, local residents and stakeholders had the means – that is, the 'voices' – and a legitimate right as citizens and stakeholders to influence the outcome.

The physical setting by itself is likely to be of marginal importance only for the actual number of people attending the courtrooms. The courtroom as an institution might, in theory at least, have a silencing effect on non-professionals that is relatively greater than that of a community centre or a hotel conference room. The physical setting in itself, it should be emphasized, is subordinate to the right to speak. The physical setting as a vehicle for generating a sense of community through sharing food is another issue. At the district court in Ängelholm there was no communal consumption of food whatsoever involving the parties present. In contrast, at the environmental court, as well as at the environmental court of appeal, everyone present was treated to lunch and to free beverages in the breaks between proceedings. The host was the Swedish National Rail Administration. Sociologically, it was remarkable to observe the mixture of court members – lawyers, civil servants and government officials, representatives of interest groups, stakeholders and laymen – participating in the communal sharing of food. Although people largely kept to their own occupational groups, they also networked and lobbied – in fact, informal negotiations took place during breaks and, once back in court, these negotiations were often explicitly referenced. Mingling was unavoidable since each table accommodated more people than 'categories' of people and no tables were reserved – not even for the members of the court.

Although freedom of speech is a fundamental principle in modern democratic societies, it is not customary that a courtroom audience possesses the actual right to speak. This is, however, not as strange as it might seem. The task of both the environmental court and the environmental court of appeal, it has been mentioned, is, first of all, to decide whether or not to grant a permit requested by the National Rail Administration (a necessary condition to continue building the tunnel). But another task is to state the terms and conditions for the actual permit. The task of the two courts is thus to balance public *and* individual interests with environmental concerns for sustainable development. The courts have the mandate to weigh national concerns about infrastructure (in this case, rail traffic in Sweden) against a variety of public and individual concerns vis-à-vis the environment. Principal stakeholders are:

- the Swedish government, which has given priority to building the tunnel and modernizing the rail track infrastructure;
- the Swedish National Rail Administration, which is responsible for the actual implementation of this decision;
- the Swedish Environmental Protection Agency (Naturvårdsverket), a governmental organization;
- the Swedish Society for Nature Conservation (Svenska Naturskyddsföreningen), another non-governmental organization representing the interests of the public; and
- principal individual stakeholders, the owners.

Principal individual stakeholders are the owners of property within the area of impact: primarily local residents living in the geographical vicinity affected by the tunnel.[18] The environmental court has to balance the diverse interests of these various individuals and organizations against the concern for the environment – the single point of reference for which is the environmental code. It is obvious that there are a multitude of conflicting interests that must be taken into account. What particularly distinguishes the environmental court from the district court is the respective time frame within which each operates. The environmental court is concerned with the future and with questions relating to the future – that is, what is going to happen. The district court, in contrast, deals with the past – what has happened. Likewise, the environmental court is concerned with society at large and its relation to nature, whereas the district court is concerned with 'the public versus X' ('X' is not a general person or corporation, but a specific individual person or corporation). These differences between the environmental court and the district court illuminate the somewhat 'open-endedness' of the former.

Structural constraints

The (convicting) verdict of the Ängelholm District Court was, on the one hand, generally appreciated by local stakeholders; but, on the other hand, they considered the sanctions of the law to be too gentle. The sense of discrepancy between law and fairness was modest, but nevertheless it was evident, the convicting verdicts notwithstanding. From the perspective of local residents and stakeholders, it is evident that convicting verdicts were received with appreciation. However, the discrepancy was rather of an economic nature than a jurisprudential nature because the sanctions of the law in terms of monetary compensation only represented a fraction of the actual costs of restoring the environment. It should be emphasized here that local public opinion saw it as unjust towards local citizens that the National Rail Administration, as a government agency, did not have better control over the project and, as a consequence, inflicted harm on a number of citizens in the municipality.[19] Furthermore, it was generally believed that it was unjust that the National Rail Administration did not take full responsibility for the consequences of leaking groundwater and acrylamide toxic leakage. The responsibilities – understood in a broad sense – of the Swedish government towards its citizens are, however, one thing and public understanding of the law is another. Analytically, we could make a distinction, on the one hand, between what is framed as unjust conduct and the unjustness of the impact of external circumstances beyond people's own control, and, on the other, the more formal legal subtleties.[20]

It is, however, appropriate to speak of a discrepancy between law and fairness when considering the chief public prosecutor's announced withdrawal of the indictment against the Swedish National Rail Administration in 'the water issue' of the trial. In a letter to the editor in the largest morning newspaper in Sweden, a writer complains:

> The decision that the Swedish National Rail Administration shall not be indicted for lowering of the groundwater in the Hallandsås Ridge is revolting and incomprehensible. The indictment seems to collapse because of a juridical technicality as to whether authorization for lowering of the groundwater level was required or not. The Swedish National Rail Administration apparently needed authorization for lowering the groundwater level in a controlled way, but not for lowering it in an uncontrolled way. Can it be more bizarre than that? (*Dagens Nyheter*, 2001).

This experience of a discrepancy between law and fairness was not only confined to the national context. In an extensive letter to the editor of a local newspaper under the heading 'The law *has to* apply to us all' (original emphasis) the writer concludes:

> Is it not time, once and for all, to agree that the laws apply to all of us? What is a crime for us at the grassroots is also a crime for those in power (*Nordvästra Skånes Tidningar*, 2001).

Another headline, in a national morning newspaper, read: 'This is devastating for people's sense of justice.' (*Svenska Dagbladet*, 2001).

The examples are numerous, but typical of them is a farmer's comment, quoted in another newspaper article: 'Is this legal? Are you allowed to do as you please! I am shocked' (*Nordvästra Skånes Tidningar*, 2001).

This experience of a discrepancy between law and fairness is not only confined to the circumstances related. The legal frame of reference of the tunnel project comprises 'the old environmental laws', whereas the legal frame of reference for the National Rail Administration's permit to continue the tunnel project is 'the new environmental code' (The Swedish Environmental Code (Miljöbalken (SFS 1998:808))), which took effect on 1 January 1999. In other words, the situation was that obsolete environmental laws were to be applied to the past – that is, what has happened – whereas a new and relatively unproven environmental code was to be applied to the future – what is going to happen.

It is hard to reconstruct the past; but, as a general rule, the nature of such an enterprise is characterized by its factuality. The permit for the continuation of the project is, however, intentional. As a consequence, the Swedish National Rail Administration is simultaneously following one (legal) strategy in the district court – trying not to be convicted – and another (semi-legal) strategy in the environmental court – trying to get a new permit.

At the district court the arguments of the National Rail Administration are advocated by its lawyers, aiming to minimize the degree of its responsibility and that of its executives because, essentially, as they argue, 'what happened was a series of incidents and events – due to a complex situation – that was *beyond* the control of the Rail Administration'. One of the National Rail Administration's lawyers is also one of Sweden's most famous criminal defence lawyers. Prior to the defence lawyer's statement, the prosecutor 'warned' the court that they were going to listen to 'the Joe Labero of jurisprudence' (in other words, a magician or illusionist). Later, the defence lawyer replied that he was certainly not a magician; on the contrary, he was devoted to facts, not fiction. Anyway, he stated, he indeed felt 'sympathy with people living on the (Hallandsås) ridge – but now we are talking law'. Later on in his statement, the defence lawyer said: 'Morals, ethics and empathy must not lead to an extensive interpretation of the law.' In a strict legal sense, he is most likely right; but in terms of 'law' and 'fairness', there is good reason to believe that this lawyer also had the feeling of a divide between the one and the other. To sum up the situation in the district court: the lawyers talk law, and if non-legal aspects arise during the proceedings, the lawyers quickly return to the legal issues. In other words, there is a clear demarcation between law and non-law.

At the environmental court, however, the situation is the opposite. Here, the National Rail Administration primarily presents its case through representatives of its organization and through external technical experts – and only to a lesser degree through its lawyers, who in this forum primarily fulfil more of an advisory role. The important difference is that at the environmental court the National Rail Administration's argument essentially goes something like this: 'What is going to happen is the building of a tunnel though a complex geological setting; but this complex situation is within our control.' To support this line of argument or strategy, at the resumed main hearing in October 2002, the

National Rail Administration, after a short introduction, started out presenting its case from a technical point of view. First, the qualifications of the expert engaged by the National Rail Administration were validated: the expert was an internationally renowned authority on tunnel drilling and he accounted for different techniques used within this trade. The expert then continued with an exposition of how to do the actual drilling through the Hallandsås ridge. The discussion was well rehearsed and skilfully presented, although it involved translation into English. Furthermore, it was very technical in nature, as were the questions following the presentation. If the first day of the resumed hearing was devoted to technique or modus operandi, then the next day of the hearing was devoted to science, or theoretical issues.

The scientific expert was a professor and dean of a renowned university of technology. He began his presentation by explaining the differences between reality and models of reality, between differences of theory in natural science and social science, and, among other issues, the premise of Occam's razor: the scientific principle that gives precedence to simplicity. The professor characterized himself as a 'friend of (scientific) simplicity' and explained that instead of habitually making models, descriptions, analyses and surveys increasingly complex in search of how to adequately represent reality, it is actually sometimes better to do the opposite – the point being that, after a certain point, complexity becomes counterproductive at worst, and, at best, its marginal utility is negligible. These two examples will be sufficient to illuminate that non-legal issues in the environmental court prevailed over legal issues.[21]

In a strict legal sense, perhaps the National Rail Administration cannot be held responsible for what happened during the past. In a strict technical sense – due to lessons learned – the National Rail Administration can, indeed, build the tunnel within the restrictions stated by the environmental code as interpreted by the environmental court; but – and this is significant – one cannot, in reality, know a priori about the future.

The account presented in this chapter might indicate that the National Rail Administration is calculating on an optimal strategy that depends upon context and is, thus, simply following different strategies in the two courtrooms – an instance of rational choice. It is, however, *not* possible for the National Rail Administration, its lawyers and its experts to present the content of its argumentation otherwise. Its means of action are actually structurally restrained by the differentiation of institutions into specialized sub-institutions and the division of labour in society.

Regardless of whether the National Rail Administration is to be held responsible or not in a strict legal sense, the lawyers representing the client at the district court are, by default, obliged to try to keep the level of responsibility as low as possible. In other words, the lawyers' primary objective is to get their clients acquitted, and if they do not succeed in this endeavour, then their secondary strategy is to minimize the sanction of the law. Given the important reservation that the National Rail Administration (or, rather, its chief executive officers) genuinely believes that it is technically possibly to build the tunnel, it is unfeasible for the administration to present the content of its argumentation otherwise at the environmental court when trying to get a permit for continuing the project. The National Rail Administration is, in spite of everything, an expert on building tunnels, in general, and as a government agency it is commissioned by the Swedish government to build a specific tunnel. In other words, structural restrictions apply between the factual and the intentional means of argumentation available to the National Rail Administration and its representatives.

Conclusion

The structural restrictions are not discernible when observing the trials separately, but emerge only when the trials are observed and studied as a whole. On an individual level, the specialists involved are confined by the limits of their trade; they simply cannot perform beyond the limits of professional standards without the risk of disciplinary sanctions. Their behaviour is restricted by internal context. The important point is that the external context is shifting. On a structural level, the differentiation of institutions and the division of labour generate restrictions in a similar manner. Within the sphere of 'law', the institutional differentiation has as its consequence that 'the case' is treated as separate 'cases'. In reality, this means that the case is treated separately.[22] Logically, this makes no sense; but legally it appears that it does!

This is not to say that the representatives of the Swedish National Rail Administration, or any other organization, for that matter, are morally dubious by default; they are no more and no less so than the local residents. They *do* follow what they presume to be the most adequate strategy – and so do the local residents. The important difference is that the local residents live in the local context – *the lived complex reality* is not polyfurcated.[23] The administrative framework, in contrast, is more manageable if it is simplified – that is, if complex reality is polyfurcated and managed by specialized institutions and specialized professionals.

Polyfurcation might be advocated for strategic concerns, or simply for manageability, or for a number of other 'good' or 'bad' reasons. But, looking at the case(s) from a bird's eye view, it is clear that the outcome of this polyfurcation is unintentional with regard to the incentives of the law, as well as to the basic idea of 'sustainable development' (of which the environmental code is an expression) – namely, that development should be ecologically, socially and economically sustainable.[24]

In the case presented here, polyfurcation generates an unintentional outcome because the institutions involved are *not* in the relation intended by and in the social system. Polyfurcation is the effect and not the cause of the complexity of the system – that is, the differentiation of the institutions and the division of labour in the social system. The constituent parts of the social system are systematically mapped out and designed with the best intentions; but the involved components in their de facto constellation, nevertheless, generate an unintentional outcome – a discrepancy between law and fairness.

Notes

Chapter 1

1 More extensive treatments of this history are available in numerous publications (see, for example, Flynn et al, 1995; Short and Rosa, 2004).
2 As was that of the Waste Isolation Pilot Plant (WIPP), the repository built in the south-western US, in New Mexico, that began accepting transuranic waste on 26 March 1999.
3 Articles in this issue of *Risk Analysis* also agree that PA is appropriate for evaluation of storage of transuranic waste at the Waste Isolation Pilot Plant in New Mexico (see, for example, Ewing et al, 1999; Garrick and Kaplan, 1999).
4 Research suggests that *control* is a major concern, especially when health and safety are at issue.
5 Less ambitious efforts were made in other counties, most notably Nye County, in which the proposed repository is located. Here we discuss only the state and Clark County programmes.
6 James Short was chair of the PRC. The following analysis is, therefore, a reflection of his participant observation of the PRC and the Clark County programme. Short had made the county's commitment to special effects and cultural effects a condition of his agreeing to chair the PRC. His resignation was prompted following the spring 1995 PRC meeting, when the NWD director informed him that funds for continuing social impact research were no longer available. Two years later, when the DOE again funded affected units of local government, economic studies were initiated in cooperation with the state. Studies of organizations and other social effects were not reinstated, however, and the PRC was never reconvened. Eugene Rosa continued to be directly involved in the Yucca Mountain siting decision with his participation on the National Academy of Sciences Committee on Principles and Operational Strategies for Staged Repository Systems and with a current appointment on the National Academy of Sciences National Board on Radioactive Waste.
7 The PRC met twice during its first year of its existence (1991), but only annually thereafter.
8 Short confirmed this data in a telephone call to the NWD director in preparation for this chapter.
9 Examples of political interference with the NWD began to appear as early as 1992. The NWD director informed the PRC chair that 'out of the blue' a county official had required him to hire particular emergency-response staff members. Later, NWD funds that were earmarked for a geographic information system (GIS) specialist were given to another county agency. Although the specialist performed some work for the NWD, the division had no control of his activities.
10 See, also, our discussion of principles related to siting controversies (Short and Rosa, 2004).
11 Roger Kasperson (2000), in his presidential address to the Society for Risk

Analysis, inveighed against over-reliance on the 'stakeholder fixes' that now are so prominent in risk analysis.

12 Ironically, misunderstandings regarding this point arise, in part, because of successes and inappropriate uses of one of social science's most potent research methodologies: the public opinion survey. Although advances in survey methods now permit identification and study of special interest publics and divergent stakeholders, most surveys do not do so; instead, they focus on general population samples within which different publics are located. Small sample sizes of general populations rarely permit identification of special interest publics, let alone their careful study. Additionally, the focus of most surveys tends to be on individual perceptions and opinions, rather than on the contexts within which perceptions, opinions and agendas are formed and actions taken. The connections between perceptions, attitudes and actual behaviour thus remain problematic (see Clarke and Short, 1993).

13 AIDS and other health hazards activists, for example, have informed themselves with sophisticated knowledge regarding health concerns in their communities and policy alternatives (Brown, 1991; Epstein, 1996).

14 The derivation and the nature of environmental beliefs and values have occasioned considerable debate. Ironically, Mary Douglas, using a type of cultural analysis quite different from Kempton et al (1985), reached quite different conclusions. Douglas and political scientist Aaron Wildavsky (1982) explain radical disagreement concerning environmentalism (as distinct from environmental values) in terms of relative satisfaction with the status quo, as represented by traditional hierarchical institutions and market processes (whose followers are themselves often opposed to one another on other public issues). Environmentalists, they argue, adopt an oppositional sectarian worldview, which leads them to focus on environmental issues as risk *choices*.

Douglas and Wildavsky acknowledge that their typology (the 'centre' characterized by beliefs in hierarchy or individualism; the 'border' by sectarian beliefs) is abstract and their positions extreme (Douglas and Wildavsky, 1982, pp102–103, 190). Careful analysis suggests that their 'ideal typology' and the cultural consensus discovered by Kempton et al (1995) are not so much opposed to one another as they are addressed to different questions. Douglas and Wildavsky did not set out to establish the nature of environmental values among hierarchists, individualists or sectarians. Their focus was on beliefs and values concerning ways of viewing risks and responding to them. They acknowledged their 'bias toward the centre', arguing that risk choices are best made by building resilience into the institutions that inevitably choose among risks and coping strategies. Wildavsky (1988) later argued that safety (like environmental protection) is best achieved not by governmental intervention and regulation – favoured, for different reasons, by both hierarchists and environmentalists – but by encouraging risk-taking and resilience. Note that Kempton and his colleagues did not seek to determine how their respondents would address specific environmental problems – for example, through individual or corporate enterprise or by means of governmental intervention and regulation. Consensus on values, such as safety and protection of the environment, does not translate simply, directly or straightforwardly into agreed-upon social policy – hence, again, the importance of deliberative and broadly participatory decision processes.

15 Key attributes of life that Habermas (1970) refers to, *in toto*, as the 'lifeworld' and comprising the same basic values that Kempton et al (1995) was found to be widely shared among diverse groups.

16 In his complex, tightly argued paper, Rappaport (1996) advances some 18 theses on risk and the human environment.

Chapter 2

1 The term 'disposition' describes the active management of radioactive waste, either in storage facilities located at or near the Earth's surface, or in as yet unsealed underground geological repositories designed for permanent isolation of waste (NRC, 2001, p12).

2 The term 'disposal' denotes an end to the need for reliance on active management for ensuring safety and security of the waste (NRC, 2001, p12).

3 COGEMA has a 1600-tonne annual reprocessing capacity (DGEMP, 2003) and reprocesses spent fuel from Australia, Belgium, Germany, Japan, Spain, Switzerland and The Netherlands (NRC, 2001). The law forbids storage in France of the vitrified waste resulting from this service, so shipments periodically are returned to the source country.

4 A small proportion of France's HLW is stored in the southeast at COGEMA's Marcoule research and reprocessing facility (close to the 'Gard' site evaluated during 1993–1998 as a candidate for an underground laboratory; see Figure 2.1).

5 The prime minister rarely initiates a study by OPECST; that is generally a parliamentary prerogative. OPECST has a small professional staff; but its investigations are conducted by members of parliament.

6 2002 research expenditures related to underground disposal amounted to 80.9 million Euros; transmutation research cost 72.8 million Euros and packaging and surface storage studies cost 69.5 million Euros (DGEMP, 2003).

7 This role description is drawn from the mission statement and activities by CLIS for France's effective URL construction site at Bure: see www.meuse.pref.gouv.fr/developpement/clis/index.html. CLIS consists of 93 persons representing 37 townships and is supported by a scientific secretary and assistants.

8 The author is indebted to Yannick Barthe of Grenoble's Institut d'Etudes Politiques for pointing out this ambiguity, and for other conversations and exchanges on RWM.

9 A *département* is a subdivision of the French territory governed by an elected general council. It contains legislative districts, which, in turn, contain townships each governed by an elected mayor and town council. *Départements* are grouped in regions, administered by a prefect and governed by elected regional councils. These three levels of elected representation – regional, general and town councils – are the local decision authorities who deliberate upon siting proposals.

10 Not all local officials had an easy time of it. A footnote to the memory of the mayor of Chatain is due: in January 1994, in an attempt to calm rumours and press reports that this small Vienne village was designated to receive a laboratory, the mayor held a local referendum (without legal value). He committed suicide after URL opponents compared his public consultation to those conducted by Nazis. 'Such a dramatic personal gesture doubtless never should be attributed to the sole turn of outside events. However, this tragic, if isolated, occurrence serves to demonstrate that nuclear waste, no matter how well 'handled', still can produce life or death situations when it arrives on some person's doorstep' (Mays and Poumadère, 1996).

11 Barthe and Mays (2001) analyse public information and communication during the

geological evaluation phase when Andra cohabited with other actors on the local scene, and during the 1997 local public inquiries triggered by the construction permit application for three URLs. Detailed study is made of the winegrowers' position: although they had lived in peace for 40 years with the Marcoule installations, the prospect of an underground repository perceived as stigmatizing tipped them into active resistance.

12 See, for example, the French-language website of Coedra (Pays de Fougères Collective against the burial of radioactive wastes, a civil society organization formed in Brittany in 1991 in response to the first site search and active through the Granite Mission period).

13 The federation was formally constituted in October 1997 and in 2001 counted more than 600 member organizations, totalling 10,000 persons (numbers not available for 2000).

14 The mission itself on 2 February posted the map on the internet: www.environnement.gouv.fr/dossiers/risques/nucleaire/dechets/2k02-mission-granite-2-carte.htm (last retrieved 3 December 2003).

15 Note that Bataille also had encountered colourful protest at various points in his regional visits, including a farmers' escort at pitchfork-point.

16 After the failure of the Granite Mission, in July 2000 the government directed Andra to 'pursue research on two different geological sites, in conformity with the law of 1991' (CNE, 2003, p35). In response, Andra was led to intensify its scientific collaboration in foreign URL projects (in Sweden, Switzerland and Finland), 'for in the absence of an underground laboratory in granite on French territory, [this] gives Andra its sole possibility to acquire data *in situ* in that rock' (CNE, 2003, p36).

17 The REPDECH study (performed during 2000–2001) compared representations of long-lived radioactive wastes – that is, low-level uranium mill tailings (through interviews with 22 residents in the Limousin mining region of central France, recruited by a 'snowballing' method) and high-level waste resulting from the nuclear fuel cycle (interviews with 40 residents of the cities of Rouen and Bordeaux, of lower-middle to mid-level socio-economic status, recruited by a survey firm to talk about 'environmental issues'). It was originally planned to interview, as a third sample, residents of a Granite Mission site; but preliminary contacts made it clear that this was not welcomed and could have a negative effect on internal community relations. The author cordially acknowledges Sylvie Charron of IRSN's Laboratory of Social and Economic Studies, who collaborated in the study design and conduct of the urban focus group discussions and individual interviews, and who contributed to the systematic analysis and reporting of the transcripts.

18 This quote probably refers to the periodic rail shipments returning fuel waste from reprocessing in La Hague to Germany's interim storage centre at Gorleben. The media report the dramatic resistance by German activists who lie down in the train's path, and the tens of thousands of police called out to line the tracks. Note that four to six shipments of waste for treatment are sent by rail from Germany to La Hague each year. Plutonium is transported by truck one or two times per week to Marcoule from La Hague (Kempf, 2003).

19 This representation was expressed six months before the events of 11 September 2001 and the subsequent highly publicized evaluations of the vulnerability of nuclear power or waste installations.

20 Comments during the final discussion panel at the meeting 'New Perspectives on Siting Controversy', Glumslöv, Sweden, 20 May 2001.

21 Consult these exchanges on www.debat-energie.gouv.fr/site/forum/list.php?f=7.

22 Buclet and Bouzidi (2003, p168) suggest that the French national energy debate cannot even be considered to be true debate, in that its conclusion – the future basis for a draft law giving a 'recognized place' to nuclear power in the national energy mix – was announced by the prime minister at the very time of launching the process.

Chapter 3

1 The main actors in the case study of Stripa are the company (Stripa Mine Service AB), the local environmental organization (Storå-Guldsmedshyttans miljöförening) and the Swedish Environmental Protection Agency (EPA). The company and the local environmental organization have primarily been the antagonists in the debate over the plans for mercury disposal in Stripa. The Swedish EPA is an important national actor in the process to accomplish final disposal of mercury. The Swedish EPA plays no current role in the debate in Stripa, but it is part of the process of moulding and defining the suggested solution to final disposal of mercury. Today, the Swedish EPA is the main actor to convey the national political representation of a future mercury disposal policy.

The analysis is based on relevant articles and letters to the editor published in the local press, *Bergslagsposten*, from March 1994 to December 1997. The data are based on a comprehensive search for the period, and after sorting out (some minor paragraphs and irrelevant coverage were left aside), it consists of 34 news articles and 17 letters to the editor (see citations at the end of the References chapter in this volume). Representatives from the company and the local environmental organization have been interviewed. Likewise written documents from the local environmental organization have been used. The analysis of the standpoints and perceptions of the Swedish EPA is based on the report *Final Disposal of Mercury* (Swedish EPA, 1997). The data also include a video recording from an information meeting in Stripa held on 25 May 1994 and a memorandum from an information meeting in Stripa held on 20 September 1995, with representatives from the company and the local opposition; three feature programmes ('*Rakt på sak*', or 'Straight to the Point') and coverage of the 20 September 1995 information meeting in Stripa as broadcasted on local radio. The local radio programmes featured representatives from the company, the local environmental organization and the Swedish EPA commenting upon or debating the planned disposal of mercury in Stripa.

The analysis is based on the data as a whole. In the case study, references are used only in connection with quotations. The data are listed in the citations at the end of the References chapter in this volume.

2 In this text *the company* designates both the parent company and its subsidiaries. During the course of events, the ownership has changed; but the representatives have presented a common perspective on the issue.

3 Today the Swedish National Franchise Board for Environmental Protection is dissolved and replaced by environmental courts.

Chapter 4

1 The study of the conflicts concerning the construction of railroads is an exception since this is generally seen as a way of increasing the ecological sustainability of

the transport system. Here, parallels might be found with renewable energy (Boholm et al, 1998, and Boholm, 2001).

2 In Sweden the name of the network against wind power is Svenskt Landskapsskydd (Swedish Landscape Protection): see www.landskapsskydd.nu. Similar networks exist in the UK, Denmark, Germany and France.

3 See *Earthscan Reader in Risk and Modern Society* (Löfstedt and Frewer, 1998) for an introduction to the research on risk analysis and risk communication.

4 See Wolsink (1994) for a discussion about different possible local reactions to a new facility.

5 Examples of incorrect arguments were claims that it was not possible to return the dry residue to the land and what seemed to be a deliberate misunderstanding about the amount of traffic that would be generated by the facility. Examples of arguments that did not concern the environment were claims that there was not sufficient supply of manure and that there would be problems selling the gas (Letters to the county administration and the municipality from neighbours to the site and people living in Dalby, 1998–2000).

6 Farmers are vital to the biogas system since they deliver animal manure, which is an important raw material in the biogas process. They are also the recipients of the digested end product that is used as fertilizer. The local utility was involved in relation to the use of the biogas.

7 The Environmental Protection Act was replaced in 1999 by the Environmental Code; but the application continued to be handled according to the former legislation.

8 The purpose of a detailed plan is to investigate whether an area is suitable for constructing buildings or other facilities, and it is required when the new facility is expected to have a considerable impact or if there is a big demand for the land in the area. The planning procedure for a detailed plan is strictly regulated and involves extensive consultation with many parties, including neighbours and other people concerned.

9 The final location had already been mentioned as a possible alternative in an early location report from 1996, which was completed long before the developer had any specific plans to buy a property (16 September 1996, Lloyd).

Chapter 5

1 The main period of fieldwork, from January to July 1997, was funded by the Economic and Social Research Council of Great Britain (Award no R000222057, 'Planning as Metaphor: Mediating Aspirations for Community and Environment'). Additional informal fieldwork was carried out from 1994.

2 AONB is an official designation for landscape quality that carries some protection within planning regulations.

3 The authority of English mayors is demonstrated through their rights to wear ceremonial neck-chains. Many in the village thought the parish council chair was being unduly formal and pretentious in insisting on wearing these chains at parish council meetings.

4 For more detail on the use of 'identifiers' and categories of villagers, see Murdoch and Abram (2002).

5 See Grimes (2000, p13).

6 See Robertson (1984) on epistemologies of development and Abram and Waldren (1998) for examples of these in practice.

Chapter 6

1 It has been argued that sense of place may operate at different scales (Rose, 1995). Broader interconnected scales may include the town or city, region or country; we may even, as Massey (1994) has suggested, look for a global sense of place. However, the home and immediate neighbourhood or locale is typically the primary focus for a sense of place (Rutherford, 1990).

2 By 'community' we refer to a positively valued experience of interpersonal communication and ties (which may reinforce a sense of belonging and affirmation of identity and, therefore, a more general sense of ontological security) rather than to 'community' as a reified entity. This value was evident in comments made by many local residents in our case study and was compromised in some of the cases of toxically contaminated neighbourhoods referred to in the next section. On the significance of salubrity, see Rotenberg (1993).

3 Shortly after the research was completed, the company became part of the international chemicals group Ciba.

4 This view was expressed by several of the local officials to whom we spoke, as well as by many local residents in the group discussions.

5 The European Seveso directive was implemented in the UK at the time of the research by the Control of Industrial Major Accident Hazard Regulations. This legislation required companies categorized as 'upper tier' through holding large quantities of hazardous materials to produce safety reports and to provide information for local residents as part of a wider process of off-site emergency planning.

6 See Walker et al (1999), Irwin et al (1999), Simmons and Walker (1999) and Simmons (2004) for other aspects of the research project.

7 These groups were not, of course, assumed to be representative of the local population. The recruitment criteria were intended simply to include people with a range of viewpoints.

8 It is important to note that claims about impacts on house prices were contested. Some participants attributed lower prices in their street to the busy main road, while others noted that selling property for a good price was difficult everywhere. One even claimed that house sales were booming in his street (which, significantly, was not adjacent to the chemical plant).

Chapter 7

1 Twenty-nine interviews were conducted between July 1999 and January 2000 with property owners affected by the groundwater leakage and the toxic spill.

2 By the National Food Administration.

3 Today, only small amounts of acrylamide are estimated to remain in the inner parts of the tunnel.

4 Tunnel walls have been strengthened through subsequent injections of concrete and by lining the tunnel. The lining method involved casting a large waterproof pipe inside the rock, sheathed with a solid plastic membrane before the moulding of the concrete tube.

5 Local perceptions and worries received confirmation in the form of an expert report from the Swedish University of Agricultural Sciences, which predicted that both farming and forestry would be adversely affected by the tunnel construction (Florgård et al, 1999). The experts concluded that the characteristic nature of the

Hallandsås ridge would change as a result of altered plant community terms, supporting people's fears that the landscape and its flora and fauna would change in the future. The Environmental Monitoring Group, an independent group of experts established to analyse and monitor ecological and geological issues in the zone officially identified as the area of influence on Hallandsås, corroborated the assessment that agricultural yields had been affected by the lowered water table (*Årsrapport för det ekologiska kontrollprogrammet 2001*).

6 Photographs of 13 photographers will be included in the analysis.

7 All interviewees understood that this research was completely independent of Banverket and its objectives.

8 The Love Canal toxic disaster turned out to pose a threat to local community values and meanings. Here, people in the affected area began to question their surrounding environment and its meanings in relation to their community and livelihood (Fitchen, 1989).

9 'Place', as with the terms 'space' and 'landscape', is a widely contested concept. In this context, place refers to an area that, to some extent, has geographical boundaries; but at the same time I have chosen to use the definition advanced by Ingold (1993), among others, where place is the embodiment of a relational context. However, while Ingold argues that place has no boundaries, I would like to add the aspects of place put forward by Agnew (1987). Interwoven in the concept is the setting in which social relations are constituted (the locale), the geographical area encompassing the locale (the location), and sense of place, which means that there exists a 'structured feeling'.

Chapter 9

1 The initial 300,000 hectares were later reduced to 172,000ha as a result of the adoption of qualitative criteria during the 1950s, which limited irrigation to quality land and required that a good water supply per hectare be guaranteed.

2 The purpose of this dam was to substantially extend the regulation of the River Esera, which rises high up in the Aragonese Pyrenees. The justification given for this extension was the need to increase the supply of water per hectare of irrigated land in the *Riegos de Aragón y Cataluña* irrigation system, one of the three in the Aragon region. It was also intended significantly to increase the area of irrigated land existing at the time.

3 A research group has studied the consequences of the water policy prevailing in Spain, and especially in 20th-century Aragon, for almost a decade. This research has dealt particularly with the construction of risk, a phenomenon that has been one of the main consequences of this water policy, especially since the end of the Franco dictatorship in 1976 (Mairal and Bergua, 1998).

4 Considering the exception of four countries with a small population (Albania, Cyprus, Iceland and Norway), Spain has about 1500 large dams.

5 In 1999 the local population affected by the Santaliestra scheme staged a protest to prevent experts from surveying the area of the future dam. In response, they were met with police charges to break up the demonstrators, including numerous elderly villagers, who were blocking access to the site of the dam.

6 Aragon is a self-governing region with its own executive and parliament.

7 The only exception is the Jánovas dam project, where the environmental impact assessment was negative. This does not mean, however, that the Spanish government has abandoned the idea of building a new dam to regulate the Ara-Cinca

River system, and a new plan at another site is expected to be proposed in the coming months.

8 It now seems clear that the conservative Aragonese nationalism of the *Partido Aragonés*, which currently forms part of the regional government, has aligned itself with this 'promise of water', while the leftwing nationalism of the *Chunta Aragonesista*, which has considerably increased its influence within Aragonese society in recent years, is aligned rather with the position of the populations affected by major water projects. The non-nationalist parties, both conservative and socialist, have also aligned themselves with the 'promise of water', although less vehemently. However, it is also true that both positions are fairly easily confused by Aragonese public opinion.

9 This identification of Aragon based on the 'promise of water' has led Aragonese society consistently and vigorously to oppose any major transfer of water from the Ebro basin to the Mediterranean Coast for the last quarter of a century. Since a basic plank of the National Hydrological Plan currently under debate is the annual transfer of 1050 hm^3 (1 hm^3 = 1000 million litres) from the Ebro River to the Mediterranean, the plan has been met with mass opposition in Aragon. Indeed, on 6 October 2000, almost 400,000 Aragonese citizens, approximately one in three of the region's inhabitants, demonstrated in the streets of Saragossa against the National Hydrological Plan. These demonstrators were inspired not so much by the idea that the transfer of water from Aragon to other regions was a bad water management policy, than by the notion that it was a grave attack on the Aragonese people. It is significant that both the opponents and defenders of the construction of new dams in the Aragonese Pyrenees participated in this demonstration.

10 We have widely written about this issue in Mairal and Bergua (1998). Culturalism implies a cultural reconstruction from within, reinforcing what is estimated as 'ours'. It is a reinvention of identity using the collective memory and the result of this reinvention is usually a revival of tradition.

11 See Mairal and Belío (2001).

12 After a large demonstration in Saragossa by the communities affected by dam-building projects in 1999, the communities of irrigators responded by organizing their own demonstration some weeks later, which drew tens of thousands of people. This was a good occasion to show their culturalism in a very impressive way, thanks to a number of slogans, big banners and a lot of singing and shouting. As pointed out previously, the affected people have done the same before.

13 See Mairal and Bergua (1997).

14 The historical tradition of water policy in Spain has been highly state-centred, while water management has remained almost the sole preserve of the state, though subject to concessions, because surface water has been considered a public good. The possible privatization of water is currently the subject of heated debate in Spain and certain legislative reforms have been passed in order to encourage the creation of new water markets.

15 Ebro River Water Authority.

16 The communities affected have, in fact, appealed on a number of occasions.

17 *Manifiesto por la dignidad de la Montaña (Manifesto for the Dignity of the Mountains)*, distributed by the various associations of affected communities in 1998 during protests in the village of Boltaña. Amongst several documents, I have chosen this *Manifesto* as my principle source as it has remained the most popular of all public discourses.

18 One fundamental aspect of this process of maturity has been described by José Angel Bergua in an essay entitled *'Discursos y voces en el conflicto del agua'*

('Discourse and voices in the water conflict'), where arguments of this type are defined as 'voices'. These would be 'voices' in the process of growing into 'discourses' and requiring a degree of reflection, the use of one or more theories and the support of a social movement and institutionalization. Today, it seems, indeed, that these voices are becoming discourses (Mairal and Bergua, 2000).

19 See American Anthropological Association (1998).

20 This document, which was produced by the Spanish Environment Ministry and published in 1998, was intended to set out the basic doctrine underlying Spanish water policy in its approximately 1000 pages.

21 This case is well known in Spain since the multinational company behind the construction of all these projects is Spanish.

22 *Manifiesto por la Dignidad de la Montaña (Manifesto for the Dignity of the Mountains).*

Chapter 11

1 Durkheim (1997, originally published 1893) is an early, and prominent, advocate of this idea – elaborated by his no less famous nephew Mauss (1990, originally published 1924).

2 Potentiality is not to be confused with actuality: in a social system there are far more possibilities of relationships than can be actualized (see Luhmann, 1985).

3 Principally, 'post-modern society' is conceptualized in terms of either discontinuity or continuity. From the perspective of discontinuity, post-modern society is seen as a *radical* break with modernity, whereas post-modern society from the perspective of continuity is seen as a containing *both* elements of the radical new and elements of modernity. To distinguish between these two different conceptions of 'post-modern society', the latter is sometimes referred to as 'late modern society'.

4 Rhizome is a figurative term used by Gilles Deleuze and Felix Guattari (1987) to describe non-hierarchical networks of all kinds:

> A rhizome as a subterranean stem is absolutely different from roots and radicals. Bulbs and tubers are rhizomes. Plants with roots or radicals may be rhizomorphic in other respects altogether. Burrows are too, in all their functions of shelter, supply, movement, evasion and breakout. The rhizome itself assumes very diverse forms, from ramified surface extension in all directions to concretion into bulbs and tubers...The rhizome includes the best and the worst: potato and couchgrass, or the weed (Deleuze and Guattari, 1987, pp6–7).

5 One early proponent of this evolutionary model from simple to complex is Lewis Henry Morgan (1985, originally published 1877). The concepts *Gemeinschaft* and *Gesellschaft* originate from Ferdinand Tönnies (1988, originally published 1887).

6 It should be emphasized that 'simple' is anything but simple-minded. Simplifications are often wielded with great sophistication by officials (Scott, 1998).

7 Observations are based on fieldwork in various courts of law, as well as documentary study of the voluminous preliminary investigation material at Ängelholm District Court (Ängelholm tingsrätt), official documents, media reports, etc.

8 Since many terms and concepts, particularly legal ones, as well as names, are notoriously difficult to translate adequately, the Swedish terms and proper nouns appear within brackets after the English translation the first time that they appear in the chapter. For a translation of Swedish legal terms into English counterparts I have relied on Domstolsverket (2001).

9 The first explorative study of the building of a tunnel through the Hallandsås ridge was conducted by the Swedish State Railways (SJ) almost two decades earlier in 1975.

10 Rhoca Gil, manufactured by the French industrial chemistry corporation Rhone-Poulenc, contains acrylamide (C_3H_5NO), which is toxic and is also believed to be carcinogenic. The health risk of acrylamide in food has been extensively discussed recently in the media.

11 This fact is not contested by any party involved. What is contested is the *degree* of responsibility on the part of the building contractor, the Swedish National Rail Administration, and other actors, such as the municipality of Båstad and the community board.

12 Since most people living in proximity to the site do not have communal water but exclusively depend upon their private wells for water supply, this is evidently a serious matter.

13 For a detailed account, see the report of the proceedings from Ängelholm District Court (Protokoll 9 March 2001, *Muntlig förberedelse i Ängelholm* – Mål nr B41-98).

14 There are five environmental courts and one environmental court of appeal in Sweden. The environmental court within the jurisdiction relocated to the municipality of Båstad.

15 Tunnel workers had been exposed to acrylamide during the construction work – 22 of them sued Skanska as injured persons claiming damages for neuritis.

16 The district court also conducted on-site inspections – or rather, one inspection. The inspection, in contrast to the inspections by the environmental court, was not intended for public participation.

17 The hearing in the environmental court of appeal was held at the same location as the first hearing of the environmental court (with, in most respects, a similar procedure).

18 Different areas of impact have been established – to be acknowledged as a stakeholder in a juridical sense, the level of the groundwater has to be at least 1 metre below (wholly or partly within) the estate.

19 It is difficult to state exactly how many people in the local context were directly affected; but the number of out-of-court settlements between the Swedish National Rail Administration and local residents is close to 200 – each settlement involving one household.

20 It has been argued that the formal aspects of law and order have been defective because the Swedish government has been reviewing decisions of its own regarding the tunnel project (Falkemark, 1998, p55). Furthermore, a general legal problem of the case is that no rules of law are being applied to the tunnel project as a whole – different rules of law are being applied to different parts of the project (Hydén and Baier, 1998, p3).

21 The last day of the hearing was, however, *partly* devoted to legal issues – primarily in the form of individuals (either representing themselves or being represented by their lawyers) claiming various interests against the Swedish National Rail Administration.

22 A textbook case of the implications of segmentation of interwoven issues – that is, polyfurcation – is the Woburn, Massachusetts, case (for a summary of the Woburn case, see Nader 2002, p186).

23 Psychologically, people might or might not experience that life is 'fragmented'; but that is another issue.

24 More often than not, development is also presupposed to be culturally sustainable.

References

Abram, S (1998) 'Class, countryside and the longitudinal study: A response to Hoggart', *Journal of Rural Studies*, 14(2), pp369–379

Abram, S (2001) 'Amongst professionals: Working with pressure groups and local authorities', in Gellner, D N and Hirsch, E (eds) *Inside Organizations*, Oxford: Berg

Abram, S (2003) 'The rural gaze', in Cloke, P (ed) *Country Visions*, Harlow: Prentice Hall

Abram, S, Murdoch, J and Marsden, T (1996) 'The social construction of middle England: The politics of participation in forward planning', *Journal of Rural Studies*, 12(4), pp353–364

Abram, S and Waldren, J (1998) *Anthropological Perspectives on Local Development: Knowledge and Sentiments in Conflict*, London: Routledge

Adam, B (1998) *Timescapes of Modernity: The Environment and Invisible Hazards*, London: Routledge

Adam, B, Beck, U and van Loon, J (eds) (2000) *The Risk Society and Beyond: Critical Issues for Social Theory*, London: Sage Publications

Adam, B and van Loon, J (2000) 'Introduction: Repositioning risks – The challenge for social theory', in Adam, B, Beck, U and van Loon, J (eds) *The Risk Society and Beyond*, London: Sage Publications

Adelman, C (1998) 'Photocontext', in Prosser, J (ed) *Image-based Research: A Sourcebook for Qualitative Researchers*, London: Falmer Press

Agnew, J A (1987) *Place and Politics: The Geographical Mediation of State and Society*, Boston: Allen and Unwin

Agnew, J (1993) 'Representing space: Space, scale and culture in social science', in Duncan, J and Ley, D (eds) *Place/Culture/Representation*, London: Routledge

Albin, C (1993) 'The role of fairness in negotiations', *Negotiation Journal*, 9, pp223–244

Alm, C and Lindberg, E (2000) *Perceived Risk, Feelings of Safety and Worry Associated with Different Travel Modes: Pilot Study*, Stockholm: Kommunikationsforskningsberedningen

Altschuler, A and Luberhoff, D (2003) *Mega-projects: The Changing Politics of Urban Public Investment*, Washington, DC: Brookings Institute Press

American Anthropological Association (1998) *The Pehuenche, The World Bank Group and ENDESA S A: Violations of Human Rights in the Pangue and Ralco Dam Projects on the Bío-Bío River, Chile*, www.ameranthassn.org/pehuenc.htm, p18

Appadurai, A (1995) 'The production of locality', in Fardon, R (ed) *Counterworks*, London: Routledge

Arrojo Agudo, P (ed) (2001) *El Plan Hidrológico Nacional a Debate*, Bilbao: Bakeaz-Fundación Nueva Cultura del Agua

Avolahti, J (1999) 'Imaging the risks, risking the image: Social impact assessment of the final disposal facility', in Andersson, K (ed) *Proceedings, VALDOR: Values in decisions on risks, Stockholm, 13–17 June 1999*, Täby, Sweden: Karinta-Konsult

Aylesbury Vale District Council (AVDC) Director of Housing, Health and Leisure (1997) *Report of Odour Monitoring Exercise at McCormick's Factory, Haddenham*, 8 September 1997, AVDC

Banks, M and Morphy, H (eds) (1997) *Rethinking Visual Anthropology*, New Haven and London: Yale Haven Press

Barthe, Y (2000) *La Mise en Politique des Déchets Nucléaires. L'Action Publique aux Prises avec Les Irréversibilités Techniques*, PhD thesis, Paris: Centre de Sociologie de l'Innovation, Ecole Nationale Supérieure des Mines de Paris

Barthe, Y and Mays, C (2001) 'Communication and information in France's underground laboratory siting process: Clarity of procedure, ambivalence of effects', *Journal of Risk Research*, 4(4), pp411–430

Bataille, C (1994) *Mission de Médiation sur l'Implantation de Laboratoires de Recherche Souterrains. Rapport au Premier Ministre (Décembre 1993)*, Paris: La Documentation Française

Bateson, G (1973) *Steps to an Ecology of Mind: Collected Essays in Anthropology, Psychiatry, Evolution and Epistemology*, Frogmore: Paladin

Bauman, Z (1998) *Globalization: The Human Consequences*, London: Polity Press

Baxter, J and Eyles, J (1999) 'The utility of in-depth interviews for studying the meaning of environmental risk', *Professional Geographer*, 51, pp307–320

Beck, U (1992) *Risk Society: Towards a New Modernity*, translated by M Ritter, Newbury Park, CA, and London: Sage

Beck, U (1994) 'The reinvention of politics: Towards a theory of reflexive modernization', in Beck, U, Giddens, A and Lash, S (eds) *Reflexive Modernization*, Stanford: Stanford University Press

Beck, U (1996) 'Risk society and the provident stage', in Lash, S, Szerszynski, B and Wynne, B (eds) *Risk, Environment and Modernity: Towards a New Ecology*, London: Sage

Beck, U (1999) *World Risk Society*, Oxford: Polity Press and Blackwell Publishers

Beck, U, Giddens, A and Lash, S (1994) *Reflexive Modernization: Politics, Tradition and Aesthetics in the Modern Social Order*, Cambridge: Polity Press

Becker, H S (1998) 'Visual sociology, documentary photography, and photojournalism: It's (almost) all a matter of context', in Prosser, J (ed) *Image-based Research: A Sourcebook for Qualitative Researchers*, London: Falmer Press

Beck-Gernsheim, E (1996) 'Life as a planning project', in Lash, S, Szerszynski, B and Wynne, B (eds) *Risk, Environment and Modernity*, London: Sage

Bender, B (ed) (1993) *Landscape: Politics and Perspectives*, Oxford: Berg

Bickerstaff, K and Walker, G (2001) 'Public understandings of air pollution: The "localisation" of environmental risk', *Global Environmental Change – Human and Policy Dimensions*, 11, pp133–145

Binde, P (2000a) 'Tracks, trains and tunnels: Ideas and concerns about risk', in Boholm, Å (ed) *National Objectives – Local Objections: Railroad Modernization in Sweden*, Göteborg: CEFOS

Binde, P (2000b) 'Risk discourse: The rhetoric of railway hazards in siting controversy', in Cottam, M P et al (eds) *Foresight and Precaution*, Proceedings of ESREL 2000, SARS and SRA – Europe Annual Conference, Rotterdam and Brookfield: A A Balkema

Binde, P (2002) 'Risk som diskurs', in Boholm, Å, Hansson, S O, Persson, J and Peterson, M (eds) *Osäkerhetens Horisonter: Kulturella Och Etiska Perspektiv på Samhällets Riskfrågor*, Nora: Nya Doxa

Böhler, T (1998) *Vindkraftens Landskap*, Göteborg: Göteborg University

Boholm, Å (1996) 'Risk perception and social anthropology: critique of cultural theory', *Ethnos*, 61, pp64–684

Boholm, Å (1998) 'Visual images and risk messages: Commemorating Chernobyl', *Risk Decision and Policy*, 3(2), pp125–143

Boholm, Å (ed) (2000) *National Objectives – Local Objections: Railway Modernization in Sweden*, Göteborg, CEFOS

Boholm, Å (2003) 'The cultural nature of risk: Can there be an anthropology of uncertainty?' *Ethnos*, 68, pp159–178

Boholm, Å (2005) 'Greater good in transit: The unwieldy career of a Swedish rail tunnel project', FOCAAL (Special issue: Politics by other means), in press

Boholm, Å and Löfstedt, R (1999) 'Issues of risk, trust and knowledge: The Hallandsås tunnel case', *Ambio*, 28, pp556–561

Boholm, Å, Löfstedt, R and Strandberg, U (1998) *Tunnelbygget genom Hallandsås: Lokalsamhällets Dilemman*, Göteborg: CEFOS Rapport 12, Göteborg University

Bonano, E J and. Leon, A A (1999) 'Comments on the legal admissibility of a performance assessment for a radioactive waste disposal facility', *Risk Analysis*, 19, pp991–993

Bourdieu, P (1977) *Outline of a Theory of Practice*, Cambridge: Cambridge University Press

Boyle, P J and Halfacree, K (eds) (1998) *Migration into Rural Areas: Theories and Issues*, Chichester: Wiley

Brinckerhoff Jackson, J (1984) *Discovering the Vernacular Landscape*, New Haven and London: Yale University Press

Brown, P (1991) 'The popular epidemiology approach to toxic waste contamination', in Couch, S R and Kroll-Smith, J S (eds) *Communities at Risk*, New York: Peter Lang

Brox, O (2000) 'Schismogenesis in the wilderness: The reintroduction of predators in Norwegian forests, *Ethnos*, 65(3), pp387–404

Brunt, A and Spooner, D (1998) 'The development of wind power in Denmark and the UK', *Energy and Environment*, 9(3), pp279–296

Buclet, N and Bouzidi, Y (2003) 'Confidence, actors' beliefs and transparency: The case of Andra', in Andersson, K (ed) *Proceedings, VALDOR 2003: Values in decisions on risk, Stockholm, Sweden, 9–13 June 2003*, Täby, Sweden: Karinta-Konsult

Budnitz, R J (1999) 'Comments on performance assessment in support of the 1996 compliance certification application for the waste isolation pilot plant', *Risk Analysis*, 19, pp989–990

Bunge, M (1998) *Social Science under Debate*, Toronto: University of Toronto Press

Bureau of Reclamation (1946) *The Colorado River: A Natural Menace Becomes a National Resource*, Comprehensive departmental report on the development of the water resources of the Colorado River basin for review prior to submission to Congress, Washington, D C: United States Department of the Interior, Bureau of Reclamation

Bush, J, Moffatt, S and Dunn, C (2001) 'Even the birds round here cough: Stigma, air pollution and health in Teesside', *Health and Place*, 7, pp47–56

Callon, M, Lascoumes, P and Barthe, Y (2001) *Agir dans un Monde Incertain: Essai sur la Démocratie Technique*, Paris: Seuil.

Camacho, D E (ed) (1998) *Environmental Injustices, Political Struggles: Race, Class and the Environment*, Durham and London: Duke University Press

Campbell, A, Converse, P and Rodgers, W (1976) *The Quality of American Life: Perceptions, Evaluations and Satisfactions*, New York: Russell Sage

Capek, S M (1999) 'Institutional failure and the demise of Carver Terrace', *Research in Social Problems and Public Policy*, 7, pp139–162

Caplan, P (ed) (2000) *Risk Revisited*, London: Pluto Press

Carlman, I (1992) *Att Acceptera Eller Inte Acceptera*, IMIR 1992: 1, Stockholm: Åmyra förlag

Carlman, I (1993) *TÄNKOM – Studier av svenska miljökonflikter och deras orsaker*, Uppsala: IMIR

Carsten, J and Hugh-Jones, S (1995) 'Introduction', in Carsten, J and Hugh-Jones, S (eds) *About the House: Lévi-Strauss and Beyond*, New York: Press Syndicate of the University of Cambridge

Castells, M (1996) *The Information Age: Economy, Society and Culture, Volume I: The Rise of the Network Society*, Malden, Massachusetts: Blackwell Publishers

Casti, J L (1997) *Would-be Worlds: How Simulation Is Changing the Frontiers of Science*, New York: Wiley

Cernea, M (ed) (1991) *Putting People First*, New York: Oxford University Press

Cernea, M and Guggenheim, S (eds) (1993) *Anthropological Approaches to Resettlement: Policy, Practice and Theory*, Boulder, Colorado: Westview Press

Charron, S, Mansoux, H and Milochevitch, A (2002) *Perception des Risques et de la Sécurité: Résultats du Sondage de Novembre 2001*, Note SEGR 02/02, Janvier 2002, Fontenay-aux-Roses: Institut de Radioprotection et de Sûreté Nucléaire (IRSN)

Chess, C (1999) 'A model of organizational responsiveness to stakeholders', *Risk: Health, Safety and Environment*, 10, pp257–267

Chess, C (2001) 'Organizational theory and the stages of risk communication', *Risk Analysis*, 21, pp179–188

Chess, C, Tamuz, M and Greenberg, M (1994) 'Organizational learning about environmental risk communication: The case of Rohm and Haas' Bristol plant', *Society and Natural Resources*, 8, pp57–66

Cheyne, G J G (1972) *A Bibliographical Study of the Writings of Joaquín Costa (1846–1911)*, London: Thames Collection

Cilliers, P (1998) *Complexity and Postmodernism: Understanding Complex Systems*, London: Routledge

Clarke, J (1854) *History of Haddeham, Bucks* (transcribed by D Alderson, 1926), Private Collection

Clarke, L and Short, J F Jr (1993) 'Social organization and risk: Some current controversies', *Annual Review of Sociology*, 19, pp375–399

CNE (Commission Nationale d'Évaluation Relative aux Recherches sur la Gestion des Déchets Radioactifs) (2003) *Rapport d'Évaluation no 9 (Juin)*, Paris: CNE

Cohen, A (ed) (1982) *Belonging: Identity and Social Organisation in British Rural Cultures*, Manchester: Manchester University Press

Cohen, A (ed) (1986) *Symbolising Boundaries: Identity and Diversity in British Cultures*, Manchester: Manchester University Press

Cohen, M (ed) (2000) *Risk in the Modern Age: Social Theory, Science and Environmental Decision-making*, London: Macmillan

Conseil d'Etat (1997) *Conclusions du Commissaire du Gouvernement, Séance du 27 Novembre 1997, Lecture du 5 Décembre 1997*, Paris: Conseil d'Etat

Corvellec, H (2000) *Talks on Tracks: Debating Urban Infrastructure Projects*, Göteborg: GRI

Corvellec, H (2001) 'Talks on tracks: debating urban infrastructure projects', *Studies in Cultures, Organisations and Societies*, 7, pp25–53

Couch, S R and Kroll-Smith, S (1994) 'Environmental controversies, interactional resources and rural communities: Siting versus exposure disputes', *Rural Sociology*, 59, pp25–44

Couch, S R and Kroll-Smith, S (1998) 'Environmental movements and expert knowledge: Evidence for a new populism', *International Journal of Contemporary Sociology*, 34, pp1–28

Croll, E and Parkin, D (1992) 'Cultural understandings of the environment', in Croll, E and Parkin, D (eds) *Bush Base, Forest Farm: Culture, Environment and Development*, London: Routledge

Cvetkovich, G and Löfstedt, R E (eds) (1999) *Social Trust and the Management of Risk*, London: Earthscan

Cvetkovich, G, Siegrist, M, Murray, R and Tragesser, S (2002) 'New information and social trust: Asymmetry and perseverance of attributions about hazard managers', *Risk Analysis*, 22(2), pp359–367

Dagens Nyheter (2001) Letter to the editor 'Upprörande att inte åtala Banverket' [It is outrageous not to indict the National Rail Administration], *Dagens Nyheter*, 3 September 2001

Dake, K (1991) 'Orientation dispositions in the perception of risk: An analysis of contemporary worldviews and cultural biases', *Journal of Cross-cultural Psychology*, 22, pp61–82

Davies, A R (1999) 'Where do we go from here? Environmental focus groups and planning policy formation', *Local Environment*, 4, pp295–316

Deleuze, G and Guattari, F (1987) *A Thousand Plateaus: Capitalism and Schizophrenia*, Minneapolis: University of Minnesota Press

Deloria, V Jr and Lytle, C (1984) *The Nations Within: The Past and Future of American Indian Sovereignty*, New York: Pantheon Books

Desvousges, W H, Kunreuther, H, Slovic, P and Rosa, E A (1993) 'Perceived risk and attitudes toward nuclear wastes: National and Nevada perspectives', in Dunlap, R E, Kraft, M E and Rosa, E A (eds) *Public Reactions to Nuclear Waste: Citizens' Views of Repository Siting*, Durham, NC: Duke University Press

DGEMP (Direction Générale de l'Énergie et des Matières Premières [French Ministry of Industry]) (2003) *L'Énergie Nucléaire, l'Aval du Cycle (la Gestion des Déchets)*, www.industrie.gouv.fr/energie/nucleair/f1e_nuc.htm

Directive 1999, No 104 (Government directive) *Samordning av det fortsatta arbetet med slutförvaring av kvicksilver* [*Coordination of the Continuing Work with Final Disposal of Mercury*], Sweden: Miljödepartementet [Ministry of the Environment]

Domstolsverket [National Courts Administration] (2001) *Ordlista för Domstolsväsendet*, 2nd revised edition, Sweden: Domstolsverket

Donahue, J M and Johnston, B (eds) (1998) *Water, Culture and Power: Local Struggles in a Global Context*, Washington, DC: Island Press

Dorshimer, K R (1996) 'Siting major projects and the NIMBY phenomenon', *Economic Development Review*, (Winter 1996), 14(1), pp60–63

Douglas, M (1986) *How Institutions Think*, New York: Syracuse University Press

Douglas, M (1987) *How Institutions Think*, London: Routledge

Douglas, M (1992) *Risk and Blame: Essays in Cultural Theory*, London: Routledge

Douglas, M and Wildavsky, A (1982) *Risk and Culture: An Essay on the Selection of Technological and Environmental Dangers*, Berkeley, California: University of California Press

Drottz-Sjöberg, B-M and Sjöberg, L (1991) 'Trains and transports: Perceived and real risks', *Rhizikon: Risk Research Reports*, 2, Stockholm: Centre for Risk Research, Stockholm School of Economics

DTLR (2002) *Planning Green Paper: Delivering a Fundamental Change*, www.planning.dtlr.gov.uk/consult/greenpap/02.htm

Dunlap, R E, Kraft, M E and Rosa, E A (eds) (1993) *Public Reactions to Nuclear Waste: Citizens' Views of Repository Siting*, Durham, North Carolina: Duke University Press

Dupuis, A and Thorns, D C (1998) 'Home, home ownership and the search for ontological security', *Sociological Review*, 46, pp24–47

Durkheim, E (1982) *Rules of Sociological Method and Selected Texts on Sociology and Its Method (Les Règles de la Méthode Sociologique, 1895)*, Westport, Connecticut: Free Press

Durkheim, E (1997, originally published in 1893) *The Division of Labor in Society*, New York: Free Press

Earle, T and Cvetkovich, G (1995) *Social Trust: Toward a Cosmopolitan Society*, Westport, CT: Praeger

Easterling, D (1997) 'The vulnerability of the Nevada visitor economy to a repository at Yucca Mountain', *Risk Analysis*, 17(5), pp635–647

Easterling, D (2001) 'Fear and loathing in Las Vegas: Will a nuclear waste repository contaminate the imagery of nearby places?' in Flynn, J, Slovic, P and Kunreuther, H (eds) *Risk, Media and Stigma: Understanding Public Challenges to Modern Science and Technology*, London: Earthscan

Edelstein, M R (1988) *Contaminated Communities: The Social and Psychological Impacts of Toxic Residential Exposure*, Boulder, Colorado: Westview Press

Edelstein, M R (1991) 'Ecological threats and spoiled identities: Radon gas and environmental stigma', in Couch, S R and Kroll-Smith, J S (eds) *Communities at Risk: Collective Responses to Technological Hazards*, Worcester: Peter Lang

Edelstein, M R (1998) *Contaminated Communities: The Social and Psychological Impacts of Residential Toxic Exposure*, Boulder, Colorado: Westview Press

Eisenberg, N A, Lee, M P, McCartin, T J, McConnell, K I, Thaggard, M and Campbell, A C (1999) 'Development of a performance assessment capability in the waste management programs of the US Nuclear Regulatory Commission', *Risk Analysis*, 19, pp989–990

Ekström, M (1993) 'Sociologiska förklaringar och variabelanalysens gränser' ['Sociological explanations and the limits of analysis of variable'], *Sociologisk Forskning*, 2, pp26–57

Entrikin, N J (1991) *The Betweenness of Place: Towards a Geography of Modernity*, Baltimore, MD: John Hopkins University Press

Epstein, S (1996) *Impure Science: AIDS, Activism, and Politics of Knowledge*, Berkeley: University of California Press

Erikson, K (1994) *A New Species of Trouble: Explorations in Disaster, Trauma and Community*, New York: Norton

Eriksson, B (2001) *Det Sociologiska Institutionsbegreppet* [*The Concept of Institution in Sociology*], Örebro: Department of Social Science, Örebro University

Ewing, R C, Tierney, M S, Konikow, L F and Rechard, R P (1999) 'Performance assessments of nuclear waste repositories: A dialogue on their value and limitations', *Risk Analysis*, 19, pp933–958

Eyles, J (1985) *Senses of Place*, Warrington: Silverbrook Press

Falkemark, G (1998) 'Hallandsåsen och höghastighetens pris', in SOU (ed) *Miljö i grund och botten: Erfarenheter från Hallandsåsen. Slutrapport från tunnelkommissionen. statens offentliga utredningar*, Stockholm: Fritzes offentliga publikationer, p137

Federal Highway Administration (2001) *US 93 Hoover Dam Bypass Project: Final Environmental Impact Statement and Section 4(f) Evaluation*, (FHWA-AZNV-EIS-98-03-F), www.hooverdambypass.org/

Ferreira, C (2004) 'Risk, transparency and cover up: Media narratives and cultural resonance', *Journal of Risk Research*, 7(2), pp199–212

Ferreira, C, Boholm, Å and Löfstedt, R (2001) 'From vision to catastrophe: A risk event in search of images', in Flynn, J, Slovic, P and Kunrether, H (eds) *Risk, Media and Stigma: Understanding Public Challenges to Modern Science and Technology*, London: Earthscan

Firey, W (1945) 'Sentiment and symbolism as ecological variables', *American Sociological Review*, 10, pp140–148

Fischhoff, B (1995) 'Risk perception and communication unplugged: Twenty years of process', *Risk Analysis*, 15, pp137–145

Fischhoff, B, Lichtenstein, S, Slovic, P, Derby, S L and Keeney, R L (1981) *Acceptable Risk*, New York: Cambridge University Press

Fitchen, J M (1989) 'When toxic chemicals pollute residential environments: The cultural meanings of home and homeownership' *Human Organization*, 48(4), pp313–324

Fitchen, J M (1991) *Endangered Spaces, Enduring Places: Change, Identity and Survival in Rural America*, Boulder, Colorado: Westview Press

Fitchen, J M, Heath, J S and Fessenden-Raden, J (1987) 'Risk perception in community context: A case study', in Johnson, B B and Covello, V T (eds) *The Social and Cultural Construction of Risk*, New York: D Reidel

Florgård, C, Linnér, H, Olsson, M and Wiklander, G (1999) *Grundvattensänkning och natur på Hallandsås – Effekter av tunnelarbeten på natur och på jord-och skogsbruk*, Uppsala: Sveriges Lantbruksuniversitet. Institutionen för landskapsplanering Ultuna

Fluëler, T (2003) 'Robust decision making in radioactive waste management is process oriented', in Andersson, K (ed) *Proceedings, VALDOR 2003: Values in Decisions on Risk, Stockholm, Sweden, 9–13 June 2003*, Täby, Sweden: Karinta-Konsult

Flynn, J, Chalmers, J, Easterling, D, Kasperson, R, Kunreuther, H, Mertz, C K, Mushkatel, A, Pijawka, K D and Slovic, P (with Dotto, L) (1995) *One Hundred Centuries of Solitude: Redirecting America's High-Level Nuclear Waste Policy*, Boulder, Colorado: Westview Press

Flynn, J, Slovic, P and Kunreuther, H (2001) *Risk, Media and Stigma: Understanding Public Challenges to Modern Science and Technology*, London: Earthscan

Flyvbjerg, B, Bruzelius, N and Rothengatter, W (2003) *Megaprojects and Risk: An Anatomy of Ambition*, Cambridge: Cambridge University Press

Flyvbjerg, B, Skamris Holm M and Buhl, S (2002) 'Underestimating costs in public works projects: Error or lie?' *Journal of the American Planning Association*, 68(3), pp279–295

Fowler, D and Fowler, C (1971) *Anthropology of the Numa: John Wesley Powell's Manuscripts on the Numic Peoples of the Western North America 1868–1880*, Washington, DC: Smithsonian Institution Press

Fowlkes, M R and Miller, P Y (1987) 'Chemicals and community at Love Canal', in Johnson, B B and Covello, V T (eds) *The Social and Cultural Construction of Risk*, New York: D Reidel

Fradkin, P L (1968) *A River No More: The Colorado River and the West*, Berkeley: University of California Press

Freudenburg, W R (1993) 'Risk and recreancy: Weber, the division of labor, and the rationality of risk perceptions', *Social Forces*, 71, pp909–932

Freudenburg, W R (1996) 'Risky thinking: Irrational fears about risk and society', *Annals of the American Academy of Political and Social Science*, 545 (May), pp44–53

Freudenburg, W R and Pastor, S K (1992) 'NIMBYs and LULUs: Stalking the syndromes', *Journal of Social Issues*, 48, pp39–62

Freudenburg, W R and Rosa, E A (1984) *Public Reactions to Nuclear Power: Are There Critical Masses?* Boulder, Colorado: Westview/American Association for the Advancement of Science (AAAS)

Garrick, B J and Kaplan, S (1999) 'A decision theory perspective on the disposal of high-level radioactive waste', *Risk Analysis*, 19, pp903–913

Giddens, A (1990) *The Consequences of Modernity*, Stanford, CA: Stanford University Press

Giddens, A (1991) *Modernity and Self-Identity*, Cambridge: Polity Press

Giddens, A (1994) *Beyond Left and Right: The Future of Radical Politics*, Cambridge: Polity Press
Giddens, A (2000) *Runaway World: How Globalization Is Reshaping Our Lives*, New York: Routledge
Giddens, A and Pierson, C (1998) *Conversations with Anthony Giddens: Making Sense of Modernity*, Stanford: Stanford University Press
Goffman, E (1963) *Stigma: Notes on the Management of Spoiled Identity*, Harmondsworth: Penguin and Englewood Cliffs, NJ: Prentice-Hall
Goldman, L R (ed) (2000) *Social Impact Analysis: An Applied Anthropology Manual*, Oxford, New York: Berg
Gottlieb, R (1988) *A Life of Its Own: The Politics and Power of Water*, New York: Harcour Brace Jovanovich
Government Bill (1990–1991), No 90, *En God Livsmiljö* [*A Good Environment*], Sweden: Ministry of the Environment
Government Bill (1993–1994), No 110, *Bättre Kontroll över Miljöfarligt Avfall* [*Better Control over Hazardous Waste*], Sweden: Ministry of the Environment
Government Bill (1996–1997) No 84, *En Uthållig Energiförsörjning*, Stockholm: Ministry of Industry, Employment and Communications [Näringsdepartementet]
Government Bill (2001–2002) No 143, *Samverkan för en Trygg, Effektiv och Miljövänlig Energiförsörjning*, Stockholm: Ministry of Industry, Employment and Communications [Näringsdepartementet]
Grabill, J T and Simmons, W M (1998) 'Toward a critical rhetoric of risk communication: Producing citizens and the role of technical communicators', *Technical Communication Quarterly*, 7(4), pp415–442
Granite Mission [Mission Collégiale de Concertation Granite] (2000) *Rapport*, www.environnement.gouv.fr/granite
Gregory, R, Flynn, J and Slovic, P (1995) 'Technical stigma', *American Scientist*, 83, pp220–223
Gregory, R and Satterfield, T A (2002) 'Beyond perception: The experience of risk and stigma in community contexts', *Risk Analysis*, 22(2), pp347–358
Gregory, R, Slovic, P and Flynn, J (1996) 'Risk perceptions, stigma and health policy', *Health and Place*, 2(4), pp213–220
Grimes, M (2000) 'Trends in research on siting controversy', in Boholm, Å (ed) *National Objectives – Local Objections*, Göteborg: CEFOS
Gurney, C M (1999) 'Lowering the drawbridge: A case study of analogy and metaphor in the social construction of home-ownership', *Urban Studies*, 36, pp1705–1722
Gustafson, P (2001) 'Meanings of place: Everyday experience and theoretical conceptualizations', *Journal of Environmental Psychology*, 21, pp5–16
Gutteling, J M and Wiegman, O (1996) *Exploring Risk Communication*, Dordrecht: Kluwer Academic Publishers
Habermas, J (1970, 1968) *Toward a Rational Society*, Boston: Beacon Press
Habermas, J (1996) *Kommunikativt Handlande: Texter om Språk, Rationalitet och Samhälle*, Göteborg: Daidalos
Halbwachs, M (1992, originally published 1952) *On Collective Memory* (edited by L Coser), Chicago: University of Chicago Press
Hallands Nyheter (1996) 'Letter to the editor', *Hallands Nyheter*, 21 September 1996
Hallands Nyheter (1999) 'Letter to the editor', *Hallands Nyheter*, 3 July 1999
Hammarlund, K (1997) *Attityder till vindkraft*, Göteborg: Göteborg University
Hansson, S O and Peterson, M (2001) 'Rights, risks and residual obligations', *Risk Decision and Policy*, 6, pp157–166
Harden, J (2000) 'There's no place like home – The public/private distinction in

children's theorizing of risk and safety', *Childhood – A Global Journal of Child Research*, 71, pp43–59

Hargreaves, D (1996) *An Investigation into Risk Communication Issues Surrounding a Proposal to Site a 20MW Straw-burning, Electricity Generating Plant at Calne, Wiltshire*, Guildford, UK: Department of Psychology, University of Surrey

Harrington, M R (1929) 'The mystery pit', *The Masterkey*, 3(2), pp28–30

Harrington, M R (1933) *Gypsum Cave, Nevada*, Southwest museum papers, no 8, Los Angeles, California: Southwest Museum

Harrington, M R (1970) *Ancient Tribes of the Boulder Dam Country (reprint)*, Nevada: The Silver State, and Carson City, Nevada: Western States Historical Publishers

Hastrup, K (ed) (1992) *Other Histories*, London: Routledge

Hay, R (1998) 'Sense of place in developmental context', *Journal of Environmental Psychology*, 181, pp5–29

Hayden, K E (2000) 'Stigma and place: Space, community and the politics of reputation', *Studies in Symbolic Interaction*, 23, pp219–239

Health and Safety Executive (1994) *The Fire at Allied Colloids Ltd*, Sudbury: HSE Books

Hechanova, A E and Singh, A K (1999) 'Comments on performance assessment in support of the 1996 compliance certification application for the waste isolation pilot plant', *Risk Analysis*, 19, p987

Heimer, C (2001) 'Solving the problem of trust', in Cook, K (ed) *Trust in Society*, New York: Russell Sage Foundation

Helton, J C and Anderson, D R (1999) 'Performance assessment for radioactive waste disposal', *Risk Analysis*, 19, pp759–761

Henning, A (2000) *Ambiguous Artefacts: Solar Collectors in Swedish Contexts – On Processes of Cultural Modification*, Stockholm Studies in Social Anthropology, 44, Stockholm: Almqvist and Wiksell

Hetherington, K (1998) *Expressions of Identity: Space, Performance, Politics*, London: Sage

Hilgartner, S (1992) 'The social construction of risk objects', in Short, J F and Clark, L (eds) *Organisations, Uncertainties and Risk*, Boulder, Colorado: Westview Press

Hinton, L and Watahomigie, L J (1984) *Spirit Mountain: An Anthology of Yuman Story and Song*, Tucson, Arizona: Sun Tracks and University of Arizona Press

Hirsch, E (1995) 'Landscape: Between place and space', in Hirsch, E and O'Hanlon, M (eds) *The Anthropology of Landscape*, Oxford: Oxford University Press

Hirsch, E and O'Hanlon, M (eds) (1995) *The Anthropology of Landscape: Perspectives on Place and Space*, Oxford: Oxford University Press

Holmberg, S (2000) 'Kärnkraften – En stridsfråga även under 2000-talet?' in Holmberg, S and Weibull, L (eds) *Det Nya Samhället*, Göteborg: SOM-institutet, Göteborg University

Hood, J E (1996) 'Social relations and the cultural landscape', in Yamin, R and Metheny, K B (eds) *Landscape Archeology: Reading and Interpreting the American Historical Landscape*, Knoxville: University of Tennessee Press

Hornborg, A (1994) 'Environmentalism, ethnicity and sacred places: Reflections on modernity, discourse and power', *Canadian Review of Sociology and Anthropology*, 31(3): pp245– 267

Hunold, C and Young , I M (1998) 'Justice, democracy, and hazardous siting', *Political studies*, 46, pp82–95

Hydén, H and Baier, M (1998) 'När kunskapen blir onödig – Om normativ asymmetri i fallet hallandsåsen', in SOU (ed) *Miljö i grund och botten: Erfarenheter från Hallandsåsen. Slutrapport från tunnelkommissionen. Statens offentliga utredningar*, Stockholm: Fritzes offentliga publikationer

Inglis, F (1977) 'Nation and community: A landscape and its morality', *The Social Review*, 25, pp489–514
Ingold, T (1993) 'The temporality of the landscape', *World Archaeology*, 25(2), pp152–174
Irwin, A (1995) *Citizen Science: A Study of People, Expertise and Sustainable Development*, London: Routledge
Irwin, A, Allan, S and Welsh, I (2001) 'Nuclear risks: Three problematics', in Adam, B, Beck, U and van Loon, J (eds) *The Risk Society and Beyond: Critical Issues for Social Theory*, London: Sage
Irwin, A, Simmons, P and Walker, G (1999) 'Faulty environments and risk reasoning: The local understanding of industrial hazards', *Environment and Planning A*, 31, pp1311–1326
Jackson, T and Löfstedt, R E (1998) *Renewable Energy Sources: A Background Paper for the Royal Commission on Environmental Pollution*, Guildford, UK: Centre for Environmental Strategy, University of Surrey
Jaeger, C, Renn, O, Rosa, E A and Webler, T (eds) (2001) *Risk, Uncertainty and Rational Action*, London: Earthscan
Jasanoff, S and Wynne, B (1998) 'Science and decisionmaking', in Rayner, S and Malone, E (eds) *Human Choice and Climate Change*, Columbus, Ohio: Battelle Press
Jasper, J M (1990) *Nuclear Politics: Energy and the State in the United States, Sweden, and France*, Princeton, New Jersey: Princeton University Press
Jay, M (1986) 'In the empire of the gaze: Foucault and the denigration of vision in twentieth-century French thought', in Hoy, D C (ed) *Foucault: A Critical Reader*, Oxford: Basil Blackwell
Jay, M (1993) *Downcast Eyes: The Denigration of Vision in Twentieth-century Thought*, Berkley: University of California Press
Jiménez, M (2001) 'National policies and local struggles in Spain: Environmental politics over industrial waste policy in the 1990s', Paper presented at the ECPR Joint Sessions of Workshops, Grenoble, 6–11 April 2001
Kahneman, D, Slovic, P and Tversky, A (eds) (1982) *Judgment under Uncertainty: Heuristics and Biases*, Cambridge: Cambridge University Press
Kaltenborn, B J (1998) 'Effects of sense of place on responses to environmental impacts: A study among residents in Svalbard in the Norwegian high Arctic', *Applied Geography*, 18, pp169–189
Kasperson, R (2000) 'Risk and the stakeholder express, President's message', *Risk Newsletter*, 4 Quarter, p3
Kasperson, R E, Golding, D and Truler, S (1992) 'Siting hazardous waste facilities and communicating risks', *Journal of Social Issues*, 48(4), pp161–172
Kasperson, R E and Kasperson, J X (1996) 'The social amplification and attenuation of risk', *Annals of the American Academy of Political and Social Science*, 545(May), pp95–105
Kasperson, R E, Renn, O, Slovic, P, Brown, H S, Emel, J, Goble, R, Kasperson J X and Ratick, S (1988) 'The social amplification of risk: A conceptual framework', *Risk Analysis*, 8(2), pp177–187
Kempf, H (2003) 'Le transport des matières nucléaires, critiqué par les écologistes, relève du "secret défense"', *Le Monde*, 3 September, p12
Kempton, W, Boster, J S and Hartley, J A (1995) *Environmental Values in American Culture*, Cambridge, Massachusetts: MIT Press
Khan, J (2003) 'Wind power planning in three Swedish municipalities', *Journal of Environmental Planning and Management*, 46(4), pp563–581
Klintman, M (1995) 'The social–psychological conditions and obstacles to environmentally responsible agency – A theoretical perspective', *Sociologisk Forskning*, 32, pp82–100

Knodt, E M (1995) 'Foreword', in Luhmann, N (ed) *Social Systems*, Stanford, California: Stanford University Press

Kopytoff, I (1986) 'The cultural biography of things: Commoditization as process', in Appadurai, A (ed) *The Social Life of Things: Commodities in Cultural Perspective*, Cambridge: Cambridge University Press

Kroeber, A L (ed) (1970, originally published 1925) *Handbook of the Indians of California*, Bureau of American Ethnology Bulletin No 78, Washington, DC: Government Printing Office

Kunreuther, H, Easterling, D, Desvousges, W and Slovic, P (1990) 'Public attitudes toward siting a high-level nuclear waste repository in Nevada', *Risk Analysis*, 10, pp469–484

Kunreuther, H, Fitzgerald, K and Aarts, T D (1993) 'Siting noxious facilities: A test of the facility siting credo', *Risk Analysis*, 13(3), pp301–318

Laird, C (1976) *The Chemehuevis*, Banning, California: Malki Musesum Press

Lash, S, Szerszynski, B and Wynne, B (eds) (1996) *Risk, Environment and Modernity: Towards a New Ecology*, London: Sage

Latour, B (1993) *We Have Never Been Modern*, New York: Harvester Wheatsheaf

Latour, B (1996, originally published 1993) *Aramis, or the Love of Technology*, Cambridge, Massachusetts, and London: Harvard University Press

Le Bars, Y (2000) *Pour un Inventaire National de Référence des Déchets Radioactifs. Rapport de la Mission sur la Méthodologie de l'Inventaire des Déchets Radioactifs (ANDRA)*, Paris: La Documentation Française

Le Bars, Y (2002) Personal communication, 20 March

Le Monde (1993) 14 January 1993

Leiss, W (1996) 'Three phases in the evolution of risk communication practices', *Annals of the American Academy of Political and Social Science*, 545, pp85–94

Lidskog, R (1994) *Radioactive and Hazardous Waste Management in Sweden*, Uppsala: Almqvist and Wiksell

Lidskog, R (2000) 'Det korroderade samhället? Lokala responser på teknologiska katastrofer' ['The corroded society? Local responses to technological catastrophes'], in Lidskog, R, Nohrstedt, S-A and Warg, L-E (eds) *Risker, Kommunikation och Medier* [*Risks, Communication and Media*], Lund: Studentlitteratur

Linneroth Bayer, J and Fitzgerald, K B (1996) 'Conflicting views on fair siting processes: Evidence from Austria and the US', *Risk: Health, Safety and Environment*, 7, pp119–134

Löfstedt, R E (1996a) 'The use of biomass energy in a regional context: The case of Växjö Energi, Sweden', *Biomass and Bioenergy*, 11(1), pp33–42

Löfstedt, R E (1996b) 'Risk communication: The Barsebäck nuclear plant case', *Energy Policy*, 24, pp689–696

Löfstedt, R (1997) 'Evaluation of two siting strategies: The case of two UK waste tire incinerators', *Risk, Health, Safety and Environment*, 8(1), pp63–77

Löfstedt, R E (1998) 'Sweden's biomass controversy: A case study of communicating policy issues', *Environment*, 40(4), 16–45

Löfstedt, R (1999) 'The role of trust in the north Blackforest: An evaluation of a citizen panel project', *Risk Health, Safety and Environment*, 10(1), pp7–30

Löfstedt, R E (2000) 'Samhällsvetenskaplig riskforskning – en kort historik' ['Risk research in social science – a short history'], in Lidskog, R, Nohrstedt, S-A and Warg, L-E (eds) *Risker, Kommunikation och Medier* [*Risks, Communication and Media*], Lund: Studentlitteratur

Löfstedt, R E (2003) 'Regulatory negotiation: The case of International Paper's hydro dam re-licensing procedure', *Risk Management: An International Journal*, 5(4), in press

Löfstedt, R and Boholm, Å (1999) 'Off track in Sweden', *Environment*, 41(4), pp16–44

Löfstedt, R and Frewer, L (eds) (1998) *Earthscan Reader in Risk and Modern Society*, London: Earthscan

Löfstedt, R E and Horlick-Jones, T (1998) 'Environmental regulation in the UK: Politics, institutional change and public trust', in Cvetkovich, G and Löfstedt R E (eds) *Social Trust*, London: Earthscan

Löfstedt, R E and Renn, O (1997) 'The Brent Spar controversy: An example of risk communication gone wrong', *Risk Analysis*, 17(2), pp131–136

Lovell, N (ed) (1998) *Locality and Belonging*, London: Routledge

Lowe, P, Murdoch, J and Cox, G (1995) 'A civilised retreat? Anti-urbanism, rurality and the making of an Anglo-Centric culture', in Healey, P (ed) *Managing Cities*, Chichester: Wiley

Luhmann, N (1985) *A Sociological Theory of Law*, London: Routledge and Kegan Paul

Luhmann, N (1995) *Social Systems*, Stanford, California: Stanford University Press

Macgill, S M (1987) *The Politics of Anxiety*, London: Pion

Mairal, G and Belío, C (2001) *Agua para los Monegros: Antropología e historia de la transformación en regadío*, Huesca: Instituto de Estudios Altoaragoneses

Mairal, G and Bergua, J A (1998) 'From economism to culturalism: The social and cultural construction of risk in the River Esera', in Abram, S and Waldren, J (eds) *Anthropological Perspectives on Local Development: Knowledge and Sentiments in Conflict*, London: Routledge EASA series

Mairal, G and Bergua, J A (2000) *De Joaquín Costa al Pacto del Agua: Los aragoneses y el agua*, Zaragoza: Egido Editorial

Mairal Buil, G, Bergua Amores, J A and Puyal Español, E (1997) *Agua, Tierra, Riesgo y Supervivencia*, Zaragoza: Prensas Universitarias de Zaragoza

March, J G (1992) 'The war is over and the victors have lost', *Journal of Socio-Economics*, 21, pp261–267

Massey, D (1994) *Space, Place and Gender*, Cambridge: Polity Press

Mauss, M (1990, originally published 1924) *The Gift: The Form and Reason for Exchange in Archaic Societies*, London: Routledge

Mays, C (2002) 'Thematic report on social psychology', in OECD/NEA (eds) *Stepwise Decision Making in Finland for the Disposal of Spent Nuclear Fuel*, Workshop proceedings, Turku, Finland, 15–16 November 2001, NEA No 03616, Paris: OECD

Mays, C and Charron, S (2000) *Étude des Représentations Individuelles des déchets Radioactifs à Vie Longue et des Modes de Gestion Associés (REPDECH). Partie A: Aspects Méthodologiques; Guide d'Entretien*, Note technique SEGR/LSEES/00 No 65, Juin, Fontenay-aux-Roses: Institut de Radioprotection et de Sûreté Nucléaire (IRSN)

Mays, C and Charron, S (2002) *Etude des Représentations Individuelles et Sociales des Déchets Radioactifs et des Modes de Gestion Associés: Analyse des Résultats et Perspectives. Rapport final*, Note technique SEGR/02-39, Fontenay-aux-Roses: Institut de Radioprotection et de Sûreté Nucléaire (IRSN).

Mays, C, Charron S and Brenot J (2003) 'Social trust and confidence in the management of long-lived radioactive waste: Qualitative data from France', in Andersson, K (ed) *Proceedings, VALDOR 2003: Values in Decisions on Risk*, Stockholm, Sweden, 9–13 June 2003, Täby, Sweden: Karinta-Konsult

Mays, C, Mansoux, H and Charron, S (2001) 'Enquiries into the representations of long-lived waste: Recent French data', Seminar on Ethics and Dialogue for Radioactive Waste Management, jointly organized by Université Paris VI and by the Commission Nationale d'Evaluation, 25 January 2001, Paris: CNE

Mays, C and Poumadère, M (1996) 'Uncertain communication: Institutional discourse in nuclear waste repository siting', in Sublet, G, Covello, V and Tinker, T (eds) *Scientific Uncertainty and Its Influence on the Public Communications Process*, Dordrecht: Kluwer NATO Advanced Research Series

Mazur, A (1998) *A Hazardous Inquiry: The Rashomon Effect at Love Canal*, Cambridge, Massachusetts: Harvard University Press

McAvoy, G E (1999) *Controlling Technocracy: Citizen Rationality and the NIMBY Syndrome*, Washington, DC: Georgetown University Press

McBride, D (1995) *Hard Work and Far from Home: The Civilian Conservation Corps at Lake Mead, Nevada*, Boulder City, Nevada: Boulder Images

Merceron, T (2000) 'A new siting process in France for a URL in granite: Lessons learnt from the recent consultation mission', in OECD/NEA (eds) *Stakeholder Confidence and Radioactive Waste Disposal*, Inauguration, First Workshop and Meeting of the NEA Forum on Stakeholder Confidence in the Area of Radioactive Waste Management, Paris: OECD, www.nea.fr/html/rwm/reports/2000/nea2829.pdf

Meyrowitz, J (1985) *No Sense of Place*, New York and Oxford: Oxford University Press

Miller, C (2001) *Planning and Environmental Protection*, Oxford: Hart Publishing

Moore, J (2000) 'Placing home in context', *Journal of Environmental Psychology*, 20, pp207–217

Morgan, L H (1985, originally published 1877) *Ancient Society, or Researches in the Lines of Human Progress from Savagery through Barbarism to Civilization*, Tucson, Arizona: University of Arizona Press

Morphy, H and Banks, M (1997) 'Introduction: Rethinking visual anthropology', in Banks, M and Morphy, H (eds) *Rethinking Visual Anthropology*, New Haven: Yale University Press

Moscovici, S (1976, originally published 1961) *La Psychanalyse, Son Image et Son Public*, 2nd edition, Paris: Presses Universitaires de France

Moscovici, S (1988) 'Notes toward a description of social representations', *European Journal of Social Psychology*, 18, pp211–250

Mouzelis, N (1995) *Sociological Theory: What Went Wrong?* London: Routledge

Murdoch, J and Abram, S (2002) *Rationalities of Planning*, Aldershot: Ashgate

Muskens, G and Kinnear, R (1993) 'Political and multicultural constraints of the social sciences in Europe: Cultural contact, schismogenesis and institutional change', *Innovation: The European Journal of Social Science*, 6(2), pp211–229

Nadel, J H (1984) 'Stigma and separation: Pariah status and community in a Scottish fishing village', *Ethnology*, 23, pp105–115

Nader, L (2002) *The Life of the Law: Anthropological Projects*, Berkeley: University of California Press

Nevada Commission on Nuclear Projects (2000) *Report to the Governor and Legislature*, Carson City, Nevada: Agency for Nuclear Projects

Newby, H (1980) *Rural sociology*, London: Sage

Newby, H (1988) *The Countryside in Question*, London: Hutchinson

Nordvästra Skånes Tidningar (2001) Letter to the editor, 'Lagen ska gälla alla!' [The law must apply to all!], *Nordvästra Skånes Tidningar*, 12 August 2001

Nordvästra Skånes Tidningar (2001) Letter to the editor, 'Nedlagt åtal väctar kritik' [Withdrawn indictment called into question], Nordvästra Skänes Tidningar, 31 August 2001

North, P (1998) 'Save our Solsbury! The anatomy of an anti–roads protest', *Environmental Politics*, 7(3), pp1–25

Norton, B G and Hannon, B (1997) 'Environmental values: A place-based theory', *Environmental Ethics*, 19, pp227–245

Norton, B G and Hannon, B (1998) 'Democracy and sense of place values in environmental policy', in Light, A and Smith, J M (eds) *Philosophy and Geography III: Philosophies of Place*, Lanham: Rowman and Littlefield

NRC (National Research Council) (2001) *Disposition of High-level Waste and Spent Nuclear Fuel: The Continuing Societal and Technical Challenge*, Committee on Disposition of High-level Radioactive Waste through Geological Isolation, National Academy of Sciences, Washington, DC: National Academy Press

OECD and NEA (Organisation for Economic Co-operation and Development and Nuclear Energy Agency) (1985) *Technical Appraisal of the Current Situation in the Field of Radioactive Waste Management: A Collective Opinion by the Radioactive Waste Management Committee*, Paris: OECD and NEA

OECD and NEA (2000) *Stakeholder Confidence and Radioactive Waste disposal: Inauguration, First Workshop and Meeting of the NEA Forum on Stakeholder Confidence in the Area of Radioactive Waste Management*, Paris: OECD and NEA, www.nea.fr/html/rwm/reports/2000/nea2829.pdf

Official Letter from the Swedish Parliament (1990–1991), No 338

OPECST (Office Parlementaire d'Evaluation des Choix Scientifiques et Technologiques) (1990) *Rapport sur la Gestion des Déchets Nucléaires à Haute Activité* (C Bataille), Paris: La Documentation Française.

Ostrom, E (1990) *Governing the Commons: The Evolution of Institutions for Collective Action*, Cambridge: Cambridge University Press

Owens, S (2004) 'Siting, sustainable development and social priorities', *Journal of Risk Research*, 7(2), pp101–114

Owens, S and Cowell, R (2002) *Land and Limits: Interpreting Sustainability in the Planning Process*, London: Routledge

Parenteau, R (1988) *Public Participation in Environmental Decision Making*, Montreal: University of Montreal Press

Pate-Cornell, M E (1999) 'Conditional uncertainty analysis and implications for decision making: The case of WIPP', *Risk Analysis*, 19, pp995–1002

Peterson, M and Hansson, S O (2004) 'On the application of rights-based moral theories to siting controversies', *Journal of Risk Research*, 7(2), pp269–275

Petts, J (1992) 'Incineration risk perceptions and public concern: Experience in the UK improving risk communication', *Waste Management and Research*, 10, pp169–182

Petts, J (1995) 'Waste management strategy development: A case study of community involvement and consensus-building in Hampshire', *Journal of Environmental Planning and Management*, 38, pp519–536

Petts, J (2001) 'Evaluating the effectiveness of deliberative processes: Waste management case-studies', *Journal of Planning and Management*, 44(2), pp207–226

Petts, J (2004) 'Barriers to participation and deliberation in risk decisions: Evidence from waste management', *Journal of Risk Research*, 7(2), pp115–134

Pidgeon, N, Kasperson, R E and Slovic, P (eds) (2003) *The Social Amplification of Risk*, Cambridge: Cambridge University Press

Piller, C (1991) *The Fail-Safe Society: Community Defiance and the End of American Technological Optimism*, New York: Basic Books

Pink, S (2001) *Doing Visual Ethnography: Images, Media and Representation in Research*, London: SAGE Publications

Poumadère, M, Mays, C, Slovic, P, Flynn, J and Johnson, S (1994) 'What lies behind public acceptance? Comparison of US and French perceptions of the nuclear power option', in IAEA (ed) *Proceedings of the International Topical Meeting on 'The Nuclear Power Option' (October)*, Vienna: International Atomic Energy Agency

Pred, A (1983) 'Structuration and place: On the becoming of sense of place and structure of feeling', *Journal for the Theory of Social Behaviour,* 13, pp45–68

Prosser, J (ed) (1998) *Image-based Research*, London: Falmer Press

Pyne, S J (1998) *How the Canyon Became Grand: A Short History*, New York: Viking, Penguin

Rabe, B G (1994) *Beyond NIMBY: Hazardous Waste Siting in Canada and the United States*, Washington, DC: Brookings Institution

Rappaport, R A (1996) 'Risk and the human environment', *Annals of the American Academy of Political and Social Science,* 545 (May): pp64–74

Rayner, S and Cantor, R (1987) 'How fair is safe enough? The cultural approach to societal technology choice', *Risk Analysis,* 7, pp3–9

Rechard, R P (1999) 'Historical relationship between performance assessment for radioactive waste disposal and other types of risk assessment', *Risk Analysis,* 19, pp763–807

Reisner, M (1986) *Cadillac Desert: The American West and Its Disappearing Water,* New York: Viking Penguin Books

Renn, O (1991) 'Risk communication and the social amplification of risk', in Kasperson, R E and Stallen, P M (eds) *Communicating Risks to the Public: International Perspectives*, Dordrecht: Kluwer

Renn, O (1998) 'Three decades of risk research: Accomplishments and new challenges', *Journal of Risk Research*, 1(1), pp49–71

Renn, O, Burns, W J, Kasperson, J X, Kasperson, R E and Slovic, P (1992) 'The social amplification of risk: Theoretical foundations and empirical applications', *Journal of Social Issues*, 48(4), pp137–160

Renn, O and Levine, D (1991) 'Credibility and trust in risk communication', in Kasperson, R E and Stallen, P M (eds) *Communicating Risks to the Public: International Perspectives*, Dordrecht: Kluwer

Renn, O, Webler, T and Wiedemann, P (eds) (1995) *Fairness and Competence in Citizen Participation*, Dordrecht: Kluwer

Renn, O, Webler, T and Kastenholz, H (1996) 'Procedural and substantive fairness in landfill siting', *Risk: Health, Safety and Environment,* 7(2), pp145–168

Report of the proceedings from Ängelholm District Court (Protokoll 9 March 2001 Muntlig föberedelse i Ängelholm (Mål nr B41-98))

Roberts, D (ed) (1995) *Reconstructing Theory: Gadamer, Habermas, Luhmann*, Carlton South: Melbourne University Press

Robertson, A F (1984) *People and the State: An Anthropology of Planned Development,* Cambridge: Cambridge University Press

Rootes, C, Seel, B and Adams, D (2000) 'The old, the new and the old new: British environmental organisations from conservationism to radical ecologism', Paper presented at the ECPR Joint Sessions of Workshops, Copenhagen, 14–19 April 2000

Rosa, E A (1997) 'Sociological approaches to risk: Friend or foe of the rational actor paradigm (RAP)', Paper presented at the Risk Assessment and Policy Association International meetings, Alexandria, VA

Rosa, E A (1998) 'Metatheoretical foundations for post–normal risk', *Journal of Risk Research*, 1(1), pp15–44

Rosa, E A and Clarke, D L Jr (1999) 'Historical routes to technological gridlock: Nuclear technology as prototypical vehicle', *Research in Social Problems and Public Policy,* 7, pp21–57

Rosa, E A, Riley, R E, Dunlap, R E and Kraft, M E (1993) 'Prospects for public acceptance of a high-level nuclear waste repository in the United States: Summary and implications', in Dunlap, R E, Kraft, M E and Rosa, E A (eds) *Public Reactions*

to Nuclear Waste: Citizens' Views of Repository Siting, Durham, North Carolina: Duke University Press
Rose, G (1995) 'Place and identity: A sense of place', in Massey, D and Jess, P (eds) *A Place in the World?* Oxford: Oxford University Press
Rotenberg, R (1993) 'On the salubrity of sites', in Rotenberg, R and McDonogh, G (eds) *The Cultural Meaning of Urban Space*, Westport, Connecticut: Bergin and Garvey
Roy, A (2001) *El álgebra de la justicia infinita*, Barcelona: Anagrama
Rutherford, J (1990) 'A place called home: Identify and the cultural politics of difference', in Rutherford, J (ed) *Identity: Community, Culture, Difference*, London: Lawrence and Wishart
Sagoff, M (1988) *The Economy of the Earth*, Cambridge: Cambridge University Press
Sandman, P M (1989) 'Hazard versus outrage in the public perception of risk', in Covello, V, McCallum, D and Pavlova, M (eds) *Effective Risk Communication*, New York: Plenum Press
Satterfield, T (1996) 'Pawns, victims, or heroes: The negotiation of stigma and the plight of Oregon's loggers', *Journal of Social Issues*, 52, pp71–83
Satterfield, T and Gregory, R (2002) 'The experience of risk and stigma in community contexts', *Risk Analysis*, 22, pp347–358
Satterfield, T, Slovic, P, Gregory, R, Flynn, J and Mertz, C K (2001) 'Risk lived, stigma experienced', in Flynn, J, Slovic, P and Kunreuther, H (eds) *Risk, Media and Stigma: Understanding Public Challenges to Modern Science and Technology*, London: Earthscan
Saunders, P (1990) *A Nation of Home Owners*, London: Unwin Hyman
Schwarz, M and Thompson, M (1990) *Divided We Stand: Redefining Politics, Technology and Social Choice*, Philadelphia: University of Pennsylvania Press
Scott, J C (1998) *Seeing Like a State: How Certain Schemes To Improve the Human Condition Have Failed*, New Haven and London: Yale University Press
SFS (Swedish Code of Statutes) (1998) No 944, *Förordning om förbud mm i vissa fall i samband med hantering, införsel och utförsel av kemiska produkter* [*Regulation on Prohibition, etc, Connected to Handling, Import and Export of Chemical Products*]
Shore, C and Wright, S (eds) (1997) *Anthropology of Policy: Critical Perspectives on Governance and Power*, London: Routledge
Short, J F and Clarke, L (eds) (1992) *Organizations, Uncertainties and Risk*, Boulder, Colorado: Westview Press
Short, J F Jr and Rosa, E A (2004) 'Some principles for siting controversy decisions: Lessons from the U.S. experience with high level nuclear waste', *Journal of Risk Research*, 7(2), in press
Shrader-Frechette, K (1991) *Risk and Rationality: Philosophical Foundations for Popular Reforms*, Berkeley and Los Angeles: University of California Press
Shrivastava, P (1991) 'Organizational myths in industrial crises: Obfuscating revelations', in Couch, S R and Kroll-Smith, J S (eds) *Communities at Risk*, New York: Peter Lang
Silva, M K, Rucker, D F and Chaturvedi, L (1999) 'Resolution of the long-term performance issues at the waste isolation pilot plan', *Risk Analysis*, 19, pp1003–1016
Simmons, P (2004) 'Performing safety in faulty environments', in Szerszynski, B, Waterton, C and Heim, H (eds) *Performing Nature*, London: Sociological Review Monographs Series
Simmons, P and Walker, G P (1999) 'Tolerating risk: Policy principles and public perceptions', *Risk, Decision and Policy*, 43, pp179–190
Simon, H A (1997) *Administrative Behaviour*, New York: The Free Press

Sjöberg, L (1997) 'Explaining risk perception: An empirical evaluation of cultural theory', *Risk Decision and Policy*, 2(2), pp113–130

Sjöberg, L (2000) 'Factors in risk perception', *Risk Analysis*, 20, pp1–11

Sjöberg, L and Drottz-Sjöberg, B-M (2001) 'Fairness, risk and risk tolerance in the siting of a nuclear waste repository', *Journal of Risk Research*, 4(1), pp75–101

Sjölander-Lindqvist, A (2004) 'The effects of environmental uncertainty on farmers' sense of locality and futurity: A Swedish case study', *Journal of Risk Research*, 7(2), pp185–197

Sjölander-Lindqvist, A, Boholm, Å and Löfstedt, R E (2000) 'Understanding aspects of environmental stigma: The case of Hallandsås', *Proceedings from the ESREL 2000 and SRA – Europe Annual Conference on Foresight and Precaution*, Edinburgh, UK, 14–17 May 2000

Sjöström, U (1985) *Låna varandras glasögon*, Stockholm: Pedagogiska institutionen, Stockholm University

Slovic, P (1987) 'Perceptions of risk', *Science*, 236, pp280–285

Slovic, P (1993) 'Perceived risk, trust, and democracy', *Risk Analysis*, 13(6), pp675–682

Slovic, P (2000) *The Perception of Risk*, London: Earthscan

Slovic, P, Fischhoff, B and Lichtenstein S (1981) 'Perceived risk: Psychological factors and social implications', in Warner, F and Slater, D H (eds) *The Assessment and Perception of Risk*, London: The Royal Society

Slovic, P, Flynn, J and Gregory, R (1994) 'Stigma happens: Social problems in the siting of nuclear waste facilities', *Risk Analysis*, 14(5), pp773–778

Slovic, P, Flynn, J, Mertz, C K, Poumadère, M and Mays, C (2000) 'Nuclear power and the public: A comparative study of risk perception in France and the United States', in Renn, O and Rohrmann, B (eds) *Cross-cultural Risk Perception: A Survey of Empirical Studies*, Amsterdam: Kluwer Academic Press

Slovic, P, Layman M, Kraus, N, Flynn, J, Chalmers, J and Gesell, G (1991) 'Perceived risk, stigma, and potential economic impacts of a high-level nuclear waste respository in Nevada', *Risk Analysis*, 11(4), pp683–696

Slovic, P and McGregor, D (1994) *The Social Context of Risk Communication*, Eugene, Oregon: Decision Research

Smith, A D (1991) *National Identity*, London: Penguin

Smith, E and Marquez, M (2000) 'The other side of the NIMBY syndrome', *Society and Natural Resources*, 13, pp273–280

Soneryd, L (2002) *Environmental Conflicts and Deliberative Solutions?* Örebro: Örebro University, Örebro Studies in Sociology

Sontag, S (1973) *On Photography*, New York: Ferrar, Straus and Giroux

SOU (2001) No 58 *Kvicksilver i säkert förvar* [*Mercury in Safekeeping*], Stockholm: Fritzes

Special Issue: New Perspectives on Siting Controversy (2004) *Journal of Risk Research*, 7(2), pp99–275

State of Nevada (2002) 'Agency for nuclear projects', personal communication

Stern, P C and Fineberg, H V (eds) (1996) *Understanding Risk: Informing Decisions in a Democratic Society*, Washington, DC: National Academy Press

Stevens, J E (1988) *Hoover Dam: An American Adventure*, Norman: University of Oklahoma Press

Stoffle, R (2000) 'Cultural heritage and resources', in Goldman, L R (ed) *Social Impact Analysis: An Applied Anthropology Manual*, Oxford: Berg

Stoffle, R W, Halmo, D B and Austin, D E (1997) 'Cultural landscapes and traditional cultural properties: A Southern Paiute view of the Grand Canyon and Colorado River', *American Indian Quarterly*, 21, pp229–249

Stoffle, R, Loendorf, L, Austin, D, Halmo, D and Bulletts, A (2000) 'Ghost dancing

the Grand Canyon: Southern Paiute rock art, ceremony and cultural landscapes'. *Current Anthropology*, 41, pp11–38
Stoffle, R, Traugott, M, Jensen, F and Copeland, R (1987) *Social Assessment of High Technology: The Superconducting Super Collider in Southeast Michigan*, Ann Arbor, Michigan: Institute for Social Research, University of Michigan
Stoffle, R, Traugott, M, Stone, J, McIntyre, P, Davidson, C, Jensen, F and Coover, G (1990) *Social Assessment of Siting a Low–level Radioactive Waste Storage Facility in Michigan*, Ann Arbor, Michigan: Institute for Social Research, University of Michigan
Stoffle, R, Zedeno, N, Eisenberg, A, Toupal, R, Carroll, A, Pittaluga, F, Amato, J, Earnest, T and Dewey, G (2000) *Ha'tata (The Backbone of the River): American Indian Ethnographic Studies Regarding the Hoover Dam Bypass Project*, Tucson: Bureau of Applied Research in Anthropology, University of Arizona
Stoffle, R, Zedeno, N and Halmo, D (eds) (2001) *American Indians and the Nevada Test Site: A Model of Research and Consultation*, Washington, DC: US Government Printing Office
Strandberg, U (2000) 'Contested territory: The politics of siting controversy', *Proceedings from the ESREL 2000 and SRA – Europe Annual Conference on Foresight and Precaution*, Edinburgh, UK, 14–17 May 2000
Strathern, M (1981) *Kinship at the Core: An Anthropology of Elmdon, a Village in North-West Essex in the 1960s*, Cambridge: Cambridge University Press
Svenska Dagbladet (2001) 'Det här är förödande för folks rättsmedvetande' [This is devastating for people's sense of justice'], 31 August 2001
Swedenborg, B (2002) *Skattemiljarder i trafikpolitiken – Till vilken nytta? En granskning av 2001 års infrastrukturproposition*, Stockholm: SNS Förlag
Swedish EPA (Swedish Environmental Protection Agency) (1993) *Avveckling av vårt dolda kvicksilverlager* [*Phase-out of Our Hidden Mercury Depots*], Stockholm: EPA Report No 4177
Swedish EPA (1997) *Slutförvar av kvicksilver: Huvudrapport* [*Final Disposal of Mercury: Main Report*], Stockholm: EPA Report No 4752
Szasz, A (1994) *Ecopopulism: Toxic Waste and the Movement for Environmental Justice*, Minneapolis: University of Minnesota Press
Tansey, J (2004) 'Risks as politics, culture as power', *Journal of Risk Research*, 7(1), pp17–32
Tansey, J and O'Riordan, T (1999) 'Cultural theory and risk: A review', *Health, Risk and Society*, 1(1), pp71–90
Teague, D W (1997) *The Southwest in American Literature and Art: The Rise of a Desert Aesthetic*, Tucson: University of Arizona Press
The Swedish Environmental Code (Miljöbalken (SFS 1998:808))
Thompson, B G J (1999) 'The role of performance assessment in the regulation of underground disposal of radioactive wastes: An international perspective', *Risk Analysis*, 19, pp809–846
Thompson, M, Ellis, R and Wildavsky, A (1990) *Cultural Theory*, Boulder, Colorado: Westview Press
Toke, D and Elliott, D (2000) 'A fresh start for UK wind power?' *International Journal of Ambient Energy*, 21(2), pp67–76
Tönnies, F (1988, originally published 1887) *Community and Society*, New Brunswick, New Jersey: Transaction Publishers
Trafikutskottets betänkande 2001/2002: TU2 (2001–2002) 'Infrastruktur för ett långsiktigt hållbart transportsystem', The Swedish Government Standing Committee on Transport and Communications

Treichel, J (2000) 'How to achieve public participation in nuclear waste decisions: Public relations or transparent adversary science', *Risk: Health, Safety and Environment,* (Summer), pp221–231

Turner, B (1978) *Man-made Disasters*, Oxford: Butterworth Heinemann

Tversky, A and Kahnemann, D (1973) 'Availability: A heuristic for judging frequency and probability', *Cognitive Psychology,* 4, pp207–232

US Department of Health and Human Services (2002) *Communicating in a Crisis: Risk Communication Guidelines for Public Officials*, Washington, DC: Center for Mental Health Services, Substance Abuse and Mental Health Services Administration

US EPA (US Environment Protection Agency) (2000) *Social Aspects of Siting RCRA Hazardous Waste Facilities*, EPA530-K-00-005

US National Research Council (1989) *Improving Risk Communication*, Washington, DC: National Academy Press

US National Research Council (1996) *Understanding Risk in a Democratic Society*, Washington, DC: National Academy of Sciences

Van Dyke, J C (1901) *The Desert*, New York: Gibbs-Smith, Peregrine Smith Books

van Erp, F (1996) 'Siting processes for wind energy projects in Germany: Public participation and the response of the local population', *Forschungszentrum Julich Heft*

von Winterfeldt, D and Edwards, W (1984) 'Patterns of conflict about risky technology', *Risk Analysis,* 4, pp55–68

Wakefield, S E L, Elliott, S J, Cole, D C and Eyles, J D (2001) 'Environmental risk and (re)action: Air quality, health, and civic involvement in an urban neighbourhood', *Health and Place*, 7, pp163–177

Walker, G P, Simmons, P, Irwin, A and Wynne, B (1999) 'Risk communication, public participation and the Seveso II Directive', *Journal of Hazardous Materials*, 65, pp170–190

Walters, H (2001) 'Culture gets hoovered: Bypass plan paves over tribes' concerns about spiritual site', *Las Vegas City Life: News and Culture Weekly*, 5–11 April 2001, p8, www.lvcitylife.com

Weart, S (1988) *Nuclear Fear: A History of Images*, Cambridge, Massachusetts: Harvard University Press

Whitley, D S (ed) (2001) *Handbook of Rock Art Research*, Oxford: Altamira Press

Whitley, D S and Nabokov, P (2000) *Hoover Dam Bypass Project: Ethnohistoric Overview and Assessment*, Simi Valley, California: WandS Consultants

Wildavsky, A (1988) *Searching for Safety*, New Brunswick, New Jersey: Transaction Books

Wildavsky, A and Dake, K (1990) 'Theories of risk perception: Who fears what and why?' *Daedalus*, 112, pp41–50

Winston, B (1998) 'The camera never lies: The partiality of photographic evidence', in Prosser, J (ed) *Image-based Research: A Sourcebook for Qualitative Researchers*, London: Falmer Press

Wolsink, M (1990) *The Siting Problem – Wind Power as a Social Dilemma*, Amsterdam: Department of Environmental Sciences, University of Amsterdam

Wolsink, M (1994) 'Entanglement of interests and motives: Assumptions behind the "Nimby–theory" on facility siting', *Urban Studies*, 31(6), pp851–866

Wolsink, M (1996) 'Dutch wind power policy: Stagnating implementation of renewables', *Energy Policy,* 24(12), pp1079–1088

Wolsink, M (2000) 'Wind power and the NIMBY-myth: Institutional capacity and the limited significance of public support', *Renewable Energy*, 21, pp49–64

Wynne, B (1987) *Risk Management and Hazardous Wastes: Implementation and the Dialectics of Credibility*, Berlin, New York: Springer

Wynne, B, Grove-White, R and Waterton, C (1993) *Public Perceptions and the Nuclear Industry in West Cumbria*, Lancaster: Centre for the Study of Environmental Change, Lancaster University

Yoffee, N (2001) 'The evolution of simplicity', *Current Anthropology*, 42, pp767–769

Young, H P (1994) *Equity: In Theory and Practice*, Princeton: Princeton University Press

Zeiss, C and Atwater, J (1991) 'Waste disposal facilities and community response: Tracing pathways from facility impacts to community attitude', *Canadian Journal of Civil Engineering*, 18, pp83–96

Zonabend, F (1993, originally published 1989) *The Nuclear Peninsula*, Cambridge: Cambridge University Press

Årsrapport för det ekologiska kontrollprogrammet (2001) Miljögranskningsgrubben, Banverket

Additional references for Chapter 3

Articles, *Bergslagsposten*

1994 'Planer på miljöfarligt avfall i Stripa gruva' ['Plans of hazardous waste in Stripa Mine'], 15 March

1994 'Naturvårdsverket tar inte ställning' ['EPA does not take stand'], 24 March

1994 'Om allt går enligt planerna: Miljöfarligt avfall i Stripa gruva om 3 år' ['According to the plans: Hazardous waste in Stripa Mine within three years'], 24 March

1994 'Planerna på att förvara tungmetaller i gruvan: Visst finns det motstånd i Stripa!' ['The plans to store heavy metals in the mine: Certainly there is resistance in Stripa!'], 2 April

1994 'Stripabor vill hindra giftigt avfall i gruvan' ['Stripa inhabitants will hinder hazardous waste in the mine'], 13 April

1994 'Kommunfullmäktige: vill ha mer information om förvaring av miljöfarligt avfall' ['The Municipal council: want more information on hazardous waste disposal'], 19 April

1994 'Informationsmöte om miljöfarligt avfall i Stripa' ['Information meeting about hazardous waste in Stripa'], 19 May

1994 'Ortsbornas budskap till företagen bakom avfallsplanerna – Nej, vi vill inte ha hit er' ['The message from the local inhabitants to the companies behind the waste plans – No, we do not want you here'], 27 May

1994 'Planerna på miljöfarligt avfall i Stripa gruva – Mycket större utsläpp från vanlig soptipp' ['The plans for waste in Stripa Mine – More leakage from ordinary refuse dump'], 7 June

1994 'Forskningsledaren dömer ut Stripa gruva' ['Director of research rejects Stripa Mine'], 8 June

1994 'Folkviljan avgör om det blir avfallsförvaring' ['The will of the people decides about future waste disposal'], 11 June

1994 'Tre frågor i den första frågestunden' ['Three questions in the first opportunity to ask questions'], 22 June

1994 'Carlsson vill ha folkomröstning' ['Carlsson wants a referendum'], 24 June

1994 'Nej, Nej, Nej, 125 emot deponeringsplanerna – 1 för' ['No, No, No, 125 against the plans of disposal – 1 in favour'], 15 July

1994 'Planerna på miljöfarligt avfall i Stripa ännu aktuella' ['The plans for hazardous waste in Stripa still urgent'], 10 November

1994 'Urberget sprickfyllt visar Umeå-forskning' ['Research from Umeå shows that the bedrock is full of cracks'], 8 December
1995 'Klart med ansökan om miljöfarligt avfall i Stripa' ['Application for hazardous waste in Stripa ready'], 14 September
1995 'Heta känslor på möte om avfall i Stripa gruva' ['Feelings ran high on meeting about waste in Stripa mine'], 21 September
1995 'Chef på Naturvårdsverket: För tidigt att söka tillstånd för avfallslagring' ['Manager at EPA: Too early for authorisation to store waste'], 26 September
1995 'Förening mot avfallsplaner' ['Movement against plans on waste disposal'], 4 October
1995 'Ansökan om avfall i Stripa försenas' ['Application on waste in Stripa delayed'], 19 October
1995 'Förening ska kämpa mot avfallsplaner' ['Movement will fight against plans on waste'], 20 October
1995 'Folkpartiets medlemmar diskuterade budgeten' ['Members of the Liberal party discuss the budget'], 26 October
1995 'Miljöföreningen uppvaktade politiker' ['The environmental organization call on the politicians'], 8 December
1996 'Stripa-ansökan blir försenad' ['The Stripa application will be delayed'], 30 January
1996 'Fortsatta planerna på miljöfarligt avfall i Stripa' ['Continuous plans for hazardous waste in Stripa'], 27 February
1996 'Ansökan om miljöfarligt avfall i Stripa skjuts upp' ['Application for hazardous waste in Stripa will be postponed'], 25 March
1996 'C reserverat mot kvicksilveravfall' ['The Centre party against mercury waste'], 8 June
1996 'Är fullmäktige redo att säga nej?' ['Is the municipal council ready to say no?'], 19 June
1996 'Axplock ur svaren' ['Extracts from the answers'], 19 September
1996 'Miljöföreningen efter läsningen av remissvaren: Ytnära bergförvar tillräckligt om kvicksilvret förbehandlas' ['The environmental organization after reading of the responses to proposals for comment: Surface disposal sufficient if the mercury is treated'], 19 September
1996 'Ansökan om koncession i mitten av oktober' ['Application for concession in the middle of October'], 19 September
1997 'Stripa kan bli slutlager för kvicksilveravfall' ['Stripa might be final disposal for mercury waste'], 2 December
1997 'Både förespråkare och motståndare: Utredningen stärker vår sak' ['Both proponents and opponents: the investigation strengthens our cause'], 2 December

Letters to the editor, *Bergslagsposten*

1994 'Miljöfarligt avfall i Stripa' ['Hazardous waste in Stripa'], 17 March
1994 'Ta lärdom av mänsklighetens misstag' ['Learn from the failures of humanity'], 14 April
1994 'De trettons brev' ['Letter of the thirteen'], 19 April
1994 'Avfallsförvaring i Stripa skall diskuteras nu!' ['Waste disposal in Stripa must be discussed now!'], 21 April
1994 'För tidigt ta ställning om avfall i Stripa' ['Too early to decide on waste in Stripa'], 23 April
1994 'Dumpning igen' ['Dumping again'], 3 May

1994 'Avfallsdeponi i Stripa gör bygden fattigare' ['Waste disposal in Stripa makes the district poorer'], 2 June
1994 'Folket vill inte ha miljöfarligt avfall i Stripa' ['The people do not want hazardous waste in Stripa'], 2 June
1994 'Vad tycker partierna om avfallsförvaringen?' ['What do the political parties think about the waste disposal?'], 15 June
1994 'Politiker måste agera' ['Politicians must act'], 22 July
1994 'Stripa gruva – i mörk eller ljus framtid?' ['Stripa mine – a dark or bright future?'], 19 November
1995 'Miljöfarligt avfall i Stripa gruva' ['Hazardous waste in Stripa mine'], 9 September
1995 'Inför kommunalt veto mot avfall' ['Inaugurate local veto against waste'], 23 September
1995 'Kompakt motstånd mot avfallsplanerna' ['Solid resistance to the plans for waste disposal'], 7 December
1996 'Avfallsplanerna lägger sordin på vårglädjen' ['The plans for waste disposal put damper on the joy of spring'], 12 March
1996 'Dödskallebygden' ['Death's-head district'], 22 November
1997 'Fel och farligt att förvara giftiga metallsopor i Storå' ['Mistaken and dangerous to store toxic metal waste in Storå'], 27 January

Radio broadcasts, Radio Örebro (local radio)

1995 'Rakt på sak' ['Straight to the Point'], 14 September
1995 'Rakt på sak' ['Straight to the Point'], 21 September
1996 'Rakt på sak' ['Straight to the Point'], 7 May

Information meetings

Video recording, Stripa Mine Service, 25 May 1994
Memorandum, Rolf Lidskog, 19 September 1995

Documents from Storå-Guldsmedshyttans Miljöförening (local environmental organization)

Annual Report 1995/1996
Regulations 19 October 1995
Records 19 October 1995–23 November 1997

Interviews

Managing director at Stripa Mine Service, 7 February 2001
Chairperson of Storå-Guldsmedshyttans miljöförening (local environmental organization), 23 February 2001

Additional references for Chapter 4

Written documentation

The developer

16 September 1996, Ola Lloyd, 'Utvärdering av olika lokaliseringsalternativ för behandling av biologiskt nedbrytbara material', EnerChem, Sysav Utveckling AB, Lund

30 January 1997–1 September 1997, Memoranda notes about the progress of the joint planning between the developer, the municipality and other stakeholders (received from Kjerstin Ekwall, Sysav AB)

13 October 1997, Kerstin Ekwall and Ola Lloyd, 'Fortsatt utvärdering av lokalisering, teknik och ekonomi för en biogasanläggning i Lunds kommun', Sysav Utveckling AB, Lund

16 September 1998, Application for an environmental permit to build a biogas plant, Sysav AB

16 October 1998, Supplementary information for the biogas application, Sysav AB

30 September 1999, Supplementary information for the biogas application, Sysav AB

The municipality and the county administration

1998–2000, Planning office and planning committee, Municipality of Lund: Statements about the application; Notes from meetings and decisions concerning the biogas plant

1998–2000, County administration: Decisions about the need for supplementary information

The public

1998–2000, Letters to the county adminstration and the municipality from neighbours to the site and people living in Dalby (some letters contained protest lists)

1998–2000, Debate articles sent to the following newspapers: *Sydsvenska Dagbladet*, *Sydskånksa Dagbladet* and *Arbetet*

Newspapers

1998–2000, Articles from the following newspapers: *Sydsvenska Dagbladet*, *Sydskånska Dagbladet* and *Arbetet*

Interviews

Politicians

27 June 2000 Sven Tufvesson, member of the environmental delegation until December 2000 (Social Democrat), Municipality of Lund

11 January 2001 Gunnar Jönsson, member of the planning committee (Social Democrat), Municipality of Lund

16 January 2001 Göran Brinck, chairman of the planning committee (Conservative), Municipality of Lund

1 December 2001 Cecilia Wadenbäck, member of the planning committee (Left party), Municipality of Lund

Civil servants

20 July 2000 Bengt Aronsson, Planning Office, Municipality of Lund
15 November 2000 Christer Källqvist, Planning Office, Municipality of Lund

Representative of the developer

9 May 2000 Kjerstin Ekwall, executive planner at Sysav AB

Members of the opposition group

30 May 2000 Neighbour to the site (confidential)
6 June 2000 Neighbour to the site (confidential)
13 June 2000 Dalby resident (confidential)
22 November 2000 Dalby resident (confidential)

Internet homepages

Svenskt Landskapsskydd (Swedish Landscape Protection), 8 March 2001, www.landskapsskydd.nu/

Index

For Product Safety Concerns and Information please contact our EU
representative GPSR@taylorandfrancis.com
Taylor & Francis Verlag GmbH, Kaufingerstraße 24, 80331 München, Germany

www.ingramcontent.com/pod-product-compliance
Ingram Content Group UK Ltd.
Pitfield, Milton Keynes, MK11 3LW, UK
UKHW011001180926
475701UK00004B/500

* 9 7 8 1 1 3 8 9 9 0 8 7 6 *